RACE AND REAL ESTATE

RACE AND REAL ESTATE

CONFLICT
and
COOPERATION
in
HARLEM,
1890–1920

KEVIN McGRUDER

COLUMBIA UNIVERSITY PRESS
NEW YORK

Columbia University Press
Publishers Since 1893
New York   Chichester, West Sussex
cup.columbia.edu
Copyright © 2015 Columbia University Press
All rights reserved

Library of Congress Cataloging-in-Publication Data
McGruder, Kevin, 1957–
    Race and real estate : conflict and cooperation in Harlem, 1890-1920 /
Kevin McGruder.
        pages cm
    Includes bibliographical references and index.
    ISBN 978-0-231-16914-1 (cloth : alk. paper)
    ISBN 978-0-231-53925-8 (ebook)
    1. Harlem (New York, N.Y.)—History.   2. African Americans—New
York (State)—New York—History.   3. Harlem (New York, N.Y.)—Race
relations.   4. Racism—New York (State)—New York—History.   5. Social
conflict—New York (State)—New York—History.   I. Title.
    F128.68.H3M295 2015
    305.8009747′1—dc23

                                                                    2014029731

∞

Columbia University Press books are printed on permanent
 and durable acid-free paper.

This book is printed on paper with recycled content.
Printed in the United States of America

c 10 9 8 7 6 5 4 3 2 1

Cover Image: Raphael Greenbaum's building at 127 West 137th Street. File
photograph from *Raphael Greenbaum v. Caroline Morlath*, Supreme Court,
New York County, Index Number 20486|1913. © Antioch College.
Overlay: 1897 map of West 135th between Lenox Avenue (6th) and Fifth
Avenue. G. W. Bromley & Co., Manhattan, Section 6.
Cover Design: Jordan Wannemacher

References to websites (URLs) were accurate at the time of writing.
Neither the author nor Columbia University Press is responsible for URLs
that may have expired or changed since the manuscript was prepared.

To my parents, Elmer and Jean McGruder
And to the memory of my twin sister,
Karen Bettina McGruder

CONTENTS

ACKNOWLEDGMENTS

Many people supported me in the completion of this project. At the City University of New York Graduate Center, Judith Stein provided clear comments as well as guidance and important mentorship. I also greatly appreciate the comments and various perspectives on my work provided by Graduate Center faculty members Joshua Freeman, Thomas Kessner, and Clarence Taylor, as well as those of Elizabeth Blackmar of Columbia University, whose appreciation of the project led me to Columbia University Press.

My friends and colleagues Kristopher Burrell, Anthony DeJesus, Carla DuBose, and Carrie Pitzulo, along with Melvin Coston, provided feedback as well as equally important opportunities to commiserate regarding our research and academic adventures. My pursuit of a career in academia was motivated by my friendship with Martia Goodson, whose example as a scholar of African American history inspired me to consider doctoral study.

I appreciate the funding provided by the National Endowment for the Humanities for the Scholars-in-Residence Program at the Schomburg Center for Research in Black Culture of the New York Public Library, in which I was a participant during the 2011–2012 year. I particularly want to acknowledge the thought-provoking questions by the program's director, Colin Palmer, and assistant director, Venus Green,, and the feedback of my fellow scholars, all of whom provided important suggestions which I believe helped me to strengthen this manuscript.

A major source of documents for this project was the real estate records available at the Office of the City Register. I want to thank Dennis Nesmith of that office for providing invaluable assistance that revealed what to some may seem an arcane and obscure source actually to be a treasure trove of information.

At the very beginning of this journey, when I was searching for a viable topic, Craig Wilder provided me with valuable advice on approaching the study of Harlem, which enabled me to identify this topic and develop this project.

The friendship and fellowship of my colleagues at Antioch College has been an important source of support as well. The interest in my scholarship by my church families in New York City at the Abyssinian Baptist Church and in Yellow Springs, Ohio, at Central Chapel African Methodist Episcopal Church have been important reminders that my work has relevance beyond the halls of academia, and that the community formation efforts of a century ago that I write about in this book are continuing today and are equally important now.

Completion of this project has been a labor of love for which I especially thank my parents, Elmer and Jean McGruder, who provided my siblings and me with a love of learning that transforms projects that might seem daunting into exciting opportunities for exploration and discovery.

RACE AND REAL ESTATE

INTRODUCTION

O n a Saturday afternoon in July 1893, Marie F. Posey, an African American, sat at her kitchen window looking at workmen drilling on a rock outcropping behind her apartment building on East 122nd Street in Harlem. Her eight-year-old daughter, Marie Adel, was at her side. In the adjacent dining room Mrs. Posey's mother-in-law, Mary, watched the other three Posey children: Irma, Austin, and Reginald. In the apartment one floor below, Mary McAdam, a white woman, spoke with her neighbor Albert Graham. The Saturday routines of these neighbors were suddenly interrupted by a deafening blast that sent a boulder directly into the apartment wall where Mrs. Posey and her daughter were sitting. They were killed instantly. In the dining room, the blast threw the senior Mrs. Posey to the other side of the room and scattered the children across the floor. Downstairs, Mrs. McAdam, who had also been sitting near the window, was knocked unconscious. Her visitor, Mr. Graham, was thrown across the room. The people responsible for the blast, part of a crew working to level out one of Manhattan's many rock outcroppings to prepare the land for development, fled as soon as they saw the results of their negligent use of dynamite. They were later arrested.[1]

Marie Posey's husband, Francis, a letter carrier, was inconsolable when he arrived home from work later that afternoon to find his apartment destroyed, his wife and daughter dead, and the rest of his family injured. This family tragedy provides us with a glimpse of the fluidity in interracial relations that existed in New York City in the late nineteenth century. The Posey apartment building, at 61 East 122nd Street between Park and Madison Avenues, was in an area of Harlem that had been developed with tenement buildings in the 1870s and 1880s. The first residents had been Jewish families from the Lower East Side, soon followed by Italian immigrants. By the 1890s African Americans had begun to move into the area. Few in number, they were scattered throughout the neighborhood, and as the Posey building illustrated, they sometimes lived in the same buildings as white tenants. While race had not been a barrier to the Poseys living in the same building with Mary McAdams, when black people were subjects of news reports they were usually identified by race. The newspaper articles describing the tragedy noted that the Poseys were "colored" and that McAdams was white. Albert Graham's race was not noted; the detonators of the dynamite were identified as Italian.[2]

East 122nd Street was a new block for black New Yorkers in 1893, but the area to the south and east of the Posey apartment building had been a settlement for them for quite some time. In 1902 social worker Mary Rankin Cranston explained that "New York's oldest Negro colony, which has been in existence for twenty-five years, is situated in Harlem and is bounded by 97th and 103rd streets and 2nd and 3rd avenues."[3]

In addition to Harlem, Cranston's description included several more recent areas of black settlement in Manhattan: the area between Sixth and Seventh Avenues from 26th Street to 33rd Street; the area between 36th and 44th Streets from Seventh Avenue west to the Hudson River; and 47th Street between Broadway and Eighth Avenue. Black New Yorkers were dispersed in many parts of the city before 1900, and contrary to Cranston's observation, there were black settlements even older than Harlem, such as Greenwich Village, which was losing black population at that time. The dispersed nature of African American settlement in Manhattan before 1900 was a testament to both the diverse and somewhat fluid racial attitudes of white New Yorkers and the small number of blacks living in New York City before the twentieth century.

By 1900 the Posey family, victims of the 1893 explosion, had moved from 122nd Street, but not to another part of Harlem. In 1900 they were living on Gates Avenue in Brooklyn. There Frank Posey, who had lost his wife and his mother in the explosion, reconstructed his household. He married Elizabeth, a New Yorker whose parents were from Virginia. His children Irma and Austin were not listed in the household, suggesting that they may have died from their injuries in the explosion. Reginald, the elder son, was joined by five other siblings who may have been Elizabeth's children. Although the Poseys did not remain in Harlem, that Manhattan community became an increasingly attractive refuge for many other blacks seeking to escape the overcrowding and sporadic violence of midtown. The surge of investment activity in Harlem in the last decade of the nineteenth century transformed the community. Although newspapers at the turn of the twentieth century often characterized Harlem residents as well-to-do people, the laboring class, like the Poseys, and the poor—black and white—also lived in Harlem in the 1890s.[4] As the new century began, about 25 percent of the city's black population already lived in the Twelfth Ward of upper Manhattan, which included Harlem. These numbers would soon grow as more black residents moved to Harlem.[5] After 1900, the numbers of African Americans in New York increased substantially, and Harlem became an area of heavier concentration for this population. As black numbers increased, racial attitudes of some white New Yorkers hardened.[6]

While Harlem was developing as an urban community in the 1890s, farther south in midtown Manhattan, the growing African American population ran up against the physical limits of its enclaves in that part of the city. After the Civil War, many blacks living in the South and the Caribbean fled oppressive social conditions and sought opportunities in northern cities such as Chicago, Cleveland, and Detroit. New York, one of the key ports along the East Coast, became a primary destination. After 1900, as the existing black neighborhoods in Manhattan's midtown area became overcrowded, the northern Manhattan community of Harlem became an attractive and accessible destination for some black New Yorkers. Many African Americans would find homes in Harlem, but the process was contentious. The movement of larger numbers of blacks to Harlem threatened white control of the community, which many white Harlem residents had assumed would continue into the future. The difficulty of the community's transformation revealed the state of race relations in New York City at the turn of the century.[7]

While there are several historical studies of various aspects of Harlem's history as an African American community, the 1966 book *Harlem: The Making of a Ghetto: Negro New York, 1890–1930*, by Gilbert Osofsky, provided the most comprehensive analysis of the transition period of Harlem from a predominantly white community to one with a large black presence. Osofsky particularly emphasized interracial conflicts and the community problems of the period after 1920, in order to explain how the community became an "enduring ghetto" with a high concentration of blacks and a wide range of social problems. He described the resistance efforts of white Harlem homeowners as well as the activities of black real estate companies and churches in establishing a black residential and institutional presence in the area.[8] This book revisits this period, looking at the many ways in which the arrival of large numbers of African Americans to the upper Manhattan community of Harlem affected the community, its existing residents, and the new arrivals. It challenges the "black invasion"/"white resistance" construct often used to describe this period in New York and in other northern cities that experienced similar racial changes. While some white Harlem residents did regard African American newcomers as "invaders," this book offers a more nuanced view of the white responses, first by acknowledging that the white community in Harlem in the 1890s was very diverse, in terms of ethnicity, class, and tenure of residence. Because of this, there was a spectrum of white responses to an increasing black presence, ranging from hostile to supportive.

If one uses the definition of community as a group of "persons in social interaction within a geographic area and having one or more additional ties,"[9] turn-of-the-century Harlem was an area of many communities with associations defined by race, religion, and income, but also often crossing these boundaries to include areas of residence and common economic interests. Many white Harlem residents believed that their own interests were endangered by the arrival of larger numbers of African Americans. In early twentieth-century Harlem, the "invader" moniker was used by some of the white residents to describe blacks who, by moving there, were taking advantage of an opportunity to obtain quality housing for the first time in New York City. For some white Harlem residents, antipathy to blacks was a major reason for resistance to their presence in Harlem. And that antipathy could be driven by a subset of other reasons: concerns about a reduction in property values that could result from the black presence in a neighborhood, an assumption that all blacks were of the lower economic class and would import vice and violence to middle-class Harlem, and a broader concern that the culture of the community was about to change from what white residents had known. In many cases these motivations were intertwined and expressed simply as hostility to blacks.[10]

The group of black people who came to Harlem after 1900 was as diverse as the white residents who were already there, ranging from native New Yorkers to migrants from all parts of the country to immigrants from the Caribbean. This book explores the strategies that these black New Yorkers employed to gain entry and form a community that by the 1920s was known as the Black Capital of the World. Acquisition of real estate was the most visible symbol of their community control, but it was accompanied by the relocation or establishment of new churches and the creation of educational and recreational opportunities for youth and adults. Rather than viewing the new arrivals as the harbinger of the coming ghetto, this book examines the social status of some who were leading the movement to Harlem, and their actions to buy property and create community institutions, framing these efforts as those of people who were seeking to form a community of some permanence that they hoped would thrive.

I use real estate transactions as a critical source of information for analyzing the range of responses among white Harlem residents to the increased black population in Harlem between 1890 and 1920. This lens also provides new insight on the tactics that blacks used to counter attempts to oust them from rental properties that they already occupied, and later to attract other blacks to live in the community. The strategies used by blacks and whites to retain or acquire real estate in Harlem reveal a range of perspectives on inter-racial relations. While many whites were hostile to blacks moving to Harlem, not all were. This book reveals a previously unexamined small group of white business owners who believed that blacks should be able to live wherever they could afford to live, and who facilitated black purchases of property. The various ways in which class and ethnicity influenced interactions between blacks and whites in Harlem, particularly as they related to the settlement of blacks in the community, challenge the invasion/resistance description of black-white relations accompanying the movement of blacks into northern cities. It is quite possible that a review of real estate records and other docu-ments in other cities during the period could reveal interracial interactions in these cities that may have been more complex than has been previously understood.

While some blacks promoted what would later be called residential inte-gration, others took actions that helped to establish a uniformly black com-munity in Harlem. These diverse responses were also common in other northern cities at the time. Only a few people on either side of the color line believed that whites and blacks might live as neighbors. For many blacks and whites, the neighborhoods of Harlem would be either all black or all white. With this zero-sum vision, the only response that many whites considered to the possibility of a black "invasion" was resistance. Whites in some cit-ies, such as Chicago and Detroit, successfully defended their communities against black entrants and therefore did not experience the dramatic ra-cial change that Harlem did before 1920. When resistance failed in Harlem, whites' own fears of the black presence created the self-fulfilling prophecy of dramatic (but temporary) declines in property values and substantial white exit from the community. Black visions of a racially uniform community helped this process along. As blacks gained control of white-occupied apart-ments, they evicted the white tenants and "opened" the buildings to eager black tenants.[11]

Though the white community in Harlem was dominated by its middle- and upper-middle-class residents who lived in the brownstones that lined the streets, there were also white working-class residents who lived in tenement apartment buildings on other Harlem streets and avenues. Across these classes there was substantial ethnic diversity. Native-born residents, such as policeman John G. Taylor, who became a major figure in Harlem, shared the community with first- and second-generation whites from Sweden, England, or Germany, such as Erduin von der Horst Koch, leader of the Harlem Board of Commerce in the 1910s. The religious affiliations of these white residents ranged from Protestants (Presbyterians, Episcopalians, Methodists, Baptists) to Catholics and Jews. Each of these groups established places of worship that also served to solidify the presence of their respective communities. This diversity of Harlem whites contributed to a range of perspectives on interracial relations. While some cities, such as Chicago, had clearly dominant white voices, such uniformity did not exist in New York.[12]

Many community studies of areas to which blacks were moving in the early twentieth century also obscured the diversity of the black populations and the organized efforts by blacks to establish thriving communities in their new places of residence. Those who led the movement to Harlem after 1900 were entrepreneurs or higher-status wage workers who paid a premium to live there. The African Americans who were principals in the transition in Harlem, such as realtor Philip Payton or minister Hutchens Bishop, were a new, post–Civil War generation of the black middle class. With some assistance from accommodating whites, this group and other, lesser-known people led the black expansion in Harlem, joining the working-class blacks who by the late nineteenth century had established a small Harlem community. As blacks secured a more visible presence in Harlem, other lower-income blacks followed, often needing to double up in apartments to meet the premium rents.[13]

Black New Yorkers moved to Harlem from other parts of Manhattan and brought their religious institutions with them, ranging from Episcopalians to Methodists and African Methodists to Baptists. Blacks who came from outside of New York infused some of these established congregations with fresh energy, but they also founded new churches. The new residents shared a desire for adequate housing in an environment free from threats of violence and intimidation, factors that had motivated southerners to move north, but had also influenced some New Yorkers as well, in the aftermath of a 1900 race riot in midtown Manhattan.[14]

In moving to Harlem blacks began to create a community in which they owned property and also could elect some of their own to public office. With population concentrations that for the first time made them more than an afterthought in New York City's political calculations, black residents of Harlem believed that black elected officials would be better able to convey their views on the management of the community and ensure that they benefited from political patronage.[15]

The large numbers of blacks arriving in Harlem after 1900 came with raised expectations, but their arrival generated other kinds of responses from longtime white residents. For the first time, some white Harlemites articulated residential segregation as a desired goal. Before their movement to Harlem at this time, New York City's black population had been so small and dispersed that it had not warranted concern from white residents either in Harlem or in other parts of New York City. But by the 1910s white neighborhood improvement associations began to articulate a new goal of residential segregation. Some promoted the use of restrictive covenants in deeds to enforce prohibitions against selling properties to blacks. The covenants were ambitious, collective undertakings. Although the restrictions were placed in the deeds of individual properties, the agreements typically required the consent of the majority of property owners on a block. This substantial organizing effort was undertaken primarily by the Property Owners' Protective Association of Harlem under the leadership of a retired police officer, John G. Taylor. While developing the agreements required a collective effort, adhering to the commitment not to sell or rent to blacks required an even greater effort of community pressure. Each signer pledged not to sell or rent his or her property to blacks for a given period of time (after which, it was assumed, the instability in the real estate market caused by the entry of blacks in Harlem neighborhoods would have subsided). An owner who broke the agreement could be sued. With the hardening of segregation traditions in New York City after 1900, the increasing numbers of blacks coming to New York found that few other residential areas were available to them and therefore they continued to seek housing in Harlem. As white residents began to leave Harlem in advance of what to some of them seemed like a black tide, many covenant signers were left with the choice of adhering to the covenant and having empty buildings, or breaking their commitments and renting to blacks at premium rents. Many whites chose economics over racial solidarity, and the movement of blacks into Harlem continued.[16]

After 1900 African American settlement in Harlem developed differently than that of earlier black communities in New York City. For one thing, the scale of the black population that settled in Harlem by 1920 was dramatically larger. Harlem's black population growth was spurred by both black migration into the city and segregation practices within the city that restricted blacks' housing choices. In addition to larger overall numbers, the period from 1910 to 1920 also witnessed a growth in the black middle class nationally as a small but significant number of blacks gained access to teaching, medicine, and other professions and also developed businesses to serve the growing black populations in cities. In New York, it was this new black middle class that played an important role in distinguishing Harlem from previous black communities in New York,[17] which were primarily in declining neighborhoods, with properties in the hands of absentee white owners who viewed them as good investments. Because of limited housing options, blacks usually paid premium rents for substandard properties that were often poorly maintained by their owners. While black renters were the most visible group of blacks moving to Harlem, there were also a significant number of blacks who became property owners themselves, sometimes purchasing the buildings that the black renters occupied. The housing stock in Harlem was often quite new and of much better quality than that in previous declining areas. But Harlem also had substandard housing as well. By 1913 black real estate broker John Nail appealed to white Harlem businessmen to encourage white landlords to keep their properties that were occupied by black renters in good repair.[18]

Black ownership of real estate in Harlem reflected the aspirations and achievements of these residents, but it was also a strategic response to white hostility. Whites followed an unsuccessful 1904 attempt to evict black tenants from Harlem with the decade-long restrictive covenant movement. At a 1913 meeting of Harlem property owners, building owner Henry Holding observed: "Nothing we can say can convince me that the situation is bearable. . . . The negroes are negroes and that's all there is to it. They are objectionable. Their mode of living is not the same as ours, and the two races cannot live together in peace. Drive them out, and send them to the slums where they belong and don't let them turn our beautiful Harlem into a cheap settlement district."[19]

Racially hostile rhetoric such as this was an important tool in the covenant mobilization efforts. Such comments had the potential to rally white residents to defend their neighborhoods against black invasion and also to discourage blacks considering a move to Harlem. But rather than dissuade blacks from pursuing residences in Harlem, the white hostility motivated them to expand their presence there from renters to owners in order to provide an anchor in the community. This ownership movement came at a time when a larger number of blacks had the means to realize the goal of ownership. Black property ownership was a critical element in the transition of Harlem from an area with small African American enclaves to one with a very visible, more permanent black community. The African American owners/residents had a long-term interest in their new community, and the ownership movement in Harlem created leaders who articulated the desires of black residents to have a voice, through elective office, in the administration of the areas where they lived and owned property. This level of black real estate ownership in Harlem was more significant than has been recognized in other studies. Gilbert Osofsky's detailed review of the activities of Philip Payton's Afro-American Realty Company in *Harlem: The Making of a Ghetto* leaves the impression that once Payton's company folded in 1908, black property ownership in Harlem ended as well. In reality, many other blacks, most of them without Payton's flair for publicity, continued to purchase property. Even Philip Payton created a new company that engaged in real estate ownership and management in Harlem.[20] The ghetto framework of previous studies may have prevented some researchers from even looking for a black ownership class, which was a small but significant influence on perceptions among African Americans of Harlem as a black-controlled community.

In contrast to the situation in cities such as Detroit or Chicago, in New York the diversity of Harlem's white residents and their relatively short residency in the community help to explain the range of their responses to blacks who moved in, and the absence of major violence as a response to the racial changes that occurred there between 1890 and 1920. Those in Harlem who opposed the black presence used newspaper stories, neighborhood improvement associations, and ultimately the law in the form of restrictive covenants in deeds to attempt to stem the black tide. When the white resisters' efforts were unsuccessful in keeping blacks out, many whites, lacking decades-long attachments to the area, chose to flee rather than to fight their new black neighbors.

Most of the principals on both sides of the color line in Harlem during the period 1890 to 1920 were known locally, but beyond mentions in newspaper articles, they left no papers or other documents that conveyed their beliefs and the motivations for their actions during the period of racial change. For this reason, real estate records are particularly important. Documents that indicate who purchased a particular property from whom, and on what terms, provide surprising insights regarding the goals of the buyers, the sellers, and in the case of restrictive covenants, the broader community. This book confirms the well-known hostile responses of some whites to the increased black presence in Harlem, but it also illustrates less well-known nuances within these responses. The neighborhood organizations and restrictive covenants were more genteel expressions of hostility to blacks, certainly when compared to the bombs used against some blacks in Chicago.[21]

The growth of Harlem as a large black community between the years 1890 and 1920 exemplifies a trend that occurred in many northern cities as blacks left the South in increasing numbers. The timing varied, as did the level of conflict that accompanied the movement of blacks into predominantly white communities. The ethnic diversity of Harlem's white residents, the middle-class status of the dominant leaders, and the brief tenure of many whites resulted in a transition in which the hostility toward blacks was verbalized at public meetings, in the press, and through deed restrictions rather than acted out through violence. The class uniformity of whites that inspired strong violent reactions to black arrivals in some cities did not exist in Harlem. The middle-class status of the blacks who led the influx of black residents into Harlem after 1900 provided them with access to whites of similar class status who did not share the hostile feelings of their neighbors toward blacks, and assisted middle-class blacks in purchasing properties that provided an anchor for the black residential area in Harlem to develop a cultural, political, and economic presence with an endurance that far exceeded that of previous New York City black communities.

1

BLACK AND WHITE
NEW YORKERS

—⸱⟨⟩⸱—

H enry C. F. Koch, twenty-one years old in 1851 when he arrived in the
United States from Hanover, Germany, eventually established a series of dry goods stores in New York City. John G. Taylor came to
New York from Maryland and joined the New York City police force. Hutchens Bishop, a native of Baltimore living in South Carolina, was called to New
York in the 1880s to serve as pastor of St. Philip's Episcopal Church, New
York's first African American Episcopal congregation. Philip Payton arrived
in New York in the final months of the century from Massachusetts, seeking his fortune. These four men, two white, two black, would eventually make
their homes in the upper Manhattan community of Harlem, where each
would play an important role in its development as an urban community.
The differences that these men represented individually, by race, class, ethnicity, and place of origin, reflected the variety of residents who would live
in Harlem at the turn of the century. These differences would become both
the source of the community's ambition and vitality and the root of tensions
that the neighborhood would experience in the first decades of the twentieth
century.[1]

Koch, Taylor, Bishop, and Payton exemplified the fact that nineteenth-
century New York City was a city of immigrants and migrants. The

transportation and industrial advances of the 1820s and 1830s had solidified the city as both an industrial center and a financial center. Railroad lines
brought goods and passengers to and from the city from various parts of the
nation, while New York's location as an East Coast port made it a convenient
destination for international and interstate travelers. As a result, from the
1840s through the end of the nineteenth century, the foreign-born population in New York was more than 30 percent of the total population, supplemented by migrants from other states seeking to benefit from the opportunities available in the nation's capital of commerce.[2]

Henry C. F. Koch arrived in New York in a tremendous wave of immigrants who sought to escape the political and economic upheaval sweeping
Germany, France, and other regions of Europe in the late 1840s and early
1850s. During this period Europeans migrated throughout the world, but for
those destined for the United States, the East Coast was particularly appealing. The port of New York City was the busiest in the nation, and the city's
continuing need for labor provided work opportunities for many of the immigrants. New York was seen as a city of refuge for people who would eventually be described in Emma Lazarus's poem as "those yearning to breathe
free."[3] By the time of Henry Koch's 1851 journey, New York City's German-
born population had grown dramatically, from 24,416 in 1845 to 56,141 in
1850. On the Lower East Side of Manhattan, the community where many
Germans began settling in the 1840s was known as Kleindeutschland or
"Little Germany." It was a tight-knit neighborhood held together by German
restaurants, theaters, beer gardens, and fraternal organizations.[4]

The settled city of New York in the 1850s was primarily below 59th Street
in Manhattan, but the city's population was continuing to increase as New
York became an industrial center. In contrast to Irish immigrants, most of
whom were escaping abject poverty in their home country, German immigrants came from a variety of income and skill levels. Because of this, some
German immigrants had access to opportunities beyond the low-skilled occupations. Henry Koch planned to enter the button trade in New York, but
after six months in the city he decided to go to Australia to seek his fortune
in the gold fields there. Meeting with some success, he returned to New York
after two years.[5]

In 1859 Koch joined with his father-in-law, John Heath, in a dry goods store (John Heath—"Dry Goods for the Millions") at 15 Carmine Street near Bleecker Street in Greenwich Village. As New York's population grew, so did the retail trade. In 1846 A. T. (Alexander Turney) Stewart opened the nation's first department store at Broadway and Chambers Street, one mile south of Heath's store. By the time Koch joined his father-in-law's business, the retail trade was beginning to move north to Sixth Avenue, above 14th Street. In 1858 R. H. (Rowland Hussey) Macy opened a store at 14th Street and Sixth Avenue, and in 1862 A. T. Stewart moved his store to the area. Heath's store in Greenwich Village thrived, and after Heath's death in 1867, Koch assumed control of the business. In 1875 he followed his retail colleagues and relocated to Sixth Avenue near 20th Street. By this time the area was known as "Ladies' Mile" and was lined with multi-storied, cast-iron-front stores catering to women.[6]

New York City's development continued to move northward, assisted by improved transportation. In the 1880s elevated train lines were built along Third and Eighth Avenues from lower Manhattan to the upper Manhattan neighborhood of Harlem. Henry Koch's store on Sixth Avenue continued to prosper. In the 1880s he joined forces with a partner, Adolf Riesenberg, and in the spring of 1891 he again moved his store, by then known as H. C. F. Koch & Company, from Sixth Avenue and 20th Street. The new "Magnificent Fire-Proof Building" on 125th Street between Lenox and Seventh Avenues in the upper Manhattan community of Harlem represented an investment of more than $500,000 (more than $11 million in 2012 dollars). Koch was clearly adept at anticipating the trends in Manhattan development. With each move of his dry goods store he had settled into a bigger building to meet the increasing demand from New York City's growing population. With the move to 125th Street, at the age of sixty-one, Koch cast his lot with the future of Harlem as the next up-and-coming area in New York City.[7]

By 1891 Harlem had been settled for more than two hundred years. Dutch farmers were the initial European inhabitants of the area in the 1630s. The village of New Haarlem was founded in 1658 with an ordinance stating that its purposes were "the further promotion of agriculture, for the security of this Island and the cattle pasturing thereon, as well as the further relief and expansion of this City Amsterdam."[8] After the English gained control of the city in 1664, a charter was granted to the settlers establishing the boundaries of Harlem as upper Manhattan from "Kingsbridge (the northern end of Manhattan) south, as far as Manhattanville on the west side, and Seventy-fourth Street on the east."[9] In the following decades, the name Harlem was used more broadly, often to refer to all of upper Manhattan. Harlem continued to grow as a farming community, and in the late eighteenth century it also became the site of estates of wealthy New Yorkers. In 1765 British colonel Roger Morris built a summer house near what would eventually become 160th Street. In 1802 The Grange, the residence of Alexander Hamilton's thirteen-acre estate at what is now Convent Avenue and the 140s was completed.[10] In 1811 a survey of the island of Manhattan up to 155th Street was completed and a grid pattern was established to designate plots of land. Since the city was concentrated in lower Manhattan at the time, most of this grid applied to large portions of undeveloped land. The establishment of the grid was an important step in preparing land in Manhattan for sale and development. At the time of the survey, the geography of Manhattan was extremely irregular, marked by streams, ponds, and rock outcroppings. The city's street commissioners recognized the obstacle that these irregularities would pose to potential developers, and steps were taken in the years following the survey to fill in the streams and ponds with landfill and to explode some of the rock outcroppings. The result was the creation of a uniform commodity of land that could be considered for purchase when the appropriate conditions arose.[11]

The 1891 move to Harlem by Henry Koch was risky. In the 1890s, Harlem was sometimes called "Goatville," a reference to the animals that grazed on undeveloped land or scampered up the rock outcroppings that were prevalent in the area. In upper Manhattan, 125th Street was still a residential street. There were small shops, but some businesses on the street had already come and gone. Besides Koch's new store, one of the few other large businesses on the street was another department store, D. M. Williams & Co., on the east side of 125th Street at Third Avenue.[12] An 1891 newspaper advertisement announcing the arrival of H. C. F. Koch & Co. on 125th Street conveyed the mixed environment of the street. The advertisement included small drawings of the previous locations of H. C. F. Koch & Co. along with a large drawing of the new 125th Street building, which was flanked by other commercial buildings to its west and a residential row house with a generous front yard to its east.[13]

The Harlem location of H. C. F. Koch & Co., on 125th Street between Seventh and Lenox Avenues, contained more than two acres of floor space on four floors. Henry Koch was confident that he could entice into his store the upper-middle-class white residents of the newly constructed brownstones lining many Harlem blocks. There they would find "the finest and most varied stock ever exhibited in New York above 23rd Street." His vision was accurate. Two years after the move to Harlem, in the middle of the 1893 national depression, H. C. F. Koch & Co. announced that due to overwhelming demand it would add a two-story extension to its Harlem store.[14] Henry Koch noted that the extension "was part of the original plan of the building, but we did not anticipate such an early necessity of carrying out the plan. It is, of course, very gratifying to us that our business is increasing in all directions and justifies our policy of offering the best line of goods at down town prices."[15]

By the time the store extension was built, Henry Koch was a Harlem resident. Soon after opening the 125th Street store, he bought 224 Lenox Avenue, a townhouse where he lived with his wife, Anna, and his sons, Erduin and William, six blocks away from the store.

In the 1890s when Koch was moving his business to 125th Street, John G. Taylor was in his second decade of work with the New York City Police Department. He had joined the force at the age of twenty-eight, in 1876, a period of labor turmoil across the nation. During those times of strikes, violence, and threats of violence, New York's police force, with a rank and file drawn from the white working class, had demonstrated its ability to maintain order among workers as well as common criminals. For Taylor, a native of Maryland, the police force had proven to be a more likely means of upward mobility than his previous occupation as a carpenter. By the 1880s, patrolmen's salaries of $1,200 per year were twice the wage of the average worker. When Taylor joined the force, politically connected references went a long way in a city dominated by the Democratic Party's Tammany Hall machine. Applicants were required to have five people "certify from personal knowledge to his sobriety, industry, and good conduct." In 1884 a civil service examination by a board of police officials was instituted for policemen, but Tammany connections remained important.[16]

In the early 1890s Taylor and his wife, Agnes, lived at 709 Washington Street on the western edge of Greenwich Village with their daughter, Mary, but in 1892 they moved to 152 Waverly Place, a four-story building between Sixth Avenue and Grove Street in the heart of Greenwich Village. The Taylors paid $17,500 (more than $400,000 in 2012 dollars) for the building and operated it as a rooming house. By 1900 they housed nine male lodgers along with a twenty-four-year-old maid. Residents of the buildings on the Sixth Avenue end of Taylor's Waverly Place block were a diverse mix of whites, most native New Yorkers, but a substantial number from Germany and Ireland. The building numbers increased as one moved west on the block from Sixth Avenue toward Seventh Avenue. The building at 142 housed two black families, with all the adults born in the southern states during or directly after the Civil War. To the west after 142, the white residency resumed, but a few doors past the Taylors' residence, beginning at 158, the residents of the remainder of this side of the block were all black. Within this enclave, at 166, was the Abyssinian Baptist Church, which by that time had an African American congregation of more than one thousand.[17]

When John and Agnes Taylor moved to Waverly Place in the 1890s, Greenwich Village had long since ceased to be the center of African American life in Manhattan. By that time African American residential groups were sprinkled on blocks from the numbered streets in the low 20s northward into the 40s west of Fifth Avenue and east of Eighth Avenue. Hutchens Bishop lived in the center of this area with his wife and seven young children, at 127 West 30th Street. Bishop was the rector of St. Philip's Episcopal Church, a black congregation founded in 1809 by African Americans who had been dissatisfied with the discriminatory treatment they experienced in worship at Trinity Church, the first Episcopal church in Manhattan.[18]

People of African descent lived in Manhattan as early as 1626, when eleven African slaves arrived under the ownership of the Dutch West India Company. At that time the heart of the city of New Amsterdam was in lower Manhattan, with farms to the north of it. When the English assumed control of New Amsterdam and renamed the city New York in 1664, 375 Africans were living there.[19]

After the Revolutionary War, as the boundaries of New York City moved north, settlements of free people of African descent moved as well. Some had been granted their freedom by former owners, others arrived free from other states, and some ventured to New York in flight from southern slavery. Some northern states abolished slavery soon after the Revolution. New York passed the "Act for the gradual abolition of Slavery" in 1799, but full freedom was not available to all enslaved African Americans in New York until 1827.[20]

St. Philip's was established during this period, with the congregation initially worshipping in a school, and then in a loft over a carpenter's shop. The church's first permanent building was located on Collect (Centre) Street between Leonard and Anthony (Worth) Streets.[21] The world that newly free men and women entered into in 1827 included supportive institutions, but many limitations. Between the 1790s and 1810, the population of free blacks in New York City had grown from 1,011 to 8,137 through private manumissions. In addition to St. Philip's, other African American churches were established, among them Mother African Methodist Episcopal Zion and Abyssinian Baptist. All were located in lower Manhattan within a few blocks of Anthony Street and close to the area where the small community of free African Americans then lived. The existence of these institutions was as much a testament to the limitations that African American New Yorkers faced as it was to their resourcefulness. Each church was established because of restrictions on participation (seating, church governance, communion, etc.) experienced by African Americans who attended predominantly white churches.[22]

In the early 1800s Manhattan's community of free African Americans had established fraternal organizations for fellowship, burial benefits, and other methods of financial and social support. In 1808 the New York African Society for Mutual Relief was founded by a group of African American men. It eventually owned property and became a training ground for African American leaders. In 1827 *Freedom's Journal*, based in New York, became the first newspaper in the nation published by African Americans. Although it was published for only about two years, its editors, Samuel Cornish and John

Russworm, continued to play leadership roles in the community after the demise of the newspaper.[23]

The subordinate status of blacks in New York was reaffirmed in 1821 when New York State held a constitutional convention to revise its 1777 constitution. The new constitution extended the vote to all white citizens regardless of their economic status. In spite of vigorous advocacy by African Americans and their allies, the constitution restricted black voting to men who owned at least $250 worth of debt-free real property, thus disqualifying the majority of black male New Yorkers.[24]

The freedom gained by formerly enslaved black New Yorkers in 1827 did not end the subordinate status, based on race, that the group had in New York. In the first half of the nineteenth century, African Americans were restricted from entering skilled trades and were most widely represented in service work and unskilled labor. But in spite of these limitations, in the nineteenth century, black New Yorkers continued to establish organizations, including the Boyer Masonic Lodge (1812) and the Garrison Literary and Benevolent Society (1834). Shiloh Presbyterian and Bethesda Congregational were two churches that joined the ranks of black religious institutions.[25] While public schools were available for African American children, the New York City school system was segregated, maintaining a separate group of Colored Schools, with black teachers reporting to white administrators.[26]

The first decades of St. Philip's history reflected the limitations that black New Yorkers faced. Although the congregation began worshipping in 1809, its admission to the fold of Episcopal churches took decades. The word "free" in the initial name of the congregation, the Free African Church of St. Philip, acknowledged that the congregation was free of denominational affiliation. Although their choice for rector, Peter Williams, Jr., son of one of the founders of the African Methodist Episcopal Zion denomination, was identified by the congregation in 1810, he was not ordained as a minister and elected rector of St. Philip's until 1826. St. Philip's was not officially admitted to the Episcopal Diocese of New York until 1853, thirteen years after Williams's death.[27]

By the 1850s transportation had become a major factor in the development of Manhattan. At the beginning of the nineteenth century, the city's business activities were concentrated in lower Manhattan, below Chambers Street. Many businesses were housed in the same buildings in which the business owners lived. As the century proceeded, a separation of business and residential activity began, but because of poor transportation, the businesses continued to be located within walking distance of the owners' residences. In the 1820s the extension of horse-drawn omnibuses as far north as Harlem resulted in the establishment of separate residential communities at greater distances from the business districts.[28] At any given time, there was more than one area in Manhattan in which blacks lived. During the early nineteenth century African Americans were a substantial presence in the Five Points community of lower Manhattan (Orange, Cross, and Anthony Streets). In 1834 anti-abolitionist rhetoric fueled a riot that led whites to attack several African American churches, including St. Philip's, as well as the homes and businesses of abolitionists.[29]

Attempts by blacks to establish themselves in a variety of fields of work were viewed by some whites as unwelcome competition. In the first half of the nineteenth century, black New Yorkers were pushed out of trades that they had once dominated. In carting, for example, the increased competition from growing numbers of European immigrants and the hardening of racial lines inspired the changes. Accordingly, in the 1830s applications for carting licenses were denied on the grounds of race and justified as a decision that would prevent conflict with white carters. Reports considering the status of black New Yorkers during the period 1834–1846 concluded that economic opportunities were declining and in many cases African Americans were being displaced from skilled positions by European immigrants. In the 1840s and 1850s the jobs of porters, dockhands, waiters, barbers, and cooks, in which blacks had once had a strong presence, were dominated by the Irish and German immigrants who were arriving in great numbers.[30] In catering, a change in tastes toward European cuisine, and the entry of elegant hotel dining rooms and ballrooms led to a decline in the demand for black caterers.[31]

Another community with a substantial African American presence by the 1830s was Seneca Village (in what is now the west side of Central Park between 83rd and 88th Streets). The biracial settlement contained three churches, Colored School No. 3, as well as more than 250 residents. Some of the black residents owned their property and therefore may have been able to vote. Irish Americans made up about 30 percent of the settlement. The black and white settlers were all evicted in the 1850s to make way for the development of Central Park.[32] During the same time, the African American settlement developed in Greenwich Village. In 1850 more than 5,000 of New York's 13,815 African Americans lived in the four Greenwich Village wards. In these settlements African Americans were a substantial portion of the population on some blocks, but white residents and others often lived on the same streets and occasionally in the same buildings as African Americans. Residential segregation was not strictly practiced.

As the African American community moved northward in Manhattan, St. Philip's followed, in 1857 moving from Centre Street to Mulberry Street, near Bleecker Street in Greenwich Village. With a small population of blacks, many of whom were confined to the lower economic ranks, poor neighborhoods often had a mix of races. The small black middle-class population typically lived in the same neighborhoods as poor blacks. The restrictions they all faced in seeking housing were often based on the personal preferences of landlords rather than on a community-wide policy of racial segregation, a pattern that would account for the scattering of black settlements in Manhattan in the nineteenth century.[33]

The nineteenth-century moves made by African Americans in Manhattan typically took them into communities that were declining, often becoming dominated by commercial establishments. During the mid-nineteenth century, transportation improvements like horse-drawn "rail cars" and elevated railroads made it feasible for prosperous whites to seek newer, more fashionable locations, usually to the north of existing Manhattan settlements. African Americans and other poor residents took over lodgings in the previously fashionable neighborhoods.[34]

Racial tensions between black and white New Yorkers continued to flare periodically and sometimes led to the courthouse. In 1854, when Elizabeth Jennings, a black Sunday school teacher (who later in life became a member of St. Philip's), was thrown off of a horse car because of her race, she sued the privately owned railroad company. While New York City did not have Jim Crow racial segregation laws, private businesses often established their own Jim Crow policies. New York's streetcar lines in the 1850s organized cars along segregated lines, with some cars restricted to whites, displaying "whites-only" signs and other cars available to everyone. Jennings, late for a rehearsal with the church choir that she directed, had attempted to ride a "whites-only" car. Defended by future U.S. president Chester A. Arthur, she was awarded $225 in damages after the jury determined that the streetcar line's policy violated the law.[35]

The departure of African Americans from lower Manhattan communities was often precipitated by pressure from the arrival of European immigrant groups also seeking the low-cost housing available in these neighborhoods. In 1850 more than 20 percent of New York State residents were foreign born. Most of these immigrants were from Europe and remained in New York City after arriving at the port, and their numbers continued to grow in the later decades of the century.[36]

The beginning of the Civil War exacerbated racial tensions in New York City. Since the city served as the nation's financial center, as well as a shipping center, its merchants were closely tied to the plantation economy. New York was also a political stronghold of the Democratic Party, whose southern wing staunchly favored protecting the institution of slavery. When southern states began leaving the Union in late 1860 following the presidential election of Abraham Lincoln, New York mayor Fernando Wood, aware of the concerns of New York merchants, threatened that New York City would also secede from the Union and become a "free trade republic" in order to maintain slave state business. This threat was not executed, but when New York men began to be drafted in the summer of 1863 to fight for the Union, New York experienced a virulent backlash directed at African Americans.[37]

Class and race were the prevailing factors behind the racial violence experienced in several cities in connection with the draft. Draftees were given an option to pay $300 to hire a substitute to fight in their stead, confirming the popular charge that the war was "a rich man's war and a poor man's fight." Although the reason for fighting the war had initially been emphasized as the preservation of the Union, the January 1863 enactment of the Emancipation Proclamation, which freed slaves in the states in rebellion, broadened the framing of the war, enabling some to accurately describe it as a war to end slavery. In this context poor whites being drafted resented being called to fight to free enslaved people whom Democratic Party functionaries said would soon be moving to the North to take their jobs.[38]

This rhetoric resulted in an explosive reaction in New York City in July 1863, with four days of rioting during which hundreds of white men and women destroyed the draft office, broke into armories and stole weapons, and rampaged through the streets. The homes of blacks and abolitionists were attacked. Many blacks were injured or killed, and the bodies of some were burned or mutilated. Union troops had to be called from the South to reestablish order in the city. St. Philip's church on Mulberry Street was used (without permission) for weeks as a barracks to house troops. After the Draft Riots, New York was in such turmoil that a firm account of those killed was never determined. Many blacks left the city, some heading for the separate city of Brooklyn and others leaving the area completely.[39] In 1865 New York City's African American population was approximately 10,000, or 1.4 percent of the city's population. This decline from the 1860 population of 12,574 has been attributed to out-migration following the 1863 Draft Riots.[40]

After the Civil War, the status of African Americans continued to be challenged in New York, where the Democratic Party's dominance persisted. Challenges to Reconstruction policies and proposals to expand the rights of blacks were not only centered in southern states. New York's political leaders weighed in on both sides of the debate regarding the impact of new federal laws and the impact of the Fourteenth Amendment on life in New York. In 1866 New York State Republicans gained enough support for a constitutional convention, with one of its stated goals being to expand voting rights for blacks, which since 1821 had been restricted to those who owned property valued at $250 or more, resulting in a very small number of eligible voters statewide. Democratic opponents adopted the language of their southern colleagues, stating that black enfranchisement would lead to black dominance. Shifts in the statewide political fortunes over the thirty months during which the convention was held led to the issue of enfranchisement being separated from the constitutional revision process and put to a referendum. In 1869 a statewide referendum to end the $250 property requirement for black male voters was defeated. The Manhattan vote was 65,189 to 27,390.[41]

In 1870 when the Fifteenth Amendment to the Constitution was ratified, the barrier preventing most African American men in New York from voting was finally removed at the same time that the barrier fell in the South. The impetus for the first federal Enforcement Act, passed later in 1870 to protect "the Right of Citizens of the United States to Vote in the several States of this Union, and for other purposes," was inspired by southern opposition to black voting, but Republican New Yorkers, concerned about voting fraud associated with the selling of naturalization papers by New York City Democratic Party supporters, were among the strongest advocates of the act. The law made such fraud, if committed in a congressional election, a federal crime.[42]

The end of the Civil War witnessed a moderate movement of blacks from the South to the North. From 1870 until 1890 approximately 41,000 black people per decade migrated to the North. The destination of these black migrants was tied to efficient, affordable transportation. Because of the presence of relatives or acquaintances from communities of origin, New York City became one of several popular northern destinations, along with Philadelphia, for African Americans from eastern states particularly, as well as for people of African descent from the Caribbean.[43]

In the five years between 1865 and 1870 New York's African American population increased by 30 percent, to 13,072, making up for the population decline that had followed the Draft Riots. The city's overall population also grew by 30 percent, to 942,292, as another major wave of European immigration began. In 1870 Philadelphia had the nation's largest black population, with more than 22,000 out of a total population of 674,022. By contrast, at that same time, midwestern black communities such as Chicago and Detroit had small black populations, 3,600 and 2,200, respectively. In the succeeding decades New York's African American population continued to grow dramatically. Between 1870 and 1880 the population increased by almost 6,600, or 50 percent, to 19,663, reflecting the movement of blacks from the South as well as from the Caribbean. New York City's overall population was also increasing. Therefore, even though the black population increased, it never exceeded 2 percent of New York City's total population.[44] Brooklyn, a separate city until the 1898 consolidation of Greater New York, also had a thriving African American population, which increased after the 1863 Draft Riots as more of New York City's black population moved there. By the late nineteenth century, Brooklyn was the center of the black elite in the region.[45]

The northern movement of blacks continued within Manhattan in the later decades of the nineteenth century. By 1880 African Americans were concentrated in settlements from the old neighborhood of Greenwich Village to a new district from 23rd Street to 69th Street on the West Side. The southern part of this midtown area was known as the Tenderloin; in addition to providing residences, it was a cultural hub of the African American community. While these areas had significant numbers of residents and several community institutions, blacks still lived throughout Manhattan. In 1880 blacks lived in each of the city's twenty-two wards.[46]

In 1885 Hutchens Bishop became the fourth rector of St. Philip's Episcopal Church. A year later, following its congregation north, St. Philip's moved from Mulberry Street, purchasing church building on 161 West 25th Street, in the heart of the Tenderloin district, which by then had a large concentration of black residents.[47] The two successors to Peter Williams, St. Philip's first rector, had served for relatively short periods—William Preston from 1872 until his death in 1874 and Joseph Atwell from 1875 until his death in 1881. Hutchens Bishop's tenure would be considerably longer, to the benefit of St. Philip's and African American New Yorkers.[48] A native of Baltimore, Bishop was born free in 1858, the son of a barber, a high-status occupation for African Americans. He grew up in the Episcopal churches of Baltimore and was the first African American student admitted to General Theological Seminary, the seminary of the Episcopal Church in New York City. Following his 1881 graduation, Bishop became rector of St. Mark's Church in Charleston, South Carolina, where he served until he was called to lead St. Philip's.[49]

The location of black churches in 1880s New York is an indicator of the range of residential locations of black New Yorkers for the period. Abyssinian Baptist Church was located on Waverly Place in Greenwich Village. Zion African Methodist Church was located on Bleecker and 10th Streets, also in Greenwich Village. Illustrating the northern movement, St. Philip's was located on West 25th Street, and Shiloh Presbyterian Church on West 26th. Little Zion Methodist Church was much farther north, on East 117th Street, in East Harlem. The widely dispersed black population illustrates

that while restrictions based on race and economics existed, the small numbers of black residents did not threaten white homeowners or renters to the
point that blacks were consigned to one neighborhood. The number of black
residents of Manhattan was not large enough to change the character of most
neighborhoods, but black New Yorkers were concentrated in several areas
throughout the city.[50]

White owners of rental properties in the 1880s rightfully believed that
they could control the movement of New York's black residents, who were
primarily renters. While overt residential segregation practices or laws did
not exist in New York City at the time, black New Yorkers seeking housing
did experience limitations. In April 1889, a few weeks before the annual
May 1 Moving Day, when New York renters' leases traditionally expired, the
New York Times presented two long articles with titles that described the
state of black New Yorkers' housing choices: "Prejudices of Landlords" explained that the "privilege of selecting their quarters wherever they please
consistent with their ability to pay the rents ordinarily demanded is denied"
to black New Yorkers. The article noted that blacks were charged premium
prices for the worst quarters, made available to them typically when whites
were no longer interested. "The Northern Color Line," which appeared two
weeks later, included the observation from Hutchens Bishop that "since the
Civil Rights bill was declared unconstitutional [in 1883] by the United States
Supreme Court, it appears to me that the spirit of intolerance of the colored
people has been on the increase in the North." The federal Civil Rights Act
of 1875 had been passed to enforce the provisions of the Fourteenth Amendment to the Constitution. The act outlawed discrimination in public accommodations and called for fines for violators. Agitation against the act began
immediately after its passage and focused on what critics claimed was its attempt to "legislate against prejudice" that was claimed to be part of human
nature. The 1883 Supreme Court decision focused on the limits of the government to interfere with private decisions.[51]

Federal census records in the late nineteenth century suggest that the
movement of African Americans in Manhattan might more accurately be
described as expansions due to population increases rather than wholesale
migrations. While new settlements of African Americans developed, older

black areas continued to retain residents. For example, as the neighborhood between 26th and 40th Streets was becoming a new area of relatively high African American concentration in the 1880s, the older community of Greenwich Village continued to be a black enclave as well. In the next ten years, this expansion of black areas of settlement grew to include Harlem.

In 1893, while mature adults like Henry C. F. Koch, and John G. Taylor were drawing on their life experiences to chart new courses, and younger men such as Hutchens Bishop were getting settled in their careers, teenager Philip Payton, Jr., was on the move. The oldest son of African American entrepreneurs in Westfield, Massachusetts (his father was a barber, his mother a milliner and hairdresser), at seventeen he was on his way south. After he had fallen in with the "wrong crowd" in Westfield, his father had decided that Payton Junior needed the discipline of an African American institution. James C. Price, president of Livingstone College in Salisbury, North Carolina, and a friend of Payton Senior, facilitated the son's entry into Livingstone in the fall of 1893.

Livingstone College traced its roots to the church, in this case the African Methodist Episcopal Zion church. The denomination grew from the 1796 founding of a church in New York City by African American members of the predominantly white John Street Methodist Episcopal Church, who could no longer tolerate the requirements of restricted seating and other limitations placed on them during worship services As schools were being established in the aftermath of the Civil War, the AME Zion denomination pooled its resources to establish several schools in the South. The Zion Wesley Institute was founded in Concord, North Carolina, in 1879 by the denomination to train ministers. Named after John Wesley, the English founder of the Methodist Church and a lifelong opponent of slavery, the institute struggled through three sessions and then closed. The institute's former leaders did not give up on the idea, however, and continued fund-raising efforts, which bore fruit in 1881 when the town of Salisbury, twenty miles northeast of Concord, invited the institute to relocate there and provided it with a $1,000 contribution. The college reopened in 1882, and later in the decade the name of the school was changed to Livingstone College to honor the British missionary and abolitionist David Livingstone.[52]

The arrival of Philip Payton, Jr., at Livingstone was not meant to prepare him for the ministry but to curtail missteps in his high school career. Payton's father hoped that the close supervision of the Livingstone faculty would help Payton to find some direction in his last years of secondary school. Payton Senior wanted all of his children to attend college. His son's profligate ways and association with the wrong type of people in Westfield in recent months had led the father to take drastic action in order to keep alive this goal for his eldest son.

Philip Payton, Sr.'s barbering skills and Ann Payton's hair businesses and millinery enterprises were complementary. Throughout the 1870s and 1880s they ran advertisements in the Westfield City Directory promoting their products and services. Through thrift and hard work they built thriving businesses that served Westfield's black and white residents. By the late nineteenth century the Payton name was well regarded by both white and African American residents of Westfield. In considering the decision to send his eldest son to school in North Carolina, Payton Senior clearly understood the lasting impact that youthful indiscretions could have on the future of a young African American man in a small town.[53]

In the summer of 1893, when Payton Junior arrived at Livingstone, a cloud of racial segregation was descending upon the South, and North Carolina was not spared. African American voting in most southern states was prohibited through various mechanisms such as poll taxes and literacy tests added to state constitutions, as well as by violent intimidation. Segregated public education was firmly entrenched, and African American schools often followed schedules designed to ensure that their students would be available for farmwork. Schooling for African Americans rarely went beyond the eighth grade in any but the largest southern cities. Therefore, colleges such as Livingstone had a critical role in filling this void through their high school sections, which enabled some African American students from across the region to gain the necessary education by leaving their hometowns. Upon completion of the high school course, a few would then have the option of continuing their education by attending college, at either Livingstone or another similar school.[54]

After the year in North Carolina, Payton had satisfactorily demonstrated to his father that he was becoming more serious-minded, and he was allowed to return to Westfield to complete his senior year of high school. Unfortunately, a football injury left him unable to attend school, so he did not attain that goal.

"After recovering from the football accident, I went in the barbershop to work and remained until April, 1899, when realizing I was not making much of myself, and that I was not growing any younger, and that if I intended to do anything in this life, I had better get started, I decided to try a new field. So, on Sunday morning, April 10, 1899, I left Westfield, pack and baggage for New York City, much against the wishes of both parents."[55]

In New York, after working as a department store attendant and barber, Payton eventually found work as a porter in a real estate office, where he made eight dollars a week. In 1900, he married Maggie Ryans, a native of North Carolina, and soon decided to go into the real estate business. With a partner he opened an office at 32nd Street and Eighth Avenue in Manhattan, approximately ten blocks from the 25th Street location of St. Philip's Episcopal Church, in the heart of the black community. The Paytons rented an apartment on West 67th Street in the San Juan Hill African American enclave. Payton's real estate business struggled. In less than a year, his partner left, and Payton decided to go it alone in a small office in the Temple Court building at the corner of Nassau and Beekman Streets in lower Manhattan. For a time he continued to struggle, sometimes walking from his office to his home because he did not have the carfare.[56]

In 1900 Philip Payton and his wife moved from their West 67th Street apartment to an apartment on West 134th in the middle of a small African American area east of Lenox Avenue that had existed for several years. A few months later they were evicted for nonpayment of rent, but Payton was able to secure another apartment on the same block. He later recounted:

Seemingly this was the turning point in my business career. Things began to pick up. I began to get charge of more houses. One fine day I made a deal that netted me more than $1,150. I could hardly believe it true. My wife refused to credit it, until I showed her the checks. From that time things grew better. I opened an office on 134th Street, still keeping my office in Temple Court. I bought the flat house in which I was living. I bought two more flats and kept them five months when I sold them at a profit of $5,000. I bought another, kept it a month, and made $2,750, another and made $1,500, another and made $2,600 and so on.[57]

In March 1903, four years after arriving in New York, Philip Payton, at the age of twenty-seven, was able to purchase a row house in Harlem, at 13 West 131st, assuming a mortgage of $9,000 (approximately $190,000 in 2012 dollars) on the property. Payton purchased from David Klein, but in 1900 the occupants had been Ernest and Elizabeth Rothchild, a manager of a cracker factory and a homemaker, both thirty-five-year-old immigrants from England who shared the home with their three children. At that time all residents on the block were white (the African American enclave was tightly restricted to West 135th and 134th Streets), the majority natives of New York, but some were born in Germany, Scotland, Italy, England, and other parts of the United States.[58]

In 1890 the *Harlem Local Reporter* had acknowledged the development taking place in Harlem with this observation: "The growth of Harlem within the past four or five years has been as if by magic. Blocks and blocks, flats and flats have been built, and the cry continues, 'Give us some more.'"[59]

This development continued through the decade and past the turn of the century. The dramatic change in Payton's fortunes can most likely be attributed to the steady increase in the value of Harlem real estate that occurred after the construction of the city's first subway line got under way in 1900. Builders continued to construct row houses on vacant land on the east-west numbered streets and apartment buildings on the north-south avenues, marketing the light and air available to residents seeking to escape the congestion of other areas of Manhattan south of Harlem.

Two months after the Paytons purchased their home on West 131st Street, John and Agnes Taylor also moved to Harlem, purchasing a row house at 213 West 136th between Seventh and Eighth Avenues. Rather than a building for commerce, like their Waverly Place rooming house, the 136th Street property became their home (they sold the Waverly Place property to the Sisters of Charity of St. Vincent De Paul). Completed in the 1890s along with a group of similarly constructed houses, the house had a brown brick facade on the upper floors and a brownstone facade on the lower floor. The roofline sloped away from the street, giving the property a slightly different look than the usual Manhattan brownstone townhouse. To purchase the property, the Taylors assumed the payments on an existing $10,000 mortgage from the Equitable Life Assurance Society. For them, the move from Waverly Place to Harlem represented a significant step up, in terms of both the quality of their home and the social class of their neighbors. Clerks, business owners, and professionals, many of them the children of Irish and German immigrants, lived on their new block. The only black residents were servants.[60]

In contrast to Philip Payton and John G. Taylor, both of whom moved to Harlem after the turn of the century, Henry C. F. Koch had moved there in the 1890s. His business prospered, and by 1900 he was sixty-nine years old and well established in the community, serving as a director of the Harlem Board of Commerce, president of the Retail Dry Goods Association, a member of the Harlem Club, and one of the oldest members of the Liederkranz Society, a German singing group. In 1897 he had run for city council, placing last in a field of nine candidates. In the summer of 1900 Henry Koch began to experience heart problems, and in July he traveled to the upstate New York resort of Saratoga Springs with his wife to recuperate. On the evening of Tuesday, September 4, with his health improving, he attended the nearby state Republican convention. That night, after returning to Saratoga Springs, he awoke complaining of illness. He died an hour later. On September 7, 1900, funeral services were held for Henry C. F. Koch at his Lenox Avenue home. In the morning hundreds of H. C. F. Koch & Co. employees paid their respects. Rev. C. B. Young, pastor of the Church of the Puritans, at Fifth Avenue and 130th Street, officiated at the service, where a quartet from the Liederkranz Society sang several of Koch's favorite hymns, which he had selected several years before, when he had planned his funeral. A year before his death, Koch had brought his sons, Erduin and William, then twenty-eight and twenty-six years old, into the firm. In the coming years, in addition to inheriting the leadership of H. C. F. Koch & Co., Erduin von der Horst Koch would also inherit his father's leadership role in the Harlem community.[61]

The surge of investment activity in Harlem in the last decade of the nineteenth century transformed the upper Manhattan community. With the construction of apartment buildings and townhouses, as well as the establishment of businesses such as Koch's, Harlem changed from "Goatville" into an urban community that attracted middle- and upper-middle-class white New Yorkers as residents. Harlem's businesses were beginning to compete with downtown enterprises. These same amenities were also appealing to black New Yorkers and blacks from other parts of the United States and the Caribbean, who were arriving in the city in greater numbers. Erduin v. d. H. Koch, John G. Taylor, Hutchens Bishop, and Philip Payton would all play pivotal roles in the changes that the community would experience in the coming decade.

2

THE END OF THE AFRICAN AMERICAN WELCOME IN HARLEM

———◦——◈—◈——◦———

By the spring of 1904, H. C. F. Koch's son Erduin was settled in as president of Koch & Co. on West 125th Street, living nearby in a Lenox Avenue townhouse. John G. Taylor had been living at his West 137th Street home for approximately one year, as had Philip Payton, in a West 131st Street townhouse eight blocks from Taylor. The year was pivotal for African Americans then living in Harlem. Their unremarkable coexistence with the white residents, marked by fluid, informal practices with regard to residential movement, was about to come to an end. In New York, as in other northern cities, what it meant to be black was changing. The increased presence of African Americans was accompanied in most cases by growing hostility from white residents, which often resulted in policies that attempted to restrict the residential movement of blacks. In Harlem, the range of white responses to the black presence demonstrated a diversity of views, as well as the importance of real estate ownership for African American community formation and permanence.

In the 1890s the Koch family had been attracted to Harlem as they sought business opportunities and convenient residency. A decade later, police officer John G. Taylor and real estate broker Philip Payton had also relocated to Harlem. But Harlem was just as attractive to individuals on the lower rungs of the economic ladder, both black and white. In the 1890s families such as that of forty-five-year-old James Holden, an African American cook and porter, married, with two daughters, moved from Manhattan's "Little Africa" area of Greenwich Village to West 135th Street in Harlem. Holden and his twelve-year-old daughter were born in New York. His wife and sixteen-year-old daughter were born in Washington, D.C. Far from the increasingly crowded black district in midtown, Harlem was still viewed by black and white New Yorkers as the suburb that it had been until 1873 when it was annexed by the city. The area was sparsely developed, with open fields on some blocks. While brownstones and apartment buildings lined some streets, the broad north-south avenues and the modest building heights gave residents access to the light and air that progressive reformers were beginning to emphasize as essential for healthy urban communities.[1] In moving to Harlem, the Holden family may have been seeking a more respectable neighborhood in which to raise their children. While Harlem's white property owners sought the "respectable" class of black tenants (and charged them premium rents), black renters wishing to escape Little Africa or the Tenderloin sought this class as neighbors.[2]

By the late 1890s, the south side of West 135th Street, where the Holdens moved, between Lenox and Fifth Avenues, was almost fully developed with small apartment buildings (fig. 2.1). Only six vacant parcels of land were scattered along this side of the block. The north side of the same block was quite different: except for fifteen buildings on its eastern edge, the north side was totally vacant. By 1900 the buildings on the south side of 135th Street were occupied by both white and black residents, usually, but not always, in separate buildings. With regard to the racial characteristics of the occupants of the twenty-two buildings on the block (table 2.1), nine buildings were occupied exclusively by African Americans, and ten properties were occupied exclusively by white residents. The remaining three properties were occupied by tenants from both groups.[3]

For many New York City renters of the nineteenth century, April 30 was traditionally the day that annual leases expired, for both residential and commercial spaces. Therefore, the following day, May 1 of each year, was known as Moving Day. On this day the streets of the city were filled with vehicles

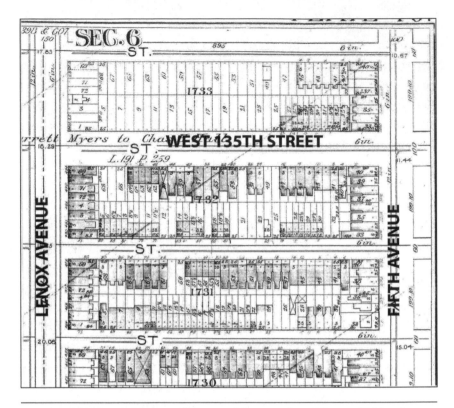

FIGURE 2.1. 1897 map of West 135th between Lenox Avenue (6th) and Fifth Avenue. G. W. Bromley & Co., Manhattan, Section 6.

loaded down with furniture and other belongings, in some cases followed by residents carrying things that would not fit on the vehicles or things that the renters preferred to carry for safekeeping. For low-income New Yorkers, moving was an annual ritual, sometimes instigated by landlords but often by tenants seeking the greener pastures of slightly lower rents or better living environments.[4] The Holdens' housing tenure reflected this tradition. From 1895 to 1900, they moved each year, between Greenwich Village and different buildings on West 135th Street.[5]

By 1900 building number 26, to which the Holdens had moved that year, was occupied by ten black households, some of them multi-generational and some including boarders. While the bonds of family or friendship might

TABLE 2.1 Race of Residents of the South Side of 135th Street (between Fifth and Lenox Avenues), 1900

Building address	Race of	Number of households in building[a]	Purchased in 1903–1904 by
2 West 135th Street	White	10	
4	Black	9	
6	White	5	
8	White	4	
10	White	5	
12	Black	11	
14	Black	8	
16	African American and white[b]	6 (1 white)	
18	African American and white	6 (1 white)	
24	African American and white	8 (1 white)	
26	Black	10	
30	White	10	James and Ella Thomas; Philip Payton; Afro-American Realty
32	White	5	James and Ella Thomas; Philip Payton; Afro-American Realty
34	Black	9	
40	Black	10	Hudson Realty
42	Black	15	Hudson Realty
44	Black	13	Hudson Realty
46[c]			Mercy Seat Baptist
48	Black	1	
50	White	1	
52	White	1	
54	White	4	
56	White	1	

SOURCE: TWELFTH CENSUS, SCHEDULE NO. 1, POPULATION, NEW YORK CITY, WARD 12, ENUMERATION DISTRICT NO. 617, SHEETS 7A–13B (WASHINGTON, D.C.: U.S. DEPARTMENT OF COMMERCE, 1900).

[a] Households represented by the number of people recorded as the "Head" of a household on the census schedule at a particular address.

[b] Two white boarders within a household headed by an African American.

[c] Not on census.

have made living in close quarters more manageable, the fact that at least one household contained seventeen people, most of whom were adults or young adults, illustrates the reality of limited housing choices and the struggle to meet premium rents that black New Yorkers faced. The residents of the other six apartments at 26 West 135th Street, all African Americans, were a mix of people born in the South, in New York, or in other northern states.[6]

Although midtown Manhattan continued to house substantial numbers of blacks, by the end of the 1890s an African American enclave, to which the Holden family had moved, had developed at 135th Street and Lenox Avenue in Harlem. The black residents of this area rented apartments owned by white investors who viewed their presence in the "Negro Colony" as a source of revenue, not unlike their presence in other black enclaves in Manhattan such as Greenwich Village or the midtown Tenderloin and San Juan Hill districts. A distinction from these earlier settlements, to which blacks gained entry as they declined, was that the Harlem district was relatively new. The buildings occupied by the black tenants were recently built.[7]

A building comparable to number 26, but separated from it by a vacant lot, was 30 West 135th Street. It was occupied by ten white families who reflected the wider occupational choices—such as mechanic, seamstress, and electrician—available to white New Yorkers. Some also included large families, for example the family of Joseph Wilbur, with six children.[8]

Like earlier black neighborhoods in Manhattan, some buildings on the block did have tenants of both races, and in one building tenants of different races shared an apartment. At 16 West 135th Street, Sallie Tagwell, a forty-year-old African American, lived with two boarders: Jamie Lee, a thirty-year-old white woman born in "Carolina" whose parents were born in Ireland, and her husband, Henry Lee, a white, twenty-nine-year-old builder, also born in Carolina. Most of the white heads of household on West 135th Street held skilled jobs, which allowed them to rise above the level of poor whites in Manhattan's midtown district. Harlem's black residents of the 1890s were also striving for middle-class status within the occupational constraints of the period. Porters, cooks, and other service workers, whose incomes were supplemented by the work of their wives, were the core of New York's nineteenth-century black middle class. On 135th Street, by living in large groups of families and with unrelated individuals who were mainly laborers, residents could combine their incomes in crowded conditions to meet the cost of better housing in Harlem.[9] While African Americans sought better living conditions, white property owners sought better returns on their investments, initially by charging blacks premium rents, but eventually by promoting development that would disrupt the placid relationships that had existed between blacks and whites in the area.

In 1900 the community of Harlem had vague northern and southern boundaries. The area north of 96th Street was often called Harlem, referring to the village of New Harlem whose boundaries had once extended even farther south, to 72nd Street, before it was annexed by New York City. The northern boundary of Harlem was also vague, ranging from 155th Street to streets in the 170s (fig. 2.2).[10]

Decade by decade, since the city's establishment at the tip of Lower Manhattan in the 1600s, development in Manhattan had moved northward and consumed land that had been either vacant or previously used for farming. An 1897 map of New York City, then consisting of only Manhattan, a year before it was joined with Brooklyn, the Bronx, Queens, and Staten Island into Greater New York, illustrates that the vacant land in the upper Manhattan community of Harlem was disappearing as development moved to the north.[11] But there were still substantial areas of vacant land. Between Seventh and Eighth Avenues, 110th and 111th Streets were almost totally vacant. Northward from that point, partial rows of brownstones began to fill blocks like 112th and 113th Streets. Most of Seventh Avenue between 110th and 116th Streets was vacant. Many of the streets east of Seventh Avenue were vacant or sparsely developed with apartment houses. Above 116th Street traveling northward to 135th Street, the blocks were more densely developed, but areas of vacant land remained in the middle of blocks or along avenues. Above 135th Street, many of the blocks were totally vacant.[12]

For many New Yorkers the development of upper Manhattan could not happen soon enough. An 1890s article expressed embarrassment at the grass that was growing in 125th Street, Harlem's main commercial thoroughfare, implying that its presence suggested a country village rather than a neighborhood in a large city. Harlem real estate investors and residents had long

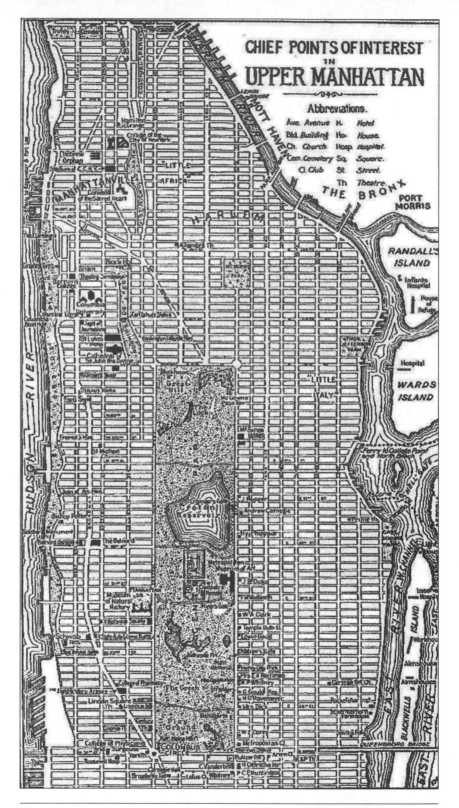

FIGURE 2.2. Map of Harlem. Automobile Club of Rochester, 1920, Florida Center for Instructional Technology.

agitated for the construction of better transportation routes, arguing that without such links their investments would not grow and neither would Harlem.[13]

The growth in developed areas of Harlem coincided with an increase in the black presence in upper Manhattan. From 1890 to 1900 the African American population in Manhattan grew by 41 percent, from 25,674 to 36,246. Behind these numbers was the exodus of blacks from southern states. Seeking to escape racial violence, declining economic opportunities, and legalized segregation, African Americans moved to northern cities like New York.[14]

The real estate transactions of African Americans in Harlem during the first decade of the twentieth century, as well as the reactions of white Harlem residents and property owners to the black presence in the community, provide a unique view of the hardening of the color line in a northern city. In cities such as Cleveland, Chicago, and Philadelphia, as well as in New York, when the black populations increased, racial lines that had previously been somewhat flexible hardened, sometimes resulting in conflict between black and white residents. Given this atmosphere, an examination of the access of African Americans to Harlem real estate, as renters and as owners, reveals examples of increased racial hostility, but also instances of cooperation between blacks and whites.[15]

Although African Americans lived throughout Manhattan, the dramatic increase in population during the 1890s resulted in greater visibility in some districts. Their largest concentration was in the midtown area. By 1900 Assembly District Nineteen (the West Side from 59th to 72nd Streets) contained the largest population of African Americans—4,982, or 14 percent of the borough's total black population (table 2.2 and fig 2.3). Four other midtown districts each contained more than 2,500 African American residents. In upper Manhattan, the Twenty-Third District, east of Fifth Avenue between 86th and 96th Streets, housed more than 3,000 African Americans. During the 1890s African Americans in upper Manhattan, previously concentrated in the area east of Third Avenue, began to move west, settling in relatively substantial numbers on 135th Street as well as on some of the blocks south of that, all east of Lenox Avenue. In 1900 the Thirty-First District in East and Central Harlem between 110th and 135th Streets was

TABLE 2.2   Distribution of the African American
Population in Manhattan, 1900

Assembly district	Total	Negro	% of total district population	% of total Negro population
1	25,959	132	0.51%	0.36%
2	52,768	261	0.49%	0.72%
3	47,295	965	2.04%	2.66%
4	76,852	22	0.03%	0.06%
5	37,951	1,378	3.63%	3.80%
6	64,286	68	0.11%	0.19%
7	41,979	793	1.89%	2.19%
8	72,125	9	0.01%	0.02%
9	42,346	1,673	3.95%	4.62%
10	70,785	18	0.03%	0.05%
West Side 14th–34th 11	*41,247*	*3,756*	*9.11%*	*10.36%*
12	72,897	4	0.01%	0.01%
West Side 34th–40th 13	*37,572*	*2,584*	*6.88%*	*7.13%*
14	54,847	25	0.05%	0.07%
15	38,911	842	2.16%	2.32%
16	73,834	2	0.00%	0.01%
17	40,975	1,214	2.96%	3.35%
18	45,197	86	0.19%	0.24%
West Side 59th –72nd 19	*65,025*	*4,982*	*7.66%*	*13.74%*
20	42,596	113	0.27%	0.31%
West Side 86th–125th 21	**89,055**	**1,135**	**1.27%**	**3.13%**
22	48,796	244	0.50%	0.67%
above 86th 23	**78,536**	**3,169**	**4.04%**	**8.74%**
24	51,209	379	0.74%	1.05%
14th–34th 25	*36,800*	*2,950*	*8.02%*	*8.14%*
26	56,882	458	0.81%	1.26%
34th–42nd 27	*36,984*	*3,318*	*8.97%*	*9.15%*
28	46,123	192	0.42%	0.53%

Assembly district	Total	Negro	% of total district population	% of total Negro population
29	51,674	957	1.85%	2.64%
East Harlem 68th–86th 30	*58,728*	*345*	*0.59%*	*0.95%*
East/Central Harlem	*78,013*	*1,483*	*1.90%*	*4.09%*
East Harlem 86th–110th 32110th–135th 31	**80,379**	**1,680**	**2.09%**	**4.63%**
33	58,112	147	0.25%	0.41%
34	38,296	862	2.25%	2.38%
Manhattan	1,855,034	36,246	1.95%	100.00%

SOURCE: COMPILED FROM TWELFTH CENSUS, CENSUS BULLETIN NO. 88, "POPULATION BY SEX, GENERAL NATIVITY, AND COLOR, BY GROUPS OF STATES AND TERRITORIES," 9.

Note: *italic text = midtown districts*; **bold text = Harlem districts.**

home to approximately 1,600 African Americans. With these increased numbers, in some districts in Manhattan the African American population approached 8 percent of the total population of the district. Borough-wide, the black population remained at less than 2 percent of Manhattan's total population of 1.85 million in 1900.[16]

The housing patterns of blacks that existed in 1900 on West 135th Street would soon be challenged by larger forces and increasing hostility toward blacks. As African Americans became a greater presence in northern and southern cities after the end of the Civil War, policies were developed to limit their movement and access to public and private accommodations. In the South, voting restrictions and segregation laws eventually resulted. Blacks were characterized as prone to criminality and disorder, factors used to justify segregation practices, harsh treatment by the criminal justice system, anti-black violence, and restrictions on educational and employment opportunities. In the North, social and economic discrimination increased. Access to skilled occupations became even more limited. Some restaurants and other public accommodations refused service to African Americans. In employment, blacks seldom had access to the jobs that were continuing to draw unskilled European immigrants to New York City. In social interactions,

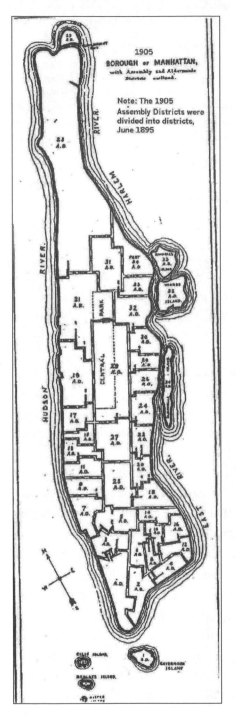

FIGURE 2.3. Manhattan assembly districts, 1905. http://bklyn-genealogy -info.stevemorse.org/Ward/1905.NYC .AD.html.

they experienced restrictions as well. The New York State Civil Rights Law of 1873 made it possible for blacks to sue if they were denied accommodations, and it did result in lawsuits related to service in bars and restaurants, but the onus was on blacks to challenge the discriminatory behavior. Many preferred to frequent places that sought their patronage rather than to challenge the hardening color line.[17]

Blacks battled against the prevailing stereotype of criminality. Journalist Ida B. Wells, in *A Red Record: Tabulated Statistics and Alleged Causes of Lynchings in the United States, 1892–1893–1894*, presented investigative reporting data on southern lynching and exposed the real reasons for the murders: they were often attempts to prevent economic competition. In *The Souls of Black Folk* (1903), William Edward Burghardt Du Bois prophesied that "the problem of the twentieth century is the color line," while celebrating the richness of black culture. In 1905 he assembled a group of black men at Niagara Falls to announce the Niagara Movement to advocate for black political rights. In Alabama, Booker T. Washington used the college he had founded in 1881, Tuskegee Institute, to promote black skills acquisition and economic development.[18]

In the late nineteenth and early twentieth centuries, progressive reformers began to look for solutions to urban problems such as vice and crime. Consistent with the developing image of black community pathology and disarray, many reformers at the time considered African Americans more prone to vice and crime than others. Black urban neighborhoods were then coming into existence or increasing in scale as African Americans migrated from southern farms to northern cities. The fact that these communities were often the locations of crime and illegal activities was considered by many to be an unavoidable natural outgrowth of racial characteristics of blacks rather than the result of restricted opportunities, racial segregation, poverty, graft, and lax law enforcement.[19]

The image of black criminality was confirmed for many New Yorkers on an August evening in 1900, when Arthur Harris, a black man, interrupted a walk with his common-law wife, May Enoch, also African American, to purchase a cigar at a corner store. Harris's wife remained on the street as he entered the store. Upon exiting the store, Harris observed that a white man was engaged in an altercation with his wife. Harris struggled with the man, and in the course of their fight Harris stabbed the man. The man was Robert Thorpe, an undercover policeman who had been attempting to arrest Harris's wife. Seeing her standing on a corner in the Tenderloin district at night, he assumed that she was a prostitute. The undercover officer was about to become the son-in-law of a senior official at the neighborhood precinct. When Thorpe died from his wounds the next day, the midtown neighborhood was swept with the fury of its white residents directed at African Americans (Harris had escaped to Washington, D.C.). In the days following the officer's death, blacks were pulled off of streetcars and beaten, their homes were damaged, and many were chased through the streets. Retaliating for the death of a colleague, police officers looked the other way as these violent acts occurred, and in some cases officers were reported to have assisted in attacks.[20]

In the aftermath of the attacks, the worst since the city's 1863 Draft Riots, area ministers organized the Citizens' Protective League, held meetings, and brought the grievances of the victims, several of whom claimed to have been attacked by policemen, to city leaders. The investigation, led by Bernard York, president of the Board of Police Commissioners (mayoral appointees), concluded that there was no evidence of wrongdoing and that "it may be that some innocent people, both black and white, were injured during the time of the trouble, but it should be borne in mind that a portion of the district in which the trouble occurred is thickly populated with a mixed class; that it calls for, at all times, extra vigilance on the part of the police."[21] For many blacks, midtown was no longer a safe area. This incident contributed to the continued movement of African Americans to Harlem.

Although the racial ideology of black criminality influenced the perceptions of whites toward blacks, the profit motive was an equally powerful factor in determining how blacks would be treated by whites. A few years after the 1900 riot, as Harlem land values increased with the first subway line nearing completion in 1904, the black residents, once sought as renters in Harlem became the targets of an organized removal effort by some white Harlem property owners. The black residents of West 135th Street were discussed on the day after Moving Day in the May 2 edition of the *New York Her-*

ald: "There is nothing but trouble in a section of Harlem where a community of negroes that has grown rapidly in a few years, is being made to disintegrate and 'move on,' through the concerted action of landlords. One hundred families will be on the move to-day, and six hundred other families are perilously near eviction."[22]

Some owners of properties on West 135th Street and nearby streets to the south had decided to exercise their Moving Day prerogative of not renewing leases. The *Herald* article suggested that the first black inhabitants of the area had arrived some twelve years previously, and were quiet, "wealthy parlor car attendants." The article noted that the motive behind the evictions was a reduction in rents in the area that attracted a more "objectionable" element of the race as evidenced by "the frequent presence of the police and the patrol wagon." The article also suggested that a rent increase, "which the parlor car porters could pay, but their colored inferiors could not," had previously been used as a strategy to remove the undesirable tenants. According to the *Herald*, the owners' target was the "colored inferiors," but the "wealthy railroad porters" were also caught in the net of the eviction effort.[23]

The black residents of West 135th Street decided to challenge this effort to oust them. An article in the May 2 edition of the *New York Times* described an "indignation meeting" of the previous evening held at Mercy Seat Baptist Church at 46 West 135th Street by "colored residents of 134th and 135th Streets, between Lenox and Madison Avenues." Those who attended the meeting complained of a "systematic campaign" to force them out of the neighborhood, noting that landlords had indicated that the black residents were "noisy and disorderly, an accusation which was denounced at last night's meeting as without foundation." Homing in on the reason for the dispossession strategy, the article noted the observation of Mercy Seat Baptist's pastor, the Reverend Norman Epps, that "the prospective opening of the subway has enhanced the desirability of the locality, and so . . . the very landlords who had once invited the negro tenants are now trying to drive them out." The language of reform was being used to veil the owners' interest in gaining unrestrained access to property that they anticipated would dramatically increase in value. No mention was made of eviction efforts targeting white tenants in the same area.[24]

Rev. Epps's analysis was accurate. The development of a subway system had been a matter of discussion in New York for many years. When construction started in 1900, Harlem property owners began to look forward to the benefits the community would experience after the announced 1904 subway opening. With a subway stop at the corner of 135th Street and Lenox Avenue, the western end of the 135th Street block, the adjacent properties then occupied by small walkup tenements and row houses were ideally located for more intensive use. The owners of the buildings were interested in obtaining higher rents from the existing buildings or constructing larger buildings to respond to the demand of residential and commercial tenants to be near the new subway stop.[25]

On May 2 African American resistance moved beyond words. Mercy Seat Baptist Church, which had hosted the indignation meeting on the previous evening, signed a five-year lease for 46 West 135th Street. The monthly rent was $100, and the lease gave the church the option to purchase the building at a price of $16,000 "at any time during the term of this lease, with the appurtenances."[26] The lessor was Louis Partzschefeld, a metalworker who lived at 4 West 136th Street.[27]

On May 12, Mercy Seat Baptist Church purchased lots at 45 and 47 West 134th Street for $16,000 from August and Mena Ruff. August Ruff was a builder who lived at 54 West 120th Street. The source of Mercy Seat's funds for the purchase cannot be determined. The sales agreement for the Ruffs' lots included a covenant, or promise, that the first building constructed on the property would be a church for Mercy Street Baptist. On the same day, the Reverend Charles Satchell Morris, pastor of Abyssinian Baptist Church, an African American congregation then located on West 40th Street, transferred to Abyssinian a building located at 61 West 134th Street that he had purchased eight months earlier, in September 1903. The church agreed to assume the payments on mortgages totaling $25,000 on the properties. On June 29, black undertaker James C. Thomas sold a half interest in his properties at 30 and 32 West 135th Street to African American real estate broker Philip A. Payton, Jr. A month later Thomas sold the other half interest to Payton. The cost to Payton for the two buildings was $200 and the assumption of a first mortgage of $30,000 and a second mortgage of $3,500.[28]

While the May 1904 newspaper articles suggested that white Harlem property owners were united in their efforts to oust blacks from 135th Street, the sales transactions noted above tell a much more complex story. The flurry of leases and purchases by African Americans that took place before and after the May eviction notices could not have happened without the cooperation of the white owners of the properties as well as others involved in real estate investing. Financing the purchase of tenement buildings in the 1890s and the first decade of the 1900s was not done by most mainstream banks. The buildings, which routinely cost between $20,000 and $40,000 ($400,000 to $800,000 in 2012 dollars), were viewed as high-risk gambles, because of both the variations in construction quality and the transient nature of the lower-income tenants who typically occupied the buildings. Banks rarely provided financing for these buildings, particularly to borrowers with modest incomes and limited social contacts. The sellers of the properties—wealthy individuals or the estates of the wealthy individuals—would have been the likely lenders for the African American purchasers of the buildings in the 135th Street area.[29]

When James C. Thomas and his wife purchased 30 and 32 West 135th Street from Charles and Katie Kroehle on May 5, 1904, they paid $100 and agreed to assume mortgages totaling $30,000 that were already on the property. The Kroehles had purchased the buildings only three weeks earlier, on April 20, from Isaac Helfer, who had purchased the property six days before that, on April 14, from George and Jennie Currier. George Currier had owned the property since the early 1890s, and in 1900 the two buildings had been occupied exclusively by white tenants. The quick series of sales suggests speculative activity connected with the increased desirability of the 135th Street area. Unfortunately there are several gaps in the record that cloud the specific terms of the transactions. In a common practice, the exact purchase price was not stated in the property records. Instead, the sale that precipitated the flurry of activity, by Currier to Helfer on April 14, was described as being for "consideration of $100 and other valuable consideration." Likewise, Helfer's sale of the property to Kroehle on April 20 was described as for "$1.00 and other goods and valuable consideration in Dollars, lawful money in the United States subject to two mortgages aggregating

$30,000 and interest theron."[30] The conveyance document for the sale by the Kroehles to James Thomas mentions only the payment by Thomas "of One hundred dollars, lawful money of the United States," with no reference to additional payment that would have been the profit over their purchase price, leaving open the possibility that the transaction was meant to facilitate the purchase by Thomas rather than to make money. The payment terms on the $30,000 mortgages on the property at the time of the purchase are not included in public records (there were two mortgages for $2,000 each placed on the property in March and April of 1890).[31] Often such a loan might call for interest-only payments for a period, followed by the payment of the principal balance, usually made either through the sale of the property or by obtaining a loan from another source to repay the first loan. For the lenders, such real estate loans were seen as another investment vehicle equivalent to bonds (which are loans that typically pay lenders interest on their funds and return the borrowed principal at a given date). Real estate loans added a level of protection for the lender, with the borrower offering property as collateral to ensure the loan payments. Although the details of the $30,000 mortgages on the property purchased by Thomas do not appear in the public records, the fact that the mortgages remained on the property through successive sales suggests that they contained provisions allowing the mortgage payments to be assumed by new owners rather than requiring a payoff upon the sale of the property. Such provisions would have minimized the Kroehles' risk in selling the property to Thomas. If Thomas had been unable to remain current with the mortgage payments, it would have been the responsibility of the original lender to start foreclosure proceedings, since the Kroehles would no longer have a legal interest in the property. Because James Thomas was a businessman with a well-established undertaking enterprise, the Kroehles most likely were confident that he would be successful in managing the buildings. Charles Kroehle owned a stable on East 55th Street and lived on East 71st Street.[32] The transaction between the Kroehles and Thomas illustrates the complex nature of the interactions between blacks and whites at the time. While some white New Yorkers were characterizing blacks as the source of problems in order to justify evicting them from Harlem, others were doing business with them for substantial sums of money, enabling these African Americans to gain a more permanent presence in Harlem.[33]

A young African American broker, Julia Liggan, also began buying property in the 135th Street area during this time. A native of Virginia, Liggan was a resident of 14 West 134th Street, where she and her widowed mother rented an apartment. Exactly one year before the 1904 eviction effort Liggan had begun acquiring nearby properties. On May 12, 1903, she purchased a property on West 134th Street. The next week, on May 20, she purchased 100 and 102 West 136th Street and agreed to make payments on a mortgage of $9,500 provided by George Chapman. On the same day Chapman also loaned Philip Payton $31,500 and $3,000. Chapman was an attorney in the office of the Astor estate. The estate at one time had extensive properties in Harlem, which may have been his link with Liggan and Payton. On June 16, 1903, Liggan sold a three-story building at 60 West 134th Street to Rev. Norman Epps, the pastor of Mercy Seat Baptist Church.[34]

With the exception of George Chapman, the white people involved in these transactions had German ancestry in common. Cornice maker Louis Partzschefeld, who leased his property to Mercy Seat Baptist Church, and his wife, Louise, were born in Germany. They had both arrived in the United States in the early 1880s. Their son, Louis Junior, attended German American Felix Adler's Ethical Culture School, which in 1904 moved into a new building at Central Park West near 59th Street, and was noted for its innovative curriculum of hands-on education.[35] August and Mena Ruff, who sold property to Mercy Seat Baptist, were also both born in Germany. August Ruff, who had arrived in the United States in 1867, was an officer in a New York City German American singing society, Schwaebischer Saengerbund, and active in Democratic politics. The wedding of his daughter was later described in the *New York Times*, suggesting that he was a successful businessman.[36] Charles Kroehle and his wife, who purchased property that they soon re-sold to James Thomas, were born in New York, but their parents were born in Germany. Like August Ruff, Kroehle was an officer of a German American singing society, New-York Maennerchor. The debut tea for his daughter was also noted in the *New York Times*.[37]

These middle-class German American households headed by craftsmen followed a generation that in the nineteenth century had supported "equal rights for all, regardless of color, religion, nationality or sex."[38] Responding to the oppressive conditions in their country, and influenced by revolutionary democratic ideology in Europe, some had supported Germany's failed 1848 revolution, and afterward fled to the United States. In America some of these Germans became vocal anti-slavery advocates. But not all Germans were of this mind. Nineteenth-century New York also had a large German American population that identified with the pro-slavery wing of the Democratic Party. The *Staats-Zeitung*, the German newspaper controlled by New York's mercantile elite and read by German mechanics and laborers, referred to its press competitors that advocated abolition as *Niggerblätter* (nigger sheets).[39]

A generation later, the actions of Partzschefeld, the Kroehles, and the Ruffs in assisting blacks to buy properties in Harlem illustrated that a different, possibly anti-racist ideology was still alive. The belief in black inferiority held by many Americans in the early 1900s had been transmitted over generations. Some new arrivals quickly adopted these beliefs as part of their efforts to Americanize themselves, but others held different understandings of the status of African Americans. Various German ideologies had ample potential to grow in New York City. In 1900, thirty-seven percent of New York's population of 3.4 million people was foreign born. German-born New Yorkers, at 322,343 (9.5 percent of the total population), accounted for the largest part of this group. Russian-born residents were a distant second at 155,102 (4.5 percent), followed by Italian-born residents at 145,433 (4.2 percent). Many German Americans lived in the lower Manhattan neighborhood of Kleindeutschland (Little Germany), but as they prospered they moved to various other areas in the city, including Harlem. This substantial population of people of German descent had developed German-language newspapers and social groups that provided the German sellers of Harlem properties with a social group that extended beyond Harlem. They were therefore less susceptible to pressure from other Harlem property owners who may not have approved of their transactions with blacks.[40]

New York newspaper accounts of the 1904 eviction efforts in Harlem illustrated that under some circumstances class distinctions among black

New Yorkers were acknowledged by whites. The reference to the welcome received by "wealthy" African American railway porters in Harlem in the 1880s and 1890s versus the twentieth-century African American "undesirables," who attracted attention from the police because of their riotous behavior, indicate that in describing the eviction the writer acknowledged such class differences. While the leaders of the eviction movement sought to portray all blacks as undesirable, other property owners, who chose to lease, sell, or lend to African Americans in 1904, were also making distinctions among African Americans. It is highly unlikely that they would have entered into what were standard sales arrangements for properties they owned if they had not believed that the African Americans with whom they were doing business were both trustworthy and financially capable of honoring their agreements. Black purchasers such James Thomas, owner of a midtown undertaking establishment, was of a similar economic class as the stable owners Charles and Katie Kroehle from whom he purchased property.

By the time Thomas had transferred 30 and 32 West 135th Street to Philip Payton, in June and July 1904, Payton had already assembled a group of African American businessmen to undertake other Harlem real estate ventures. In 1902 Payton and his wife, Maggie, had purchased a brick townhouse at 13 West 131st Street. That same year they had also purchased an apartment building at 67 West 134th Street from the trustee of an estate. For the apartment building, the Paytons assumed the payments on an existing mortgage of $23,000 and also agreed to make payments on an additional $23,000 loan that the estate had provided to them toward the purchase of the property.[41]

Payton's building at 67 West 134th Street housed the offices of the new company that he established in 1903, the Afro-American Realty Company. The company was a partnership with several African American investors, including James C. Thomas, the undertaker who had sold Payton 30 and 32 West 135th Street.[42] The term "Afro-American" was not popularly used to describe black people in the early 1900s. The terms "colored" and "Negro" were more common. The fact that Payton selected this term sent a strong signal of the ethnic identification of the company's founders and made clear the group whom they planned to serve.[43]

The May 1904 attempt to evict African Americans from the 135th Street area was of both personal and professional interest to Payton, and led him to expand his company in July 1904 by incorporating it in order to raise more capital. The pamphlet used to solicit investors noted: "When the movement was started to put the colored people out of West 135th street, this co-partnership being unable to lease any houses on this street, voted to buy and did buy two 5-story flats valued at $50,000 and thereby stemmed the tide, which had it been successful in West 135th street, would surely have extended to West 134th street, which is almost entirely given over to our people."[44]

The company's shift in focus from leasing and managing buildings to owning them required more capital, and with the incorporation the company gained the ability to raise as much as $500,000 through stock sales at $10 per share. The company's prospectus of business activity suggested broader aims than merely stopping the eviction movement: "The idea that Negroes must be confined to certain localities can be done away with. The idea that it is not practical to put colored and white tenants together in the same house can be done away with."[45] The office of the most powerful African American in the country, Booker T. Washington, gave encouraging words as early as May 3, 1904, with a letter to Payton from New York: "I have read in yesterday's *World* how you turned the tables on those who desired to injure the race, and wish to congratulate you on this instance of business enterprise and race loyalty combined."[46]

Payton had most likely met Washington through his membership in Washington's National Negro Business League, an organization created in 1900 that had local chapters of African American business leaders and held annual meetings that drew on Washington's philosophy of promoting black economic development.[47]

On July 29, 1904, Payton transferred 30 and 32 West 135th Street to the Afro-American Realty Company, along with the building housing his company's Harlem office, 67 West 134th Street. Individual blacks had been moving to Harlem in increasing numbers during the previous decade, but Payton's activities represented an organized and very visible effort. They did not go unnoticed by others outside of Harlem. The Afro-American Realty Company was the subject of a *New York Times* article and an editorial in

July 1904. Under the headline "To Make Color Line Costly in New York" the article paraphrased the company's prospectus, noting that $100,000 in capital had been paid in by investors and that most of the directors were "negro property owners and business men." In an editorial the next day the *Times* suggested that the Afro-American Realty Company, formed "to depress real estate values in order to bring desirable apartment houses into the market as homes for negroes promises to be a business mistake." The editorial predicted that white residents would leave and "that the number of unobjectionable negro tenants standing ready to take their places is not great enough to prevent neighborhood deterioration."[48]

The suspicion that the Afro-American Realty Company sought to depress real estate values was linked to a conflation of the racial beliefs of the era with the poor neighborhoods to which most African Americans were consigned in cities. Many if not most, in the real estate field believed that the presence of blacks caused the deteriorating conditions in which they lived. Implicit in this belief was the notion that African Americans lived lives of disarray marked by crime and sexual abandon. It was the common belief that property values in neighborhoods occupied by African Americans would be depressed because of their presence. This theory failed to recognize that while crime, gambling, and prostitution existed in some African American neighborhoods, it flourished under the tacit approval of corrupt police and others who benefited from the revenue generated by such activities. Although the criminals were visible in the black neighborhoods, such as midtown Manhattan, the majority of the residents who worked as domestics, deliverymen, elevator operators, or in other menial positions were unseen by critics of African Americans. The *Times* article assumed that people such as James Thomas and Philip Payton, who could enter into agreements to repay substantial loans, were intent on bringing the disarray of San Juan Hill or the Tenderloin district to Harlem. In reality Thomas and Payton were jumping at an opportunity that a generation earlier had been unavailable to African Americans. The post–Civil War increase in Manhattan's black population, from fewer than 10,000 in 1865 to more than 36,000 by 1900, not only brought potential tenants to New York, but increased the pool of potential black investors, business partners, and customers of black businesses as well. James C.

Thomas had moved to New York from Texas in the 1880s, and established his business in 1897. New York's black business class grew as the black population grew, since it was better able to sustain more viable businesses. Philip Payton was able to draw from this business class to attract the eight initial investors in the Afro-American Realty Company. A generation of growth in African American economic activity following the Civil War had resulted in a coterie of individuals who could be deemed creditworthy by white owners of properties in an area of Manhattan that was in great demand. This position would have been unimaginable decades earlier.[49]

The African Americans' efforts to remain in Harlem in 1904 represented a unique phenomenon for several reasons. While African Americans had been living in Harlem since its settlement in the 1600s, and moving there in increasing numbers after 1880, the efforts in 1904 represented an organized initiative to remain in, and continue moving to, a community that was not marginal but was being developed. The closest earlier examples in New York would be the movement to Seneca Village in Manhattan or to Weeksville in Brooklyn. Both were nineteenth-century villages rather than urban areas, but both also had high levels of black property ownership. Before Harlem, African Americans in New York City had been consigned primarily to areas that were on the way down. From Five Points, to Greenwich Village, to midtown, blacks had entered each neighborhood in the nineteenth century when that neighborhood was declining, seemingly confirming the theory that the black presence led to depressed real estate values. While some African American churches and a handful of individuals owned properties in each of these areas, they did not have to overcome resistance to their entrance to these neighborhoods. By the time these areas were made available to them, previous owners were glad to find renters or buyers for their declining properties. Ironically African Americans, desperate for housing, were charged a premium for these properties in comparison to rental rates charged to recent white occupants.[50]

The entry of African Americans into East Harlem in the 1880s could be seen as the beginning of the exception in black settlement in Manhattan, since East Harlem was then being developed. The existing black population there was small and therefore went unnoticed. The movement of blacks into the Central Harlem area of West 135th Street in the 1890s involved renters, not owners. Without the arrival of the subway, the African American presence in the area may not have been an issue even in 1904. The white property owners would have been satisfied to continue collecting their premium rents from black tenants. However, the arrival of the subway created the potential for the investors to extract dramatically more income from the properties, and transformed the desirable black renters into undesirable troublemakers who needed to be evicted. The fact that when their presence became an issue, blacks organized to acquire property for substantial sums was unique.

The removal effort on West 135th Street highlighted the differences between large and small white property owners. If Rev. Norman Epps's assessment was accurate—that the primary impetus for African American eviction was the increased value of the property—such value would be much more difficult for small property owners to exploit without selling outright to those with more capital, who could redevelop the properties. After the opening of the subway stop at Lenox Avenue and 135th Street, small property owners in the area could have increased their rental revenue by increasing rents on the properties, but there was a limit to what tenants, black or white, would pay for a tenement apartment, as the frequent annual moves of renters demonstrated. The greatest future value of the 135th Street properties would have been realized through the acquisition of the land on which the many small tenement apartment buildings and row houses stood, demolition of these buildings, and construction of buildings that could command higher rents because of their larger sizes, better designs, and more dense development. Such ambitious plans would have required access to substantial amounts of capital, unavailable to a stable owner such as Charles Kroehle, who in the face of the eviction movement sold the Thomases 30 and 32 West 135th Street, or metalworker Louis Partzschefeld, who leased 46 West 135th Street to Mercy Seat Baptist, or builder August Ruff and his wife, Mina, who sold land at 45–47 West 134th as a future site of Mercy Seat's church. The *Times* articles criticizing the Afro-American Realty Company's aims reflected national racial mores, but the purchase of Harlem properties by blacks indicated that there were other whites who viewed black businessmen as permanent fixtures in Harlem.[51]

In *Black Manhattan*, James Weldon Johnson, whose future brother-in-law John E. Nail worked for Philip Payton's Afro-American Realty Company before starting his own company, suggested that the Hudson Realty Company was the company that sought to expel African Americans from Harlem in the 1904 effort by buying the properties in which they lived. Hudson Realty was formed in 1893. Its directors included members of New York's elite such as Maximilian Morgenthau, brother of banker and diplomat Henry Morgenthau (who was an initial director), and Joseph Bloomingdale of the department store family. In comparison to small property owners, white or black, this company had access to the capital that could remake the 135th Street corridor after the removal of the black tenants. An indication of this access is the fact that in 1902 the directors of the Hudson Realty Company agreed to increase the company's capital stock from $100,000 (in $100 shares) to $1,000,000. At the same meeting at which this decision was made, the directors also voted to expand the company's purpose beyond the sale and leasing of property to include the sale of stocks, bonds, and securities, the making of mortgages, and the issuing of bonds. The fact that the renovation or construction of properties was not included in the list of expanded activities could indicate that Hudson would assemble properties for clients rather than develop properties itself.[52]

On April 5, 1904, approximately one month before the eviction effort, the Hudson Realty Company purchased seventeen vacant lots on the north side of 135th Street for $100 and assumed mortgages totaling $296,500 on the properties. Four of these lots had frontage on Lenox Avenue, and the remainder were on the north side of 135th Street. Hudson Realty also purchased six lots on the south side of 136th Street as part of this transaction. And on April 23 the company purchased three buildings, at 40, 42, and 44 West 135th Street, just to the east of 46 West 135th Street (which was eventually leased by Mercy Seat Baptist Church in May 1904).[53]

In 1900, the three buildings were occupied by African American tenants.[54] It is likely that Hudson Realty's purchase of these 135th Street buildings was followed a week later by eviction notices for residents, just in time for the May 1 Moving Day. (James and Ella Thomas's purchase of 30 and 32 West 135th Street may have been accompanied by similar eviction notices for white tenants). It is also possible that Hudson was the firm that offered to purchase Philip Payton's newly acquired buildings at 30 and 32 West 135th Street. The Afro-American Realty Company's investment pamphlet noted: "When those who had it in their minds to change the tenancy of this street found themselves circumvented by this co-partnership, known as the Afro-American Realty Company, they lost no time in putting themselves in communication with this company and made them an offer of a tempting profit, which was declined."[55]

Perhaps small property owners such as Louis Partzschefeld, August and Mena Ruff, or Charles and Katie E. Kroehle did not see a benefit to joining forces with the Hudson Realty Company (or were not provided with the opportunity to do so). These property owners might not have believed that the Hudson Realty Company would reward them any better than anxious African Americans would in a sale of their properties. Harlem's large and small property owners had very different interests, which can be seen in these different responses to the presence of blacks in the 135th Street settlement following the construction of the subway.

As the congratulatory note from the office of Booker T. Washington to Philip Payton suggested, the efforts of Payton, the Thomases, and other African Americans to gain control of 135th Street properties were viewed by Washington's followers as litmus tests of the ability of black business leaders to use economic power to secure their rights, not just in New York but across the nation. The Hudson Realty Company conceded defeat in stages: in November 1904 the company sold twelve lots on 136th Street; in February 1905 it sold 40, 42, and 44 West 135th Street; a month later, in March, it sold two lots—at the northeast corner of Lenox and West 136th Street and on Lenox Avenue between 136th and 135th Streets; finally on November 1, 1906, the company sold the remaining seventeen parcels it owned on 135th Street. Each transaction was executed with a different group of white purchasers, making it less likely that Hudson's attempt to assemble the large tract of properties on West 135th Street could be revisited by these new owners. With several unrelated new owners of the properties, a future developer would have to be very determined and patient to try to reassemble the large tract of property that Hudson Realty had relinquished.[56]

The success of black property owners in acquiring control of properties in the 135th Street area could not have occurred without the cooperation of white property owners and lenders. The white property owners had alternatives. They could have sold to white investors such as the Hudson Realty Company. The fact that all of the transactions to African Americans were not quick, with some involving initial modest cash payments and then multi-year payments, suggests complex relationships across the lines of race and ethnicity. By 1904, southern segregation laws and racial violence were popularizing notions of black pathology and inferiority, and some of these ideas were being adopted in northern cities in response to the growing numbers of African Americans. Hostile statements and actions against African Americans became increasingly visible. What was less visible, and perhaps often unspoken, was the fact that some white residents did not view the black community as monolithic, and indeed it was not. In the area of business, while some white businessmen were limiting African American access to Harlem properties, others chose to enter into real estate transactions with African Americans at a time when they could easily have dealt with white investors instead. Perhaps the white small business owners identified with African Americans such as undertaker James C. Thomas and real estate broker Philip Payton, whose economic status was comparable to that of the white property owners. It is also possible that ethnicity played a role: three of the property owners who were associated with pivotal real estate transactions in 1904, Charles Kroehle, Louis Partzschefeld, and August Ruff, and their spouses, were of German descent, either first- or second-generation immigrants. Ethnicity may have led these owners to be more receptive to striving African American buyers than to possible offers from the principals of the Hudson Realty Company, who were established members of New York's business elite. Ethnicity may have been intertwined with social class. Maximilian Morgenthau and Samuel Bloomingdale, two of the principals of Hudson Realty, were of German descent, but their families had been in the United States much longer and therefore had had a greater opportunity to absorb the increasingly hostile views toward African Americans. They were also much more established both financially and socially than the Kroehles, Partzschefelds, or Ruffs.[57]

The 1904 debates in Harlem regarding blacks and real estate also suggest that for some white New Yorkers racial rhetoric became a convenient tool to use against African Americans to justify their evictions from increasingly valuable property. But some blacks also adopted a brand of racial rhetoric, which they used strategically to create an organized movement to increase African American access to Harlem real estate. The prospectus of the Afro-American Realty Company made clear that its goal was to provide opportunities for blacks to live wherever they could afford to live. The prospectus even suggested that racial integration in housing would also be a goal. While the Afro-American Realty Company did not state that Harlem would be its focus, the community was the location of its first purchases of property. The efforts of African Americans in Harlem to secure a place in the community through property ownership in the first decade of the twentieth century were highlighted by the rhetoric that accompanied the formation of the Afro-American Realty Company. With its formation, the black movement to acquire property in Harlem shifted from being simply a reaction to eviction attempts to being an ongoing, organized effort. The change from a community of transient renters to one of owners with a long-term financial stake in the community represented a shift in social class as well. While the "wealthy" porters may have been in the vanguard of black residency in the 135th Street area in the 1890s, the group of black business owners and professionals that sought to ensure a black presence in Harlem in 1904 was near the top of the black economic ladder as it was available to black New Yorkers at that time. Some white property owners would respond to their effort with another strategy to keep African Americans out of Harlem, or at least to contain them in the area of their 1904 victory over eviction.

3
FROM EVICTION TO CONTAINMENT

❖

Through the early 1910s, real estate transactions in Harlem continued to reflect a range of interracial relations. As the first decade of the 1900s proceeded, some Harlem property owners decided that the black "invasion" of Harlem had to be confronted directly. They developed a legal strategy using racial restrictive covenants placed in the deeds of their properties to try to keep African Americans from moving into some areas of Harlem. Harlem's white business class—business owners, lawyers, and other professionals—concluded that the problem was not with the blacks but with whites in Harlem who had not effectively marketed the many desirable aspects of the community to potential white buyers. They developed their own program to market Harlem to whites. And a few white residents did not take the time to analyze the problem, choosing to use violence to attempt to oust African Americans from the community. A unified response to the black invasion continued to elude white Harlem residents because the community was ethnically and religiously diverse and was a mix of old-timers and newcomers. Even the principal resistance leader was a recent arrival.

By 1904, the year of the eviction struggle on West 135th Street, the development of the area west of Lenox Avenue as an exclusive urban residential area was proceeding quickly. Newly developed properties were built to attract middle- and upper-middle-class New Yorkers. A few townhouses and large, elevator apartment buildings were built in the 1880s, but during the 1890s townhouses were being constructed on many of the east-west numbered streets from the low 120s north to the 160s.[1]

Larger apartment buildings, for upper-income residents, distinguished from tenements by their more gracious accoutrements such as elevators, large rooms, and architectural details, were also being built, many as a result of the 1901 Tenement House Law, which created the guidelines followed by builders of new apartments in New York City. The law allowed apartment buildings to be built at heights twice as tall as the width of the streets on which they were located, and also required designs that would provide for sufficient light and air to all rooms in multi-family buildings.[2] In 1904 the completion of the Interborough Rapid Transit (IRT), the first line of the New York City subway system, which in Harlem traveled along Lenox Avenue and had stops approximately every ten blocks, solidified Harlem's position as a residential community. The subway made it possible for people who worked downtown to commute daily to homes in Harlem with a travel time of approximately thirty minutes from Harlem to City Hall in lower Manhattan.[3]

After its 1904 success in acquiring properties in the 135th Street area, the Afro-American Realty Company continued leasing and purchasing property. A construction boom in modest tenement buildings for lower-income people in Manhattan was brought on by surges in European immigration and the improved transportation provided by the new subway line. The result was a "sustained and healthy demand for real estate, both for use and for investment."[4] Real estate investment was seen as a prudent endeavor, not a speculative one. A review of the 1905 real estate market in the *Real Estate Record and Builder's* Guide, a New York City industry weekly, stated that "anybody who considers calmly the existing situation must reach the conclusion that there is no surer way of making money in the world than to purchase improved real estate which carries itself in some central but less expensive district of Manhattan."[5]

In July 1906 the Afro-American Realty Company came to citywide attention again when it entered into a five-year lease for a fifteen-unit apartment building at 525 West 151st Street between Amsterdam and Broadway. The white tenants of the building were told they would need to vacate the premises by August 1 and would be replaced by "colored" tenants. Under the headline "Negro Invasion Threat Angers Flat Dwellers," the *New York Times* reported in great detail the shocked reaction of the janitress, a Mrs. P. M. Roth, who reportedly had refused to install a sign reading "Just Opened for Colored Tenants Five Room and Bath Apartments" on the building. The indignation of other tenants who would be required to move quickly was also reported, as were the comments of adjacent property owners, one of whom suggested, "It's a trick to make us buy them out." The article ended with a quote from Afro-American Realty principal Philip Payton: "What we wish to do is to stop forced colonization. We are in earnest in this proposition. We intend to have negro families in that apartment house. Of course there is a prejudice against them, but there was once similar prejudice against the Jews and the Italians. They overcame it and we should be able to do so."[6]

Payton referred to New York's residential racial segregation tradition as "colonization" because the areas where African Americans were concentrated were often called "Negro colonies." While Payton's proposed strategy challenged residential segregation by attempting to move blacks into a building on an exclusively white street, there were limits to his mission to "stop forced colonization." He did not attempt to attract African American *and* white residents to the same building. In evicting the white residents of the building he leased, and identifying the building as one reserved for "colored" residents, he was conceding that an apartment building with residents of both races was not his goal. Although, as noted in chapter 2, West 135th Street had a few buildings with residents of both races, this pattern was not common in New York City. Mixed-race buildings were often seen as symbols of poverty, where the limited choices of the residents, both black and white, led them to overlook the social customs of racial segregation that the broader community maintained. The fact that Payton's purchase was the subject of a newspaper article suggests that the white residents of West 151st Street had no intention of leaving without a fight. In presenting the plight of the white tenants facing eviction, whether at the instigation of the residents or the *Times*, support for the white tenants could be rallied.[7]

Philip Payton did not have an opportunity to challenge the racial divide on 151st Street. In September 1906, the lease that he had entered into two months earlier for 525 West 151st was canceled. The lease had contained a clause allowing for such an outcome if a sale occurred. Before any black tenants recruited by Payton had moved in, the building was purchased by Loton Horton, the owner of Sheffield Farms Dairy. In addition to making a payment of $100, Horton assumed the payments on three mortgages on the property, which totaled $50,000. Although the transaction did not allow Payton to provide housing for African Americans on West 151st Street, he did benefit from the sale. According to the terms of the lease, he received a $1,000 payment due to the cancellation of the lease.[8]

It is quite possible that Horton's purchase was a response to the publicity that Payton's actions prompted and that Horton served both literally and figuratively as a "white knight" to retrieve the building from Payton's "clutches." This scenario would seem to corroborate the suspicion of the adjacent property owner quoted in the *Times* article. Considering the substantial fee that Payton received, the equivalent of $19,500 in 2012 dollars, his role in the transaction was more complex than that of race champion.[9] The owner of the property with which Payton negotiated the initial lease was Louis Meyer Realty Co. This company had purchased the property in May 1906, only two months before Payton leased the property. It is possible that Louis Meyer Realty Co. did want to facilitate the sale of 525 West 151st Street and saw the agreement with Payton as a likely means to bring about this result as neighbors scrambled to keep blacks off the block. Unlike the 135th Street building owners in 1904 who provided financing for blacks to purchase their buildings, Louis Meyer Realty did not provide Payton with financing to purchase the building. Payton's options for obtaining institutional financing would have been limited. Bank or insurance company financing of tenement buildings was not common, since the buildings were viewed as risky. In addition, there would have been great reluctance to facilitate black ownership, since even without Payton's prior publicity, it would have been assumed that his tenants would be black. Instead, Louis Meyer Realty offered Payton a lease. For Payton, the lease was a "win-win" agreement. If the building had not been sold during the five-year lease term, but rented by him to African Americans, it would have been another victory for the Afro-American Realty Company. Although this goal was not accomplished, the $1,000 fee he received was a significant amount of capital. But Payton's gain did have a cost in increased hostility toward blacks. The evictions of the white tenants from the building and Payton's pronouncements regarding his interest in bringing in black tenants raised sufficient concern that a *Times* reporter was assigned to the story, which could be viewed as a warning to readers. Payton's decision to ignore the mission of the Afro-American Realty Company, as stated in its 1904 prospectus, that "the idea that it is not practical to put colored and white tenants together in the same house can be done away with" was a missed opportunity to model integrated residential living in Harlem.[10] In this context the cost of Payton's gain was an increased concern regarding a black "invasion" in Harlem. Since in this scenario black entrance meant white exit, Payton's actions encouraged a more vigilant defense by whites in Harlem as well as a long-term white backlash toward blacks and the view of future black entrants to Harlem as not only undesirable neighbors but as the likely cause of the ouster of some white residents.[11]

The renting of properties to African Americans continued to be a concern in Harlem. Four months after Payton's 151st Street agreement ended, the January 26, 1907, issue of the weekly *Real Estate Record and Builders' Guide*, a local industry magazine, included an example of increased concern about the black presence. The advice column of the magazine ran a letter asking whether a lender making a loan for a property that eventually was leased to someone who planned to rent to "colored tenants" could do anything to "make his mortgage more secure" since the property was vacant (as the lessee continued to seek these tenants), but the borrower was paying the taxes and interest on the loan when due. Implicit in the letter writer's question was a desire to prevent blacks from renting the property, since the lender viewed that as a threat to the property's value. The magazine columnist explained that "the renting of the mortgaged premises to colored tenants is no ground for interference by a mortgage holder." While the question was couched in financial terms, the concern was both financial and racial. Since black tenants typically paid higher rents than whites, the plan to lease to blacks would have increased the possibility that the lender would be able to be paid from the higher rent revenue that the building would produce. The lender's financial concerns stemmed from a belief that black tenants lowered property values because they supposedly brought with them social problems. In spite of the higher rents that black tenants paid, real estate appraisers would consider the income of a building as well as values of nearby properties. If enough people believed a property was worth less, it would be worth less regardless of whether it generated higher rent revenue than it could with white tenants. An appraiser would consider these factors and possibly lower the valuation of the building. Therefore the lender's concern that the value of the property might decrease with black tenants did have merit.[12]

Ironically, in the same issue of the *Record and Guide*, the person who had become a symbol of the tactic mentioned by the letter writer, Philip Payton, had a half-page advertisement with his photograph under the heading "Colored Tenements Wanted." In the advertisement he claimed, "I can manage a 'Colored Tenement' better than any White agent in New York City." Clearly Payton had abandoned the call for integrated housing announced in his 1904 Afro-American Realty prospectus. His 1907 advertisement acknowledged that there were white real estate agents who specialized in managing black buildings, but stated that he could do it better. His photograph alluded to the competitive advantage that he implied, that being a black person, he would be able to out-manage the competition. He was clearly African American, just like the tenants whom he sought to rent to, but his conservative suit and tie and his wire-rimmed glasses conveyed an air of austerity and professionalism that was a fairly rare media image for African Americans in 1907.[13]

Soon afterward, the concern expressed by the *Record and Guide* letter writer and the heightened white hostility to black entry evolved into an organized movement to use the law to resist the "Negro invasion" in Harlem. The movement began in the 100 block of West 137th between Lenox and Seventh Avenues, two blocks north and one block east of the West 135th Street block that had been the site of the 1904 effort to evict African Americans (fig. 3.1). The 100 block of West 137th Street shared a characteristic with West 135th Street in that in 1907 it was only partially developed.

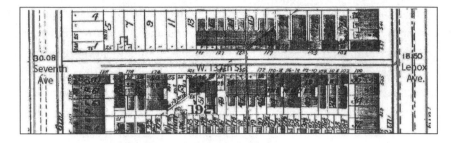

FIGURE 3.1. West 137th Street between Seventh Avenue and Lenox Avenue. G. W. Bromley & Co., Manhattan, Section 6.

On the north side of the block, sixteen of the twenty-three lots facing the street were vacant, and on the south side fifteen of the twenty-one lots facing the street were vacant. The buildings on the south side of the street were large apartment buildings and those on the north side were smaller apartment buildings. Most of the residents of the block were native New Yorkers, but a significant number were born in Ireland and Germany. A smaller number was born in Sweden, Scotland, or other parts of the United States. Many of those born in New York had parents born in Germany, Ireland, and Scotland. A few of the households included servants.[14]

The occupations of the household heads on West 137th Street were much more diverse than those of the black or white residents of West 135th Street. Several residents of West 137th Street were stenographers. One resident was a civil engineer, one was a tailor, and another was a merchant, but there were others who were janitors and servants. As suggested by their occupations, the residents of this block were of a higher social class than their neighbors on 135th Street. The racial composition was different as well. Whereas the 135th Street block had African American and white residents, there were only two African Americans residing on the 100 block of West 137th, and they were servants in two households.[15]

On February 13, 1907, twenty-three owners of properties on the 100 block of West 137th Street entered into an agreement that they hoped would protect their block from the presence of African Americans for the foreseeable future. The agreement stated that up to and including January 1, 1917, they would not

permit . . . the said premises to be used or occupied in whole or in part by any negro, mulatto, quadroon or octoroon of either sex whatsoever . . . this covenant or restriction may be proceeded on for an injunction and for damages against the party. . . . It is expressly understood and agreed that this covenant or restriction shall attach to and run with the land belonging to the respective parties herewith.[16]

At the beginning of the agreement, following the list of the owners' names and addresses, was a justification for the document: "The white tenants in the property known and described as 106 and 108 West one hundred and thirty-seventh Street . . . were dispossessed and the said premises leased and rented to tenants of the negro race . . . for the purpose of compelling adjoining and neighboring owners to purchase the same property to protect their holdings."[17]

The inspiration for the covenant was the successful rental of two buildings on the block to black tenants following the eviction of the white tenants. The authors of the covenant assumed that the move-in of blacks was a ploy to push the remaining white residents on the block to purchase the black-occupied buildings in order to oust the black tenants and thus maintain the value of their properties (as the 151st Street residents had suspected of Philip Payton's actions). There is no record of the leases for 106 and 108 West 137th Street, but in the two years before the covenant was executed, the properties changed hands four times. They were sold by Daniel Mahoney to Wolf Bomzon in May 1905 for $100 and an assumption of mortgages totaling $40,000. Fifteen months later the properties changed hands twice in the same day in transactions that belied the claim that property values were endangered by the possibility of a black presence in Harlem. First on October 17, 1906, Bomzon sold the properties to Montgomery Rosenberg for $100 and the assumption of mortgages of $53,500, an increase of $13,500 in less than two years. Later on the same day, Rosenberg sold both properties to Hannah Theobold for $100 and the assumption of mortgages of $60,000. While it was not a cash transaction, Rosenberg was able to identify a borrower willing to pay $6,500 more for property than what he had paid only hours earlier. It is likely that Theobold, who appears to have been a real estate investor, precipitated the February 1907 covenant by evicting the white tenants of 106 and 108 West 137th to bring in black tenants, in order to charge higher rents to better meet her loan payments. But Theobold, similar to Philip Payton on West 151st Street, did not have an opportunity to fully realize her plan. On January 31, 1907, she sold the properties, three months after purchasing them. Jacob Blauner purchased 106 and assumed mortgages of $30,000. Rosa Newman purchased 108 and also assumed mortgages of $30,000. Two weeks later, on February 13, the West 137th covenant was filed, signed by both Blauner and Newman, suggesting that by that time their properties no longer had black tenants. Residents of West 137th Street wanted to ensure that there would be no repeat of Theobold's actions.[18]

The scenario surrounding these properties as described in the restrictive covenant and reflected in the series of transactions is quite similar to the circumstances that residents of West 151st Street faced after the Afro-American Realty Company leased the apartment building at 525 West 151st: white tenants had been evicted by a person intent on renting to blacks. On West 137th Street, the abrupt eviction of white tenants by Hannah Theobold, who replaced them with black tenants, was viewed with fear by the remaining white residents on the block, particularly the owners of properties. The community pressure was sufficient that Theobold decided to sell the buildings at cost three months after purchasing them. The covenant signed by the property owners on West 137th Street indicated that the entry of African Americans to the block "caused or induced many of the white tenants to move and required a substantial reduction in rents to those who remained and prevented the reletting of vacant and unoccupied flats . . . except at rentals much lower than those formerly prevailing."[19]

The text of the covenant may be an exaggeration, but in the environment of fear whipped up by those predicting calamity upon the arrival of black residents to a block, it is possible that the activity described in the covenant took place within a three-month period. The property-owning residents of 137th Street were not afraid of being evicted, but they were concerned about the decline in the value of their properties. Adopting the same perspective as the property owners on West 151st Street had in 1906, the white property owners viewed black tenants on West 137th Street as being part of a larger conspiracy to induce whites to purchase the newly occupied buildings (implying that the black tenants would be removed if the buildings were purchased) to protect the values of their own properties. Although the restrictive covenant suggested that white tenants had moved from the block as a result of the African American presence, the document does not suggest that the conspiracy sought to induce the remaining property owners to sell their own properties, or that the intent of the "conspirators" was for blacks to control the block. White Harlem residents on 137th Street viewed the entry of blacks onto the block as a ploy to push whites into buying the black-occupied properties. There was no reference point in their experiences that would have led them to view the tenanting of two buildings by blacks as the vanguard of a broader settlement movement. The West 137th Street restrictive covenant was meant to maintain the stability of real estate values, and the white property owners believed that racial segregation was necessary in order to achieve that goal.

The white property owners seemed to have been certain that the aim of the parties behind the black tenants was to force a purchase of the buildings with black tenants. Although the *New York Times* had suggested in 1904 that black movement into white neighborhoods was motivated by a desire to drive down prices to facilitate more black purchases, the residents of 137th Street did not envision that such a goal that would result in their selling their homes, which were less than twenty years old. For them the logical purpose of the black presence on their block could only have been to push whites to *buy* the properties occupied by blacks in order to evict them. White residents of 137th Street were seeking a more enduring solution to the Negro problem through the restrictive covenant.[20]

The restrictive covenant signed by the residents of West 137th Street had its roots in British law. By the eighteenth century the covenants were used in England to set aside private parks for exclusive use. In the early nineteenth century the covenants also began to be employed to prevent landowners from undertaking uses that could hurt their neighbors. Covenants typically

restricted the development of slaughterhouses, tanneries, and soap factories, industries notorious for their noxious fumes and waste. Restrictive
covenants began to be used with some frequency in the United States in the
nineteenth century also in connection with park development and the building of residential subdivisions. Covenants eventually dealt not only with land
use, lot size, property setbacks, and building construction types, but also
with race and ethnicity. The deeds of the Brookline, Massachusetts, Linden
Place subdivision from 1843 stated that the residences could not be sold to
"any Negro or native of Ireland." In the late nineteenth century and early
twentieth century the covenants were widely used in developments for the
wealthy. The enforcement of long-term covenants became the province of
homeowners' associations.[21]

The 137th Street covenant was not perpetual but was designed to have a
ten-year term. Its signers viewed it as a measure that would remain in place
until the crisis—the entry of blacks onto West 137th Street and the anticipated decline in property values—subsided. The agreement noted:

> There is no desire to preclude or prevent negroes or citizens of African de-
> scent, solely because of their race and color from occupying any of the proper-
> ties owned by the parties hereto . . . the sole desire purpose and object of the
> parties hereto being to secure a resumption and continuance of the rentals
> obtained prior to the introduction of negro tenants into 106 and 108 West One
> Hundred and thirty-seventh street.[22]

The contradictory statement in the covenant suggesting that there was no
desire to exclude "citizens of African descent" was included with an eye on
potential legal challenges. There was also an assumption that a black owner
would eventually seek black tenants, so the covenants precluded purchase of
buildings by blacks as well. Concern regarding the growing African American presence in this section of Harlem continued and on May 28, 1907, seventeen residents of the 200 block of West 140th Street, between Seventh and
Eighth Avenues, executed a restrictive covenant for their block. The instrument differed from the 137th Street covenant. Instead of a lengthy preamble
outlining the parties' names and their reasons for coming together to execute
the covenant, the document quickly noted that the properties owned by the

signers would "not be used as a colored or negro tenement leased to colored or a negro tenant or tenants sold to colored or negro tenant or tenants." There was also no end date for the agreement, suggesting that the agreement would be in place in perpetuity. The agreement prohibited the occupancy, lease, or sale of properties to blacks. More densely developed than West 137th Street, West 140th Street was a block of large apartment buildings.[23]

The collective nature of the covenants, involving substantial numbers of property-owning neighbors, suggests a motivated individual or organization, capable of alerting residents of the common threat and convincing them to take legal action. As other covenants were executed in the neighborhood, John G. Taylor, the white police officer who had moved to Harlem from Greenwich Village in 1903, played a pivotal role in organizing the resistance to the black presence in Harlem.[24] Taylor had retired from the police force in November 1906 at the age of fifty-eight, after thirty years of service, having risen to the rank of paymaster. As a leader of the Property Owners' Protective Association of Harlem for the next several years, he would be a key figure in the effort to limit the movement of blacks into Harlem.[25]

The Property Owners' Protective Association had begun in 1900 with an initial goal to "do away with some of the evils which have made Harlem real estate less remunerative than it ought to be." Its initial focus had not been on the racial mix of Harlem's residents. At the time of the association's formation, owners of new Harlem apartment buildings, competing for tenants, had developed a practice of offering several months of free rent as an enticement to prospective tenants. The Protective Association argued that the practice had led to an expectation of free rent periods from tenants and had reduced the revenue that all property owners were receiving. Its initial activities focused on persuading property owners to forgo free-rent arrangements and set rents at competitive levels. By 1910 the focus of the organization had shifted to Harlem's Negro problem. In December 1910, John G. Taylor, then vice president of the association, announced that he had raised $20,000 (most likely in pledges) by canvassing property owners on two blocks of West 136th Street between Eighth and Lenox Avenues. He indicated that the funds would be used for a campaign "to keep the negroes of 'Little Africa' just east of Lenox Avenue from further encroaching upon the street." Specifically the funds would be used to buy mortgages of properties occupied by blacks and to obtain evidence against owners who the association believed were using the tenancy of blacks to induce owners of adjacent properties to buy the buildings occupied by blacks at an "enhanced price."[26]

Taylor had previously claimed to the local police that a house at 121 West 136th Street owned by Edna C. F. Minott, "a negress," was occupied by "disorderly persons." When the police informed him that no action could be taken, the fund-raising campaign was mounted. But Taylor did not give up on his previous strategy either, advising those with complaints concerning disorder in the neighborhood to take their complaints directly to police "headquarters instead of the West 125th Street station." As a retired policeman, Taylor perhaps had more influence at headquarters than at the local precinct, since he was relatively new to the neighborhood. It is also possible that the local precinct would be more likely than headquarters to be aware that the disorderly claims could not be substantiated since they disguised the real complaint regarding the black presence on some blocks in Harlem.[27]

As suggested by the Protective Association's shift in purpose, and growing concern, the black presence in Harlem had increased dramatically by 1910 (table 3.1). In 1900, 20 percent of Manhattan's African American population lived in the area above 86th Street on the east and west sides of Manhattan covered then by four assembly districts. By 1910 almost 50 percent of Manhattan's African American community resided in eight assembly districts covering a comparable area. The shift in the black residential concentration away from midtown also reflected this change. In 1900 more than 48 percent of Manhattan's African American population lived in five midtown assembly districts. By 1910, 32 percent lived in five midtown districts covering a comparable area.[28] Behind these numbers was the dramatic growth through migration in the absolute number of blacks in Manhattan from 36,000 in 1900 to 60,000 in 1910. While some of the Harlem numbers represented movement from midtown, a substantial portion were immigrants coming directly from the South or the Caribbean. The restrictive covenant movement was a response to these demographic changes, and it continued to grow as the African American presence in Harlem increased.

TABLE 3.1 Distribution of African American Population in Manhattan, 1910*

Assembly Districts	Total Assembly District population	Negro population In the Assembly District	Negro population as a % of total Assembly District population	Assembly District Negro Population as a % of total citywide Negro pop	Colored, Non-Negro population
1: clarkson, west 3rd, Broadway	75,878	529	0.70%	0.87%	59
2: Williams, Park row, Henry St.	91,509	65	0.07%	0.11%	107
3: Worth, Bway, 14th, 2nd Ave.	88,002	85	0.10%	0.14%	2,353
4: Stanton, Clinton, E. River	99,721	31	0.03%	0.05%	13
5: 8th ave, Clarkson, 18th, Hudson River	57,341	1,066	1.86%	1.76%	46
6: Ave. B, Stanton, 10th, E. River	99,223	28	0.03%	0.05%	18
7: 7th ave., 18th, 30th, Hudson River	52,483	1,850	3.52%	3.06%	63
8: Stanton, Christie, Clinton, Henry	109,107	28	0.03%	0.05%	22
9: 7th Ave, 31st, 43rd, Hudson river	54,496	5,361	9.84%	8.86%	62
10: 2nd Ave, 14th, Ave. B, Stanton	100,929	27	0.03%	0.04%	35
11: 8th Ave, 43rd, 52nd, Hudson river	52,833	1,269	2.40%	2.10%	32
12: 14th St, 3rd Ave., 23rd St.	78,010	91	0.12%	0.15%	51
13: Hudson Rvr, 52nd, 67th, Columbus Ave	52,290	9,273	17.73%	15.32%	65
14: 23rd, Lexington Ave., 42nd, E. River	63,879	86	0.13%	0.14%	100
15: Hudson Rvr, 67th, 91st, CP West	72,031	1,865	2.59%	3.08%	152
16: 42nd, Lex, 56th, E. River	61,415	693	1.13%	1.14%	62
17: Hudson Rvr, 91st, 106th, CP West	63,348	3,074	4.85%	5.08%	81

TABLE 3.1 (*continued*)

Assembly Districts	Total Assembly District population	Negro population In the Assembly District	Negro population as a % of total Assembly District population	Assembly District Negro Population as a % of total citywide Negro pop	Colored, Non-Negro population
18: 56th, 3rd Ave., 73rd, E. River	74,594	38	0.05%	0.06%	51
19: 101st, 7th Ave, 133rd, Hudson River	82,407	1,690	2.05%	2.79%	149
20: 74th, 3rd Ave, 82nd, E. River	65,821	723	1.10%	1.19%	31
21: Hudson Rvr, 127th, 141st, 5th Ave.	73,446	10,912	14.86%	18.03%	82
22: 82nd, Lex, 93rd, E. River	54,135	181	0.33%	0.30%	24
23: 141st, Lenox, Harlem River	119,799	2,092	1.75%	3.46%	130
24: 92nd, 3rd Ave, 106th, E. River	85,109	2,051	2.41%	3.39%	33
25: West 3rd, 7th, 30th, 3rd Ave.	54,282	1,407	2.59%	2.32%	137
26: 96th, 5th, 120th, Park Ave.	82,542	893	1.08%	1.48%	33
27: 30th, 8th, 57th, Lex	55,203	3,548	6.43%	5.86%	154
28: 106th, Park Ave, 116th, E. River & Randalls Island	89,802	283	0.32%	0.47%	46
29: 57th, CP West, 110th, Lex Ave	65,300	1,951	2.99%	3.22%	122
30: 117th, Madison, E. River	92,275	7,556	8.19%	12.48%	13
31: 110th, St. Nicholas, 127th, Fifth Ave	64,327	1,779	2.77%	2.94%	39
Totals	2,331,537	60,525			4,365

*Compiled from the Thirteenth Census of the United States, 1910, Bulletin, Population: "Composition and Characteristics of the Population", New York, pp. 43–45; Manhattan Assembly District Map, 1914

On June 10, 1910, three years after the West 140th Street agreement was executed, another covenant was executed by ninety-one owners of property on the adjacent 100 and 200 blocks of West 136th Street (fig. 3.2). This agreement included John G. Taylor's home at 213 West 136th Street, between Seventh and Eighth Avenues. This street differed from 135th, 137th, and 140th Streets, the areas of the earlier covenants, both in housing stock and in the characteristics of its residents. The blocks were almost entirely lined with brownstones, a housing form more likely to be occupied by homeowners in 1910. Seventy percent of the signers of the 136th Street covenant were owners who lived on the block. On 135th Street participation in the covenant by owners who lived on the block was 27 percent. Because the 137th and 140th Street covenants did not include the home addresses of the signers, a similar comparison cannot be made definitively, although on both streets apartment buildings were more prevalent, in which the owners were less likely to live.[29]

The language of the June 10, 1910, covenant for West 136th Street was similar to that of the initial West 137th Street covenant. The document noted that "various parties have been purchasing different parcels of property in and about 137th Street, West" with the purpose of renting the properties to African Americans in order to compel the adjacent white property owners to purchase the properties. The same explanation and profession of no desire to restrict African Americans' housing choices was provided. The agreement was for a ten-year term. John G. Taylor's name was noted as the witness to the signatures of all of the property owners, which included his wife, Agnes, at 213 West 136th Street.[30]

Other covenants were made in the following months and years: in December 1910, thirteen property owners in the 200 block of West 135th (between Seventh and Eighth Avenues) signed a covenant; on February 4, 1911, forty-two owners on the 200 block of West 132nd Street (between Seventh and Eighth Avenues) signed a covenant; in December 1911, sixty-six owners of properties in the 100 blocks of West 129th, West 130th, and West 131st Streets (between Seventh and Lenox Avenues) signed covenants. These three covenants all included the same language as the 136th Street covenant, and John G. Taylor served as witness of the signatures on two of the three documents.[31]

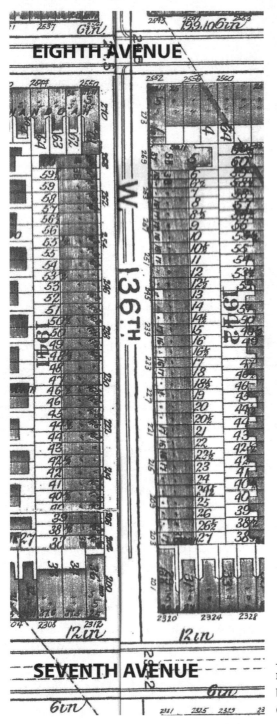

FIGURE 3.2. Map 5. 200 block of West 136th Street. G. W. Bromley & Co., Section 6.

The year 1913 proved to be a pivotal year in the effort to restrict black movement into Harlem. In March the Harlem Board of Commerce held a "conciliation meeting" and invited African American broker John Nail to speak to a group of two hundred members regarding relations between white Harlem property owners and black property owners. Formed in 1896, the Board of Commerce represented the owners of large and medium-sized businesses as well as lawyers and other professionals. The meeting was led by the board's chairman, Erduin v. d. H. Koch, owner of Koch Department Store (having inherited it from his father) on 125th Street, who stated: "The negroes have a right to live and the privilege of going on Fifth Avenue or Riverside Drive if they can pay for it. Many obnoxious things have arisen from antagonisms stirred up between the two races."[32]

This statement is remarkable since in 1913, in Harlem and other parts of the country, even many of those who favored fair treatment of blacks set clear limits, usually suggesting that African Americans should be satisfied with obtaining good housing in black neighborhoods. In going well beyond this position, perhaps Koch was concerned that racial antagonisms could lead to individual acts of violence or race riots such as had occurred in New York in 1900, Atlanta in 1906, or Springfield, Illinois, in 1908. In these confrontations lives were lost, property was damaged, and the business climate of the communities suffered. As the leader of the organization formally representing Harlem's business class, Koch may have reached his perspective by considering the manner in which racial tensions affected the economic life of a community. It also is possible that Koch held a more radical vision for race relations. Like Charles Kroehle, Louis Partzschefeld, and August Ruff, who assisted black buyers of Harlem properties in 1904, Koch was of German descent. His father, Henry C. F. Koch, founder of the family dry goods store, was born in Germany. While Erduin Koch did not assist blacks in purchasing property, his statement to the Board of Commerce is the most direct expression of the beliefs of this group of people of German descent regarding interracial relations. His statement supported the point made ten years earlier, that blacks should be able to live anywhere they could afford.[33]

At the 1913 Board of Commerce meeting, John Nail provided a snapshot of the state of blacks in Harlem as well as the challenges they were already

FIGURE 3.3. Harlem blocks with racial restrictive covenants, 1907–1911.
Automobile Club of Rochester, 1920, Florida Center for Instructional Technology.

facing in seeking housing that was of better quality than in previous enclaves.
A year before the Great Migration of blacks leaving the South for the North
would begin, unable to foresee this massive movement, Nail indicated that
blacks had sufficient property to sustain growth in the community over the
coming five years. He noted that they had vacancy rates of approximately
30 percent in their buildings. Nail added that blacks owned approximately
5 percent of the properties in the area where they resided, and asked that
white absentee owners in this area maintain their properties in good con-

dition. An African American minister who was present complained about the bars that white people were establishing in the area. Nail and the minister were both concerned that the black settlement in Harlem, which had seemed so attractive because of the better quality of housing, not become a repeat of previous deteriorated black settlements in Manhattan. It is likely that the minister was Rev. Hutchens C. Bishop, pastor of St. Philip's Episcopal Church. Two years earlier Nail and his business partner, Henry C. Parker, had facilitated the purchase of a row of ten apartment buildings on West 135th Street between Lenox and Seventh Avenues by St. Philip's Church. The purchase, linked with the sale of St. Philip's downtown rental properties, was touted in the African American press as the largest real estate transaction by African Americans. As Harlem's black settlement had grown, white residents had established Lenox Avenue as the "deadline" west of which no blacks would be allowed to settle. Located west of Lenox Avenue, the St. Philip's purchase broke through that traditional western boundary for African Americans in a dramatic manner because of its scale. The white residents of the apartment buildings were evicted and the properties were rented to African Americans.[34]

John G. Taylor, who as the principal organizer of many of the restrictive covenants in Harlem was a purveyor of some of the "antagonisms" toward blacks criticized by Erduin v. d. H. Koch, attempted to join the Board of Commerce meeting but was barred. He does not appear to have been a member of the group, but his message seems to have been one that Board of Commerce members had determined would not contribute to a productive meeting. When later asked about the meeting by a newspaper reporter, Taylor suggested that Nail's statement regarding the unlikely possibility of black territorial expansion was not sincere and that it was made to provide those present with a false sense of security. Since Nail had no way of predicting the Great Migration that, along with World War I, would soon bring even more blacks to New York, his projections to the Board of Commerce were realistic, given the information that was available to him. Even so, his presentation to the Board of Commerce of the movement of blacks as a benign activity did not convey his interest in expanding black ownership in Harlem. He had facilitated the St. Philip's apartment purchases that were followed by the eviction of the white tenants. Nail's ability to move into Harlem so aggressively, perhaps not known by the Board of Commerce members, would have rankled those attending the conciliation meeting. Taylor also criticized the Board of Commerce, claiming that the board's conciliatory measures were motivated by a desire to "control the negro vote," a point denied by Board of Commerce leaders. The numbers of blacks moving to Harlem, as potential voters, were large enough for them to become a part of the political calculations of local elected officials, but there is no evidence that this influenced the Board of Commerce members.[35]

While Harlem's white businessmen were attempting conciliation, Harlem's youth had a more direct approach. In a March 20 front page article under the headline "Gangs of White and Negro Boys Hold Stone Battles Almost Daily," the *Harlem Home News* noted that the Madison Avenue bridge at 135th Street crossing the East River to the borough of the Bronx had become such a daily battleground that police would soon have to be posted at all of the bridges leading from Harlem to the Bronx. The article claimed that the battles were started by African American youths from the "Black Belt" of Harlem defending territory against white youths from the Bronx. In addition to the youths, the report suggested, on Sundays the Madison Avenue bridge was dominated by African American loiterers who made it very uncomfortable for others to pass. This report fit the notion that black residents would bring disarray to the community, and echoed complaints at public meetings about the Negro problem. The probability that the estimates of the numbers of black youths were exaggerated is quite high because of the perception among some whites that Harlem was being invaded by blacks.[36]

Adults were also involved in violent acts. In July 1913 *New York Age* described a "race riot" that it indicated had occurred in the area of Lenox Avenue and 142nd Street, a block on which racial tensions between white and African American residents had reportedly been festering. No explanation was provided for the source of the tension, implying that the mere presence of the two races in constant, close proximity was enough to lead to unrest. The details of the riot were also not reported, but one arrest was made. Walter Brown, an African American, was charged with assault for firing two pistols during the altercation. The focus of the *Age* article was a request by the judge in Brown's trial that the jurors consider the facts of the case fairly, suggesting that the charged state of race relations in New York City required this admonition beyond what would have been the jurors' standard duty.[37]

By 1913 the hardening of racial lines in New York City affected the ways that blacks did business even in parts of the city beyond Harlem. In the first decade of the 1900s, Booker T. Washington, leader of Tuskegee Institute, and his assistant, Emmett J. Scott, traveled frequently to New York from Alabama to cultivate relationships with northern philanthropists and to attend to other aspects of the institution's political ties. On these trips they stayed at downtown hotels such as the Hotel Manhattan on 42nd Street or the Fifth Avenue Hotel on Madison Square near 23rd Street.[38] By 1913 hotel policies in New York City had changed. In late 1913 in correspondence with Bertha Ruffner, owner of the Hotel McAlpin on Broadway and 34th Street, Emmett Scott sought to negotiate a compromise regarding the hotel's racial segregation policies and inquired about the hotel manager's "attitude . . . with reference to respectable colored people who have regard for the 'natural fitness of things.' It would not be my purpose to ostentatiously parade myself—nor would it be the attitude of any thoughtful black man—about the corridors of a hotel. In fact, as a rule I have my meals always outside of rather than in hotels where I have stopped."[39]

A few days later Miss Ruffner replied: "We regret that we have been unable to secure the name of any hotel in this city, to which we can refer you. We have written and telephoned several, but their restrictions are such that they are unable to accommodate you. It is impossible for us to be of service to you in this connection."[40]

A decade earlier, because of their social class, Scott and Washington had no problems finding lodging in white-owned hotels, but by 1913 there was no hotel in New York City for Scott even if he agreed to remain out of sight. Race had become much more important than social class. Other northern cities experienced a similar hardening of racial lines. Previously dispersed residential patterns of blacks shifted to concentrations of increasing black populations in a few neighborhoods. This is the context in which the movement of blacks to Harlem was defined by whites as an invasion.[41]

The heat of the summer of 1913 brought a steady drumbeat of stories regarding racial tensions in Harlem and the responses to it. By July, John G. Taylor's Property Owners' Protective Association claimed a membership of two thousand people who had signed restrictive covenants. As the summer proceeded, complaints regarding the Harlem Black Belt increased: "The immoral practices of negro men and women have made the section of Harlem one of the most notorious resorts of the demi-monde."[42]

Newspaper reports noted incidents of "respectable women" being insulted by blacks and indicated that white women walking on streets frequented by blacks were in danger. A report in the *Harlem Home News* concluded: "The fact that real estate values are going down rapidly in this section of Harlem is fully explained by the conditions described."[43]

During July and August a series of public meetings were held by white residents in Harlem to discuss the Negro problem. Perhaps reflecting a growing concern among Board of Commerce members, at a July meeting of the board called by its Property Owners Committee, John G. Taylor was allowed not only to attend, but to make a presentation. In a stirring speech he recounted the work of his organization through the use of restrictive covenants and suggested the formation of a company to purchase properties occupied or about to be occupied by blacks. The acquired properties would be renovated and rented to white tenants, an action that he claimed would automatically result in an increase in value. Taylor's solution met opposition. Bernard Naumberg, a lawyer, stated:

> There is a well-defined colored district and we do not wish to get them out of it. I am assured by men who know that there is plenty of room for everybody. At the same time, white people can not live on the same block with negroes. To my mind, the best way to solve the problem is not by restricting the negroes but by bringing white people to live in the section. To this end we must advertise Harlem.[44]

While in March 1913 Erduin v. d. H. Koch had said that blacks should be able to live anywhere they could afford, Naumberg dismissed the then radical notion that blacks and whites could live as neighbors. Even so, he did not advocate either expulsion of the black residents or tremendous restrictions. His solution for maintaining white control of Harlem was straightforward:

get more white people to move to the area. That night speakers outlined a plan for a proactive approach to the "black invasion" in Harlem by focusing on increasing the demand for Harlem property among whites. Consistent with Koch's admonition against "antagonisms," as well as with Naumberg's perspective, the speakers suggested that it was the failure of white residents of Harlem to properly inform other whites of the benefits of Harlem that had led white property owners to resort to renting or selling to African Americans. By the end of the meeting a committee was formed to carry out the advertising plan, with Erduin Koch serving as the committee's chairman (a clear signal that he believed that some type of intervention was important). They collected more than $300 that evening to support the plan, and projected that a total of $1,500 to $2,000 would be needed for the first advertising initiative.[45]

The black newspaper *New York Age* responded to the charges made by Taylor, noting that "one J.G. Taylor, erstwhile real estate agent and always a Negro hater, is president" of the Protective Association. The *Age* stated that Taylor's charges regarding the peril that whites faced by residing in close proximity to blacks were claims that "are absolutely untrue and which could have their conception only in a depraved and distorted consciousness." The article went on to note that "the Negro as a rule has in his home such furnishings and fittings as are out of proportion to his income, and very much superior to the furnishings to be found in the homes of average white family." A list titled "A Few Whose Homes Should be Visited" included more than a dozen black lawyers, real estate agents, ministers, and other Harlem leaders. The *Age* made clear that middle-class status was not only a matter of income but also an appreciation for and possession of some of the finer things of life. The article concluded by suggesting that "if there is the immorality and depravity among Negroes of Harlem as is charged, then the white man who owns the saloon and dives in that neighborhood is responsible."[46]

At the July Board of Commerce meeting, John G. Taylor had also assured the audience of the viability of the restrictive covenant as a tool to defend their neighborhoods, noting that the strength of the covenant would soon be tested in court. He added that he expected the decision to affirm the viability of the covenant. In mid-August of 1913 a lawsuit was initiated against Caroline Morlath, the white owner of 125 West 137th Street, by her next-door neighbor, Raphael Greenbaum. Morlath was born in New York, the daughter of German immigrants. She and her husband, Charles, also a child of German immigrants, had raised their three children, Caroline, William, and Susan, first on Second Avenue (near 29th Street) and later on Madison Avenue. By 1910 Charles, Caroline, and their daughter Carrie, had moved to West 137th Street, where the family's income was derived through investments. The owner of 127 West 137th Street, Raphael Greenbaum was a seventy-eight-year-old German immigrant who lived with his forty-four-year-old son, Isidore, his daughter-in-law, and his granddaughter. He and his son worked at a butcher shop on Eighth Avenue, a few blocks from their home. This was the block where the initial February 1907 restrictive covenant in Harlem was executed by twenty-three property owners.[47] In court papers, Greenbaum complained that Morlath had rented apartments in her ten-unit building to black tenants, violating the restrictive covenant that was part of the deed for her property. He noted that Morlath's actions had endangered the value of his property, which he indicated he had purchased because of the value that the restrictive covenant had provided. He asked for "an order . . . restraining the defendant from permitting negroes, mulattoes, quadroons or octoroons to occupy a whole or a part of the said premises 125 West 137th Street."

He also asked for $10,000 in damages from Morlath.[48]

Soon after the suit was initiated, the Property Owners' Protective Association hosted a meeting to discuss the lawsuit. John G. Taylor appealed for funds to cover Greenbaum's lawyer's fees, and more than $175 was collected. In rallying the troops, Taylor noted:

> We are now approaching a crisis. It is the question of whether the white man will rule Harlem or the negro. It is up to you to say who it shall be—the black or the white. The Equal Rights law has been pronounced unconstitutional, and the courts have upheld the restrictive agreement of a group of white people in Baltimore. I have no doubt that our agreement will be upheld too.[49]

In his remarks, Taylor also criticized the Harlem Board of Commerce's advertising campaign, noting that it would not solve the race problem, since no "respectable family" would be interested in living "in this section of Harlem, next door to negroes." Taylor ended with an appeal for contributions and signatures on a document that would extend the restrictive covenant to a larger area.[50]

In 1895 New York State had enacted a Civil Rights Law that prohibited discrimination in public accommodations on the basis of race and religion. The law made violations a misdemeanor, with victims required to file a civil action to obtain damages (privately owned housing was not considered a "public accommodation"). Despite Taylor's statement, in New York State an equal rights statute had been making its way through the legislature in 1913. In March a bill sponsored by Assemblyman Aaron Levy passed, followed by a similar bill in the Senate sponsored by Robert Wagner. At the beginning of September 1913 the law went into effect. The new statute also prohibited discrimination in public accommodations but specified that violators would be subject to penalties of "not less than $100 nor more than $500 or shall be imprisoned not less than thirty days nor more than ninety days or both." The new law also prohibited owners from advertising that "persons belonging to a particular race, creed or color are not wanted or will not be accommodated."[51] Taylor's mention of the Baltimore restrictive covenant case referred to a 1911 Baltimore ordinance to maintain racial segregation by prohibiting either whites or blacks from moving onto blocks occupied "in whole or in part" by residents of the opposite race. In 1913 the Maryland Court of Appeals ruled that the law was unconstitutional, but a week later the Baltimore City Council passed a new ordinance to meet the complaints of the court. The "Baltimore idea" of residential segregation was soon adopted in other southern and border states. Until the concept was ruled unconstitutional by the Supreme Court in 1917, it was one of a variety of restrictive agreements used throughout the nation to limit the movement of blacks, and also Jews, in some cases.[52]

John G. Taylor's advocates were not the only ones watching the Harlem restrictive covenant case. The *New York Age* also reported on the case, presenting Caroline Morlath as a champion of African Americans. The *Age* indicated that

the John M. Royall firm of real estate agents has charge of the renting of this property and it is due largely to their influence that this and other properties in what is called the "restricted section" has been opened to Negro tenants. Mr. Royall has received assurances from Mrs. Morlath that she will fight this case to the court of last resort if necessary and that she will not be dictated to by any body as to whom she shall rent her houses. She has a number of other properties rented to Negroes, and their tenancy is perfectly satisfactory to her.[53]

John Royall was an African American real estate broker. The *Age* article also stated that Caroline Morlath had retained African American attorney Wilfred Smith (who had been an investor in the by then defunct Afro-American Realty Company) to represent her.

In September 1913, as the case proceeded through the court, various real estate brokers submitted depositions for the plaintiff and the defendant, describing the neighborhood. Although the suit had not been filed until August 14, three depositions had been given, on July 31, August 1, and August 6, suggesting that while the Harlem Board of Commerce was looking for an amicable solution to Harlem's Negro problem, the groundwork for the Morlath case was being laid.[54]

Morlath purchased her building in 1908. Its previous owner, Isaac Birkner, had signed the June 1907 covenant that was attached to the property.[55] In her September 4, 1913, deposition Caroline Morlath admitted renting apartments to blacks, but she indicated that the only reason she did so was because she was unable to rent to whites. She noted that she was a widow and that the apartment house, where she also lived, was her only source of income (if she owned other properties, as the *Age* article suggested, she did not mention these). She added that if she had waited for white tenants to rent, she would have been unable to pay her mortgage and would have lost her building. She indicated that the black presence in the neighborhood had become so large that white residents would no longer rent apartments on West 137th Street. Supporting her statement were affidavits submitted by various real estate brokers (including John Royall) identifying black residents of nearby buildings, some of which were under covenant, as well as black patrons of businesses on Lenox and Seventh Avenues, the avenues at each end of her block. Morlath also noted a falsehood in Greenbaum's initial deposition. He had stated that the existence of the restrictive covenant on the block had influenced his purchase, but Morlath pointed out that Greenbaum had signed the 1907 covenant and was the owner of his property before the covenant was executed. Morlath concluded by noting that her attorney had informed her that the restrictive covenant agreement that Greenbaum sought to have affirmed "is void because it is against public policy to create or maintain discrimination by the public against colored people, which is evidenced by the Civil Rights Law of this State and also by the recent amendment to the Civil Rights Law passed in the year 1913 which went into effect September 1, 1913."[56]

This latter statement was consistent with the *New York Age*'s portrayal of Morlath as a champion for the rights of African Americans. She may have been, but if she was, her deposition suggests that she also saw the need to rationalize her decision to rent to blacks as an action that was reluctantly reached because she had no other choice. Although the *Age* had stated that Morlath had retained African American attorney Wilfred Smith to represent her in the case (in keeping with its framing of Morlath's actions as those of a race champion), her attorney of record was Henry Greenberg.

Raphael Greenbaum also submitted a series of depositions from real estate brokers. John G. Taylor, leader of the restrictive covenant movement, submitted two depositions. In his first deposition, made on August 1, he explained:

> I am devoting my whole time and attention to the protection of real estate interests in the section of New York known as Harlem, which has been suffering a serious depreciation by reason of what is known as the negro invasion, that is to say the occupation of various apartments and tenements by negro tenants. This I am doing without compensation and solely for the protection of the said district in New York, and for its maintenance as a locality for the residence and occupancy of white people.[57]

In that same deposition Taylor highlighted the ways that the black presence in the neighborhood had harmed property values, and he offered examples of homes that in 1913 sold for substantially lower prices than their purchase prices when the street had been exclusively white. His argument might have supported Raphael Greenbaum's claim of the harm to his property value by Morlath's rentals to blacks, but he perhaps later realized that the facts of this deposition could also be used to support Morlath's arguments that many African Americans were in the neighborhood before she began renting to them. On September 10, 1913, Taylor was deposed again. In this deposition he attempted to offer a more nuanced representation of the black presence in the neighborhood. Admitting that African Americans lived at 107 West 137th Street and 113 West 137th Street, he stated that they moved to these premises after July 25, 1913. He added that although 178 West 137th Street and Morlath's building, at 125 West 137th Street, had African American tenants, "All other houses in this block to my intimate knowledge were occupied exclusively by white tenants." Taylor seemed to be attempting to support the justification for Raphael Greenbaum's lawsuit, even though as Caroline Morlath claimed, racial conditions in the neighborhood had changed substantially.[58]

In a deposition made the next day, September 11, 1913, Caroline Morlath refuted Taylor's claims, noting that 178 West 137th had more than a "few" black tenants, but was fully occupied by African Americans at least six months before Greenbaum's legal action. She recounted that the houses that Taylor claimed had exclusively white tenants had few tenants at all, and that their owners had indicated they would begin renting apartments to blacks. Morlath challenged Taylor's depiction of the racial composition on other nearby blocks as well. She also highlighted the contradictions between the two affidavits, concluding that "Mr. Taylor seems to be rather inconsistent." Taylor had begun by noting the large number of blacks in the neighborhood in his first deposition. In his second account, he attempted to support Raphael Greenbaum's justification for undertaking the lawsuit against Caroline Morlath (when Greenbaum had not challenged others renting to African Americans) by attempting to characterize Morlath's rentals as among the first to blacks on the block. The map in figure 3.4 depicting the presence of African Americans in Harlem in 1913 also illustrates the extent of Taylor's inconsistencies.[59]

On October 1, 1913, Caroline Morlath submitted a final document to the court that included a photograph of Rafael Greenbaum's building at 127 West 137th Street (fig. 3.5). The document showed X's that drew attention to

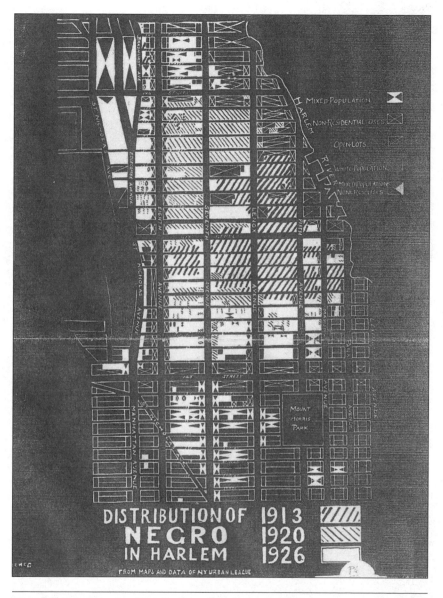

FIGURE 3.4. Distribution of black population in Harlem, 1913, 1920, 1926. New York Urban League.

FIGURE 3.5. Raphael Greenbaum's building at 127 West 137th Street. File photograph from *Raphael Greenbaum v. Caroline Morlath*, Supreme Court, New York County, Index Number 20486|1913.

Greenbaum's building and a new sign on it that read: "5 Room Apartments, All Improvements to Respectable Colored Tenants." Morlath's document requested that Greenbaum's case be dismissed "since the plaintiff is now committing a breach of the contract he seeks to enforce." It appeared that Rafael Greenbaum had succumbed to the same economic pressures that Caroline Morlath had described. On October 15, 1913, Greenbaum's motion for an injunction against Morlath's renting to African Americans was denied. The case that John G. Taylor had expected to affirm the covenant had instead further acknowledged the presence of African Americans in Central Harlem.[60]

Apart from the ironic outcome, *Greenbaum vs. Morlath* leaves several questions unanswered. If the neighborhood had such a large black presence, as indicated by the Morlath affidavits, the Urban League map, and Greenbaum's eventual actions, why did Greenbaum bring the suit? Was it because, with Morlath's actions, the black presence was right next door to him? Was there a broader dispute between the two owners, with the suit being used as a tool of retribution? Since John G. Taylor was a dominant presence in the case, submitting two affidavits, was he the primary motivation behind Greenbaum's decision to bring the case forward?

While Raphael Greenbaum's request for an injunction to prevent Caroline Morlath from renting apartments to blacks was denied and the use of racial restrictive covenants in Harlem was not affirmed because of the shifting facts of the case, there was also no decision made on a broader question of the legality of the racial restrictive covenant instrument. The effectiveness of the covenant as a tool of resistance was not clarified by the Morlath case, and no new covenants were added to those enacted during the period 1907–1911. The momentum of the resistance movement was undoubtedly hampered by the death of its leader, John G. Taylor, in January 1914. The leadership mantle was passed to Meyer Jarmulowsky, a Lower East Side banker who had invested a substantial portion of his family's assets in Harlem real estate and therefore had a vested interest in preventing a decline in property values there. The outbreak of World War I in 1914 challenged many banks serving European immigrants who sought to withdraw deposits in order to send money home. In August the Jarmulowsky Bank joined the ranks of several immigrant banks that failed when it was unable to provide funds that had been invested. Other Jarmulowsky businesses were embroiled in a series of lawsuits charging fraud, and Meyer Jarmulowsky's ability to lead the Harlem movement was hampered.[61] While there were individual efforts to resist, organized, publicized efforts were few in the last half of the decade. The restrictive covenant continued to be used effectively over the next three decades as a tool to enforce residential racial segregation in other parts of the country, from Chicago to Washington, D.C. In 1948 the Supreme Court ruled the instruments unconstitutional.[62]

Many other northern cities were experiencing similarly dramatic increases in their populations of black residents during the first decade and a half of the twentieth century. While some of the rhetoric of white Harlem residents regarding the Negro invasion was insulting to blacks, when compared to responses in other cities, it was relatively genteel. Class, relatively brief housing tenure, and white ethnic diversity influenced the responses in Harlem. There were at least three responses to the increase in black residents there: welcome based on class distinction—they should be able to live wherever they could afford; hostility manifested by the use of restrictive covenants; and hostility as evidenced by spontaneous violence. Wealthy people such as Harlem Board of Commerce chairman Erduin v. d. H. Koch may have been more liberal because of their confidence that ultimately they could control their communities. Although Koch lived at Lenox Avenue near 120th Street, some similarly minded members of the Board of Commerce may not have lived in Harlem and therefore did not feel personally threatened by the black presence in the community.[63]

John G. Taylor's response, while more vocal, could be characterized as intermediate or moderate. He was more confrontational than the business leaders, and undoubtedly was able to recruit some from the business class who believed that the Koch approach was not strong enough. In addition Taylor relied on owner-occupants and small investors, both of whom were more susceptible to concerns about the decline in their property values and less able to weather such a loss. While Taylor was able to organize large groups to sign restrictive covenants, there were obstacles to getting signers to adhere to their agreements. The short lengths of residency in the newly developed area and the diversity of ethnic backgrounds among white residents limited the commitment that residents had to the neighborhood. As noted in chapter 2, West 135th Street was a newly developed area in 1900. Many buildings had been built in the 1890s, and by the first decade of the 1900s many streets were still partially undeveloped. Beyond aesthetics, this fact could have affected the inclination of residents to consider a street as "theirs." In many cases, white residents, including covenant leader Taylor, were almost as new to the neighborhood as the blacks seeking to move onto their blocks. In addition to limited time of residency, white Harlem was ethnically diverse, with native-born whites living on the same blocks as first-generation immigrants from Germany, Ireland, and other countries. This diversity extended to religion as well, with prosperous German Jews building synagogues on Fifth Avenue and other avenues to the west, as well as purchasing brownstones on streets in the 130s, while Christians built churches in the same area. This diversity was an obstacle to a more vigorous defense of their neighborhoods. As chapter 2 illustrated, some white residents had provided financing to black purchasers of their buildings, indicating that they did not fear community sanction.

It is also possible that while some white Harlem residents were concerned enough about their property values to enter into restrictive covenants, the more salient concern of some may have been economics rather than race. Their antipathy to blacks may not have been as deep as John G. Taylor's. Before his move to Harlem, Taylor lived on Waverly Place in Greenwich Village. During the time he was there, Greenwich Village still contained vestiges of African American enclaves that earlier in the nineteenth century had earned it the name "Little Africa." The growing black congregation of the Abyssinian Baptist Church was located at 164 Waverly Place just a few doors from Taylor's home at 152 Waverly Place. To John G. Taylor his move to Harlem may have been as much an escape from the company of neighbors whom he considered undesirable as a sign of his increasing prosperity. He undoubtedly knew of the 135th Street enclave when he purchased his home on 136th Street in 1903, but he also had every reason to believe that it would remain within its boundaries, east of Lenox Avenue. This history, linked with Taylor's economic concerns, may have motivated him to lead the restrictive covenant movement in the last decade of his life. While his neighbors joined the movement by signing agreements, their commitment to maintaining Harlem as a white community was different from his. The third response to the increased number of blacks in Harlem, violence, occurred in only a few instances. The limited reports of violence reflect the lukewarm commitment of white residents to defending their community. Other than schoolboy fights and a few isolated incidents involving adults, many white residents responded to the black invasion of Harlem by moving out of the community. But even as they exited they were reluctant to relinquish their church edifices to black newcomers.[64]

4

THE BATTLE FOR
CHURCH PROPERTIES

—◦◦◦◦—

The restrictive covenant movement was clearly an example of racial conflict in Harlem related to residential property ownership in the first decades of the twentieth century. But as the African American purchases financed by white sellers Louis Partzschefeld, Charles Kroehle, and August Ruff demonstrated, with respect to residential properties there were also examples of cooperation across racial lines. This was not true for church properties. Where church properties were concerned, there were limits to cooperation with African Americans even for white Harlem residents who may not have been overtly hostile to the increasing black presence in Harlem. When African Americans attempted to purchase religious properties in Harlem during the first two decades of the twentieth century, white church officials did not directly sell properties being vacated by predominantly white congregations to black congregations. This aversion may have been grounded in attempts by remaining white property owners to retain control of the real estate in their communities even as many of the members of the white congregations moved elsewhere. An examination of the ways in which white congregations struggled to maintain control of these properties provides insight into their larger fears about the prospect of being "pushed" out of their community by the arrival of African Americans. From the perspective of many white Harlem residents, possibly even some who conceded the presence of a Negro colony there, the idea that these black newcomers would also establish churches in the community and seek to acquire buildings constructed by white congregations was going too far. Attempts by blacks to acquire Harlem churches formerly occupied by white congregations were viewed by whites as concessions of defeat as well as symbols of both black permanency and black civic participation that highlighted for whites the decline of white dominance in the community.

Church real estate represented a symbol of permanency and community for white residents in Harlem, as well as a sign of responsible citizenship. For this reason church properties were very significant for white Harlem residents. They were signs of community control. The properties were significant for black Harlem residents for the same reasons. While African Americans were not necessarily seeking exclusive control of the community, as their numbers in Harlem increased during the first decade of the 1900s, blacks sought sufficient control over the areas where they resided to ensure that they could remain there without harassment. In a period when subway transportation was in its infancy, having a church within walking distance of one's home was an important asset in the formation of a community. The church properties were also significant to African Americans as symbols of good citizenship and well-regulated behavior, at variance with the common stereotypes that characterized blacks as gamblers, drunks, and prostitutes who threatened the future peace of white Harlem.

In 1890, 36 percent of New York State residents belonged to a church, synagogue, or other religious organization (the national rate was 32 percent). The church and the synagogue remained important centers of religious faith, as well as indicators of community membership and class status. As the development of Harlem as a residential community proceeded in the second half of the nineteenth century, some downtown congregations moved north to Harlem, and new congregations were also established in the area. The completion of a church building was celebrated in the newspapers. Drawings of new church buildings highlighted the architectural designs and significant investments being made by the congregations and reinforced the church edifice as a symbol of middle-class stability. The opening of a new church was viewed as a sign of progress, strengthening the community.[1]

For African Americans, church membership had additional appeal. While church membership was a sign of respectability, the church was even more significant as a community institution. Black mutual benefit societies and literary organizations existed in some cities and towns, but with few independent institutions controlled by blacks, churches were important for African Americans in developing social networks, enforcing community mores, and seeking redress against maltreatment. The black pastor, whether full-time or part-time, receiving an income drawn from the offerings of church members, exercised a measure of independence unavailable to other African Americans most of whom worked in menial jobs.[2]

In New York City, the first predominantly African American congregation was formed in 1796 when the Zion African Methodist Episcopal Church was established by former members of John Street Methodist Church in Lower Manhattan who were dissatisfied with restricted seating and other signs of their subordinate status within the church. Similar circumstances led to the 1808 founding of the Abyssinian Baptist Church by people of African descent attending First Baptist Church (on Gold Street in lower Manhattan), and in 1809 to the founding St. Philip's Episcopal Church by a group of blacks attending Trinity Church, also in lower Manhattan. In the following decades of the nineteenth century, these churches were joined by a handful of other black congregations, typically located in the areas of black settlement in Lower Manhattan, and later in the midtown area. The churches provided social centers for concerts, lectures, and rallies, as well as places of worship. They were also the targets of anti-abolition and anti-black mobs in the 1830s and during the 1863 Draft Riots. White elites often considered black pastors to be the leaders of the African American community, and black congregants often expected their pastors to voice their grievances to the broader community. During the four-day Draft Riots, whites protested the drafting of soldiers to serve in the Civil War by killing many blacks and burning or otherwise destroying property owned by African Americans and their allies. In the aftermath of the violence, Rev. Henry Highland Garnet, pastor of the black congregation of Shiloh Presbyterian Church, and Rev. Charles Bennett Ray, pastor of Bethesda Congregational Church, a predominantly white congregation, were selected by a group of white merchants to disburse aid to African American victims. They attempted to use their positions to help those in need, but also tactfully presented to the merchants the grievances of the black community regarding past discriminatory treatment.[3]

While most African American churches were located near black enclaves in lower Manhattan and midtown in the mid-nineteenth century, black congregations in lower Manhattan recognized the need to serve African American settlements in Harlem. In 1843 Zion African Methodist Episcopal Church, then located at Church and Leonard Streets in lower Manhattan, established a Harlem mission to serve the black population in that area. Located at 236 East 117th Street between Second and Third Avenues, "Little Zion," as the church was called, continued to grow as the African American population in the area increased in the late 1800s. In 1882 Carmel Baptist Church, a congregation pastored by Rev. J. E. Raymond, was established on East 121st Street with a congregation of thirty people. In 1891 the growing congregation built a new church on East 123rd Street between Second and Third Avenues. As the African American settlement in Harlem shifted westward after 1900, the churches followed.[4]

Jewish congregations were also moving to northern Manhattan in the late nineteenth century. Incorporated in 1873, Congregation Hand-in-Hand, became the first synagogue established in Harlem. Until the early 1880s it held services in rented halls. Improved transportation to the area as a result of the extension of elevated railroad lines along Second and Third Avenues in 1879 and 1880 and the growth in apartment construction along the route led to the growth of Congregation Hand-in-Hand. In 1888 it reorganized as Temple Israel and moved into a new building at 125th Street and Fifth Avenue, "the crossroads of Harlem's wealthiest district." In 1907, as more prosperous Harlem residents moved to the west, Temple Israel built a Neo-Roman synagogue on Lenox Avenue at 120th Street. It was then considered "one of the most prestigious synagogues in the city."[5]

In 1892 St. Luke's Episcopal Church, a predominantly white congregation, celebrated the opening of its new church at Convent Avenue and 141st

Street. Founded in 1820 on Hudson Street in Greenwich Village, the church had witnessed growth and decline in the middle decades of the nineteenth century. The move to northern Manhattan had not been totally voluntary. In 1887 Trinity Episcopal Church, the oldest and largest Episcopal congregation in New York City, and long-time patron to St. Luke's and other Episcopal congregations, had informed St. Luke's that it was planning to open a chapel and school on land it owned nearby in Greenwich Village. It offered to incorporate St. Luke's congregation into the new chapel. Members of St. Luke's recognized this offer as the death of St. Luke's as an independent congregation. They decided to move to an area where they believed they would not have to compete with other churches for members and where potential for growth existed. St. Luke's requested Trinity's assistance in financing the building of a church in Washington Heights, as the area of Convent Avenue and 141st Street was then known. (Washington Heights took its name from the fact that George Washington had led Revolutionary War battles in the area and had his headquarters at the Morris-Jumel Mansion, one mile to the north.) The "Heights" referred to the steep hill that separated the area from Harlem to the east of St. Nicholas Avenue.[6]

In 1892 the area, on the northern edge of Harlem, was sparsely populated:

South of Saint Luke's Church there are no dwelling houses except two or three wooden cabins or shanties until the Convent of the Sacred Heart is reached situated at West 130th St.— . . . west of Saint Luke's Church there are some few buildings, the majority of which are unoccupied and That in all probability there will not at a near date be a large population in that section—That east of the church on St. Nicholas Avenue between 135th Street and 145th Street there is not one dwelling house and that from a population further east but few persons can be expected to attend Saint Luke's owing to the proximity of other parishes and to the steep grade of . . . 141st [Street].[7]

Although the area seemed remote, it was actually in the path of development. St. Luke's was built on a parcel that had been part of the Hamilton Grange, the estate of Alexander Hamilton. In 1887, the year that St. Luke's was informed of changes at its Lower Manhattan location, the estate had been divided into lots that were to be sold at auction. Townhouses, much larger than the standard Manhattan brownstone, were built on these lots over the next two decades. In the 1890s, as real estate developers began to position Harlem as an in-city bedroom suburb of lower Manhattan, townhouses were built on Convent Avenue north of St. Luke's and to the east on the L-shaped street named Hamilton Terrace. In 1907 the College of the City of New York moved to a new campus on land to the south of Saint Luke's, a portion of which had been the Convent of the Sacred Heart. All of these developments contributed to the growth of St. Luke's congregation after 1900.[8]

By 1913, as African American settlement in Harlem continued to move west of Lenox Avenue, and the restrictive covenant movement progressed through the courts with the Morlath case, the thriving congregation of St. Luke's experienced a Negro problem. African American children had begun to attend its Sunday School, to the dismay of some mothers of white children. The rector, Rev. George Oldham, responded to the mothers' complaints by offering to create a separate class for black children, but he suggested that the best solution would be for these children to attend a church with their own kind, and so he directed them to St. Philip's Episcopal Church, the black Episcopal congregation that had recently relocated to Harlem. No mention was made of the black children's parents, suggesting that their parents did not accompany them to Sunday school.[9]

Racial tension erupted in at least one other Episcopal congregation in 1913. St. Mary's Church, on 126th Street near Amsterdam Avenue, had requested that an African American Sunday School teacher cease teaching. Her father, Wilfred Smith, a lawyer and partner of Philip Payton in the Afro-American Realty Company, threatened to take the matter to the Episcopal bishop. There is no evidence that Smith followed up on his threat, but the fact that he believed that the bishop would hear this grievance also suggests that Smith believed that the bishop did not agree with the local priest's idea of the subordinate status of blacks.[10]

St. Philip's Episcopal Church, the church that St. Luke's pastor had suggested the black children attend, was ten years older than St. Luke's, formed in 1809 by African Americans who had been dissatisfied with the discrimination they had experienced at Trinity Church in Manhattan. After initially worshipping in a school, and then in a loft over a carpenter's shop, St. Philip's congregation secured its first permanent building on Collect (Centre) Street between Leonard and Anthony (Worth). As the African American community moved northward, St. Philip's followed, moving to Mulberry Street in Greenwich Village in 1857 and in 1886 purchasing a church building on 161 West 25th Street, in the heart of the Tenderloin district, which by then had a large concentration of black residents.[11]

By 1910 the area around West 25th Street was becoming problematic for St. Philip's. The 1900 race riot in midtown, although several blocks to the north, left a pall over the community. After the riot, black pastors organized a committee and filed grievances against the police department for brutality. The tepid official response to complaints left the community frustrated. The lack of security in the black settlements in midtown, and the Pennsylvania Railroad's acquisition of large swaths of property from 30th Street to 34th Street in preparation for the construction of Pennsylvania Station and its Hudson River tunnels made the area unsuitable for the community.[12]

During this period St. Philip's undertook a series of real estate transactions that resulted in the construction of the first new black church in Harlem. The church's move began with small steps. In January 1907 its rector, Rev. Hutchens Bishop, purchased a building at 212 West 134th Street between 7th and 8th Avenues for $100 in cash and the assumption of a mortgage of $5,000. On February 15, Bishop paid $13,500 for two more properties on 133rd Street and one on 134th Street between 7th and 8th Avenues (217 and 219 W. 133rd, 210 W. 134th). This transaction took place two days after twenty-three white owners of properties on West 137th Street between Lenox and Seventh Avenues had signed a restrictive covenant agreeing not to sell or rent to blacks for a ten-year period. On February 18 Bishop purchased two more properties on the same block, at 214 and 216 W. 134th, making a payment of $20,000 (fig. 4.1). The transactions were noted a month later in the *New York Times*, in its standard weekly listing of real estate matters. Because Hutchens C. Bishop was fair-skinned, the sellers of the properties and the observers of the transactions may not have realized that an African American had purchased properties west of Lenox Avenue, the previously implicit western boundary for the Negro Colony in Harlem.[13]

The real estate purchases of Rev. Bishop did not draw the attention of white property owners, even though the purchases had been made at the same time the restrictive covenant movement had been put into effect on

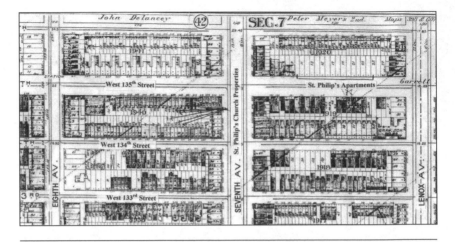

FIGURE 4.1. Rev. Hutchens Bishop/St. Philip's Harlem property purchases, 1907. G. W. Bromley & Co., Section 6.

the adjacent blocks. A letter regarding the possible plans of St. Philip's to move to Harlem, however, generated considerable discussion. In February 1907 Rev. Bishop sent a letter to Rev. Dr. George R. Van de Water, rector of St. Andrew's Episcopal Church at Fifth Avenue and 127th Street, a predominantly white congregation, informing Van de Water that St. Philip's was considering a move to Harlem. Although the two congregations served different populations, Episcopal protocol required that congregations in proximity be informed in advance of a contemplated move to an area by another congregation. The existing congregations then would have an opportunity to voice their opinions of the move to the Standing Committee, the regional governing body of the Episcopal Church.

Rev. Van de Water commented on Bishop's request in St. Andrew's newsletter, noting that he fully supported St. Philip's plans and "that it is not for the best interests of either the whites or the blacks that they should attend the same Sunday schools, or the same churches." Rev. Van de Water in an interview in the *New York Times* elaborated on his view on blacks and whites worshipping together, adding:

I repeat, that the sooner the colored people get out of St. Andrew's the better it will be for both whites and blacks. If President Roosevelt wants to eat with a colored man he can do so. I won't, and I am just as much entitled to my opinion as he is. I do not want the colored people in my church, neither do my parish-ioners for they have been a source of much trouble. In the first place, we have gentlemen ushers, Wardens, and Vestrymen and they in a manner, object to es-corting colored people up and down the aisle.[14]

Although his views reflected the views of many New Yorkers, Van De Wa-ter was denounced by some black and white New Yorkers for un-Christian racial hostility. Two days after the initial *Times* article, in a letter to its editor Rev. Van De Water repeated his position but added that any "colored person coming to my Sunday school or church will be received graciously, courte-ously. . . . All the same I hold that it is much better for all concerned that the races should worship by themselves."[15]

Hutchens Bishop continued to lay the groundwork for the move that would establish St. Philip's in Harlem. On January 31, 1910, he transferred the Harlem properties he had purchased in his name in 1907 to St. Philip's. In February 1910 St. Philip's requested permission from the Episcopal Diocese to sell its 25th Street church for $140,000 and its 30th Street property for $450,000 (an advantage of the commercialization of the area was an increase in real estate values), and also requested permission to build a church on West 134th Street in Harlem. The Standing Committee of the Episcopal Dio-cese sent a copy of the request to "the three parishes and mission districts nearest the site": St. Luke's on Convent Avenue and 141st Street, St. Mary's on 126th near Amsterdam Avenue, and Church of the Redeemer on West 136th between Lenox and Seventh Avenues. A hearing by the Standing Com-mittee on March 3, 1910, invited comment by any opponents of the move. No one appeared in opposition, and the request was approved.[16]

With the Harlem properties now in the name of St. Philip's and the ap-proval of the diocese secured, plans for the construction of the new church began. The architectural firm of Tandy and Foster was selected to prepare the design for the new building. This firm was one of the few black firms in the country. One of the partners, Vertner Tandy, a member of St. Philip's, was the first African American in New York State to be licensed as an archi-tect. For St. Philip's, he and his partner, George Washington Foster, designed a parish house on West 133rd Street, and a "spare, northern Gothic church in salmon-colored Roman brick" on West 134th Street. Construction was completed in 1911, the same year that St. Philip's most significant real estate purchase occurred. [17]

In March 1911 St. Philip's purchased a row of ten occupied, six-story walkup apartments on the north side of West 135th Street just west of Lenox Avenue for $393,000 using the proceeds from its downtown property sales.[18] The seller was the Chase Realty Group, which took back mortgages on the properties. The transaction was reported in an article in the *New York Times*, and was highlighted with banner headlines in the African American *New York Age*. The *Times* noted that the "white tenants were notified of the change yesterday, and many families are already preparing to move out." As Philip Payton had proposed to do with the leased property on West 151st Street in 1906, St. Philip's evicted the white occupants of the West 135th Street properties, and replaced them with black tenants. In one very visible move the Lenox Avenue racial "dead line" had been crossed with the construction of a significant church edifice and the acquisition of a large swath of residential properties. While St. Philip's new church building on West 134th Street was a symbol of the African American presence in Harlem, the congregation's control of substantial residential property nearby enabled it as an institution to play a significant role in the literal formation of the black community in proximity to its church. There is no record of a protest from the evicted white families, suggesting that either St. Philip's had caught them off guard or they had resigned themselves to the hard realities of New York's real estate policies in which a new owner, even a black one, could evict tenants who were white. Undoubtedly there was lingering bitterness held by those evicted as well as by white residents aware of the evictions, all of which may have contributed to the organized resistance efforts that gained visibility in 1913.[19]

By 1913 when Rev. Oldham, the rector of St. Luke's, repeated the 1907 suggestion made by the rector of St. Andrew's that it would be better for everyone if blacks at St. Luke's would consider attending their "own" church, St. Philip's was a congregation of more than one thousand people with financial assets that surpassed those of St. Luke's and several other white congregations in Harlem, some of which were struggling as white residents moved away in response to the "Negro invasion" (fig. 4.2).[20]

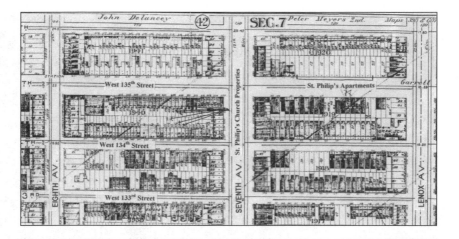

FIGURE 4.2. St. Philip's Episcopal Church Harlem properties, acquired 1907–1911. G. W. Bromley & Co., Section 6.

The struggles of the Episcopal congregation of the Church of the Redeemer illustrate the ways in which control of church real estate was linked to control of the community for most predominantly white congregations in Harlem during the first two decades of the 1900s. As the African American population increased and black congregations such as St. Philip's began moving to Harlem, white congregations made a concerted effort to prevent African American congregations from purchasing the buildings of white congregations. Founded in 1853 as part of the Episcopal Diocese of New York, the Church of the Redeemer was initially located at Park Avenue between 81st and 82nd Streets. When the church was not successful there, its building was sold in 1897 to avoid a foreclosure sale. In 1898 the Church of the Redeemer merged with the Church of the Nativity, an Episcopal congregation that had previously merged with the Church of the Holy Innocents, which had a graystone church building in Harlem at 153 West 136th Street, with a yard that extended north through to West 137th Street. The consolidated congregations, under the name Church of the Redeemer, moved to the Harlem building in 1898. These mergers reflected the challenges of maintaining small congregations not just in Harlem but across the country, even in areas where racial change was not an issue—which it was not in 1900 in Harlem. The loss

of a few key families or individuals in a congregation through death or relocation, or disenchantment with a pastor, could lead to the irreparable decline of
a congregation.[21]

After experiencing several decades of turmoil in the nineteenth century,
Church of the Redeemer had less than a decade of tranquillity at its Harlem
location. The small congregation continued to struggle to meet its expenses,
and a variety of efforts were undertaken to deal with the financial problems.
In the spring of 1910 the church received permission from the Episcopal Diocese to sell its rectory at 142 West 137th for $11,500.[22] Soon afterward the
congregation began to consider moving away from Harlem altogether. Before
long, the church received an offer of $50,000 for its building, from St. James
Presbyterian Church, an African American congregation founded in 1893 by
former members of Shiloh (First Colored) Presbyterian Church. Shiloh had
been a prominent African American congregation in the mid-nineteenth
century. From 1857 to 1864 it was pastored by abolitionist Henry Highland
Garnet, who had coordinated aid to black residents after the Draft Riots of
1863. The church had disbanded in 1891, but former members went on to establish St. James. The new church had a growing congregation that had occupied a building on 32nd Street, but was displaced by the building of Penn
Station. In 1903 St. James took over the West Fifty-first Street Presbyterian
Church at 359 West 51st Street.[23]

In responding to St. James's purchase offer, the Church of the Redeemer's
vestry (the governing body for business matters) seemed concerned that
the prospective purchaser of their building was not an Episcopal church.
Even though racial tension was growing in Harlem, membership in the denomination still inspired an affinity that could cross racial lines. At a special
meeting on May 23, 1910, the vestry passed a resolution to offer the church
to St. Philip's Episcopal Church, the black congregation led by Hutchens
Bishop, for $50,000. The resolution also provided an explanation for the sale
to a black congregation:

> WHEREAS for a number of years past the population of Harlem adjacent
> to the Church has been changing in character, and colored people have become
> residents of blocks and streets immediately adjacent to the block on which the

Church is situated, and the colored population has been growing in numbers and steadily approaching nearer to the Church and the Vestry is now reliably informed that a large number of houses on 136th Street near the Church are for sale, and the Presbyterian Church above referred to has an option on three houses nearly opposite the Church, and

WHEREAS, it appears that the street on which the Church is situated between Seventh and Lenox Avenues is certain in the near future to be entirely populated by colored persons, and

WHEREAS, the Vestry recognizing their duty to conserve the property of the Church and believing that if the present offer of St. James Presbyterian Church be not accepted it will be impossible to sell the Church Building for any price whatever, and that even the land will seriously deteriorate in value.[24]

The vestry unanimously voted for a sale to St. James to proceed if St. Philip's declined. The detailed explanation in the church's official record seemed to be in anticipation of criticism the church officers expected to receive for selling this community institution to blacks. Their concerns were well founded.

While the Redeemer vestry was struggling over selling its property to a black congregation, John G. Taylor, leader of the restrictive covenant movement, was organizing a major effort to block such transactions. Taylor lived at 213 W. 136th Street, one block west of Redeemer's church building at 153 West 136th. On June 7, 1910, the massive restrictive covenant discussed in chapter 3 was recorded with the New York City Register, covering ninety-one owners of properties on the 100 and 200 blocks of West 136th Street (between Lenox and Eighth Avenues). The agreement did not simply prohibit black residency, but broadly prohibited "use or occupancy" of the properties by people of African descent. Church of the Redeemer was not a party to this agreement, but owners to the east and west of Redeemer as well as across the street, were. The effort to get these ninety-one signatures must have been proceeding for days or weeks before the June 7 recording date. Perhaps the covenant effort was sparked by Redeemer's sales plans.[25]

In spite of the covenant, on June 13 Redeemer petitioned the Episcopal Diocese for permission to sell its buildings, outlining its options in the same manner as its May 23 resolution had. The Standing Committee of the Episcopal Diocese noted that, as required, Bishop David H. Greer had already approved the request and the committee then also approved it. Because religious institutions also needed permission from the New York County Supreme Court to mortgage or sell properties, on June 13 an application was entered to the Supreme Court requesting permission to sell the property.[26] Redeemer's financial challenges were covered in the press, with one article indicating that representatives of the church had explained that the proposed sale was due to the fact that "changes in the population in Harlem have depleted the congregation of the church to such an extent that it is no longer possible to keep it open." It was announced that the Church of the Redeemer planned to build a new church either in the predominantly white communities of Washington Heights in Upper Manhattan or University Heights in the Bronx, two areas to which congregants leaving Harlem were likely to move.[27]

St. Philip's declined to purchase Redeemer's building. By June 1910 the cornerstone for St. Philip's new building, four blocks away on 134th Street between Seventh and Eighth Avenues, had already been laid.[28] But the Redeemer vestry's contingency plan of proceeding with the sale to St. James did not occur either. Perhaps the restrictive covenant covering many properties on the block made the vestry wary of community disenchantment with such a sale. This concern may have gone as far as the bishop of the Episcopal Diocese. Lawson Purdy, who was chief warden of Church of the Redeemer, later suggested that the sale to St. James did not occur because of a change in Bishop Greer's position, noting that it was Bishop Greer "who was responsible for our not having sold out when we could have obtained $60,000 for the property. He wanted us to hold the Fort; it was against my judgment. This is not said in criticism of the Bishop who was loyal and an earnest good friend, always."[29]

By "holding the fort," or not selling to the black congregations of St. James or St. Philip's, the bishop would have been echoing rhetoric of the restrictive covenant movement, which framed the role of white residents as defending their community against the Negro invasion. In October 1910 the struggling Redeemer congregation received another destabilizing blow. Rector William Davis submitted a one-sentence note announcing his resignation, effective

November 12. It is quite likely that Redeemer's precarious financial state was a factor in the resignation. A fund-raising campaign had to be undertaken to secure a portion of the next rector's salary before a replacement was sought.[30]

In December 1910 John G. Taylor sent a letter to Redeemer in which he expressed concern about the possible sale of the church to African Americans. Chief Warden Lawson Purdy indicated that he had replied "unofficially that it was improbable that the church would be sold to colored people." At the same December 14 meeting at which Taylor's letter was discussed, the vestry passed a motion that "the clerk be instructed to write to Mr. J.R. Glide that the church of the Redeemer does not propose to sell the property at present." In all likelihood Glide represented African Americans, for this motion was followed by a motion to instruct the clerk to determine if a $39,000 purchase offer from a Mr. Knox would include a statement that "he would restrict the property for five years so it would not be used by colored people." There is no record of a response from Mr. Knox. Either he was no longer interested or perhaps was not willing to adhere to the restriction, given the racial changes occurring in the neighborhood.[31]

By the end of 1910 Redeemer was considering another plan. With an air of desperation, church leaders approached St. Luke's Church on Convent Avenue and 141st Street and proposed to

> transfer a deed of the property [its church at 153 W. 136th Street] to Saint Luke's Church on the condition that Saint Luke's should continue services in said Church of the Redeemer for a reasonable length of time, after which if the expenses exceeded the receipts there would be no objection to Saint Luke's disposing of the property in any way or manner which they saw fit.[32]

A few months after a potential $50,000 sale of its property to St. James Presbyterian did not materialize, Church of the Redeemer was proposing to give its building to St. Luke's to operate as a mission church to St. Luke's. The vestry of St. Luke's seriously considered how it might absorb Church of the Redeemer's congregation, discussing the appointment of the senior vestryman Lawson Purdy of Church of the Redeemer to the vestry of St. Luke's, and also considered "providing a special clergyman to attend to the needs of the Parish of the Church of the Redeemer." With a large building that was not fully utilized, debts from the 1892 construction still being paid, and operating expenses that were difficult for the modest-sized congregation of approximately four hundred to meet, the possibility of bringing additional members into St. Luke's must have been attractive. But these additional members would have been met with the challenge of operating buildings at two locations, one in an area of increasing racial change. In late 1910 St. Luke's informed the Church of the Redeemer that it would decline the offer.[33]

At its December meeting, the Redeemer vestry had called for a committee to secure pledges of $1,000 for two years, after which a rector would be called. In April 1911 a substantial portion of the pledges were secured and Rev. Henry Cornelius Dyer was asked to become rector at an annual salary of $1,200. During 1911, fund-raising efforts for church operations continued through a plan to develop a "mission from Paradise Endowment." By the end of the year discussions were under way to consolidate with the Church of the Holy Road, a congregation at Broadway and 181st Street. This plan also did not proceed, and for the next year other plans were considered. In March 1913 the vestry suggested that the Catholic Apostolic Church be asked to make a purchase offer. When that church declined, in June the vestry suggested that efforts begin to get the appropriate approvals (from the Episcopal bishop, Standing Committee of the Diocese, and New York Supreme Court) to convey the Church of the Redeemer to the Church of the Transfiguration, which would assume Redeemer's debts. This did not occur either.[34]

In June 1913 John G. Taylor interceded on Redeemer's behalf. Taylor proposed approaching the widow of financier Russell Sage for assistance. Taylor asked Mrs. Sage to consider purchasing the Church of the Redeemer building to establish a new congregation, "Church of the Stranger," in Redeemer's building. In 1898 a Church of the Stranger congregation had moved into a new building on 57th Street near Eighth Avenue. The church drew on the Christian ethos that all were welcome, particularly young people. Ironically John G. Taylor hoped to use this concept to prevent African Americans from controlling the Church of the Redeemer property.[35]

It appears that Mrs. Russell Sage declined to support John G. Taylor's plans. In December 1913 the Redeemer vestry agreed to accept a $19,000 offer from real estate agent Paul Friedland for the church. At a meeting on January 12, 1914, the Standing Committee of the Episcopal Diocese heard Lawson Purdy explain the sale "owing largely to the occupation of the neighborhood about the church by colored people, as well as other antecedent causes . . . it had become wholly impossible to maintain the church in the locality." An opponent of the sale, Mr. Ransome E. Wilcox, "representing property owners in Harlem," stated that the sale "would be injurious to the neighborhood if the property came into possession of colored people." The committee approved Redeemer's request. On January 19 the sale of the Church of the Redeemer to Paul Friedland's client Mildred Helm, a white Yonkers resident, was completed. Rather than move to a new location, the church's congregation disbanded. The rector, Rev. Henry C. Dyer, accepted an appointment with Metropolitan Life Insurance Company as chaplain of the company's Mount McGregor Sanitarium in Wilton, New York.[36] Area property owners speculated on the building's future: "According to one rumor, it will be turned into a moving picture theatre, though another report has it that the negroes of the neighborhood are anxious to secure it for one of their churches."[37]

Dr. Robert Bruce Clark, pastor of the Church of the Puritans on West 130th Street expressed his concern regarding the "danger of being engulfed by the negro invasion":

> The churches, more than any other organizations, are suffering from the existing conditions north of 130th St. For years we have struggled to keep our congregations and it has been an uphill fight not to allow them to scatter. . . . Under the circumstances, I wonder that [Church of the Redeemer] held out so long as they did. The site of the church is in the heart of the colored section, and it is not in the least surprising that its members did not care to remain in Harlem any longer because of the steady increase of negroes in the neighborhood.[38]

On January 22 1914, three days after the initial sale of Church of Redeemer, Mother AME Zion Church purchased the church building from Mildred Helm, agreeing to assume a $17,000 mortgage on the property. Perhaps aware of the reluctance of Redeemer to sell to a black congregation given the experience of St. James, Mother AME Zion was able to have Helm stand in to assuage Redeemer's concerns of an outright sale to blacks. Although as the quote above suggests, it was generally believed that Redeemer's building was likely to come under the control of an African American congregation, by selling to Mildred Helm, a white woman, Redeemer's loyal vestry could not later be criticized for contributing to the Negro invasion. That responsibility would fall to Mildred Helm, a woman from outside of the community, for whom such a criticism would carry less weight.[39] Other predominantly white congregations in Harlem went through similar transactions, rarely selling to an African American congregation but instead to an individual who then sold to a black congregation.[40]

The movement of African Americans into Harlem was concentrated in an area between West 130th and West 140th Streets, and therefore did not affect Harlem synagogues to the same extent as it did predominantly white churches. In the first decade of the 1900s as some synagogues moved from East Harlem to the area west of Lenox Avenue, they concentrated in an area between West 116th Street and West 125th Street. In 1900 a faction of Congregation Shaare Zedek, then located on Henry Street, built a synagogue at 23–25 West 118th Street between Fifth and Lenox Avenues. In 1914 the uptown faction reunited with the downtown faction at this location, but in 1922 they sold their building to another synagogue, Chevra Talmud Torah d Agustow. In 1908 the First Hungarian Congregation Ohab Zedek, then located on the Lower East Side (172 Norfolk Street), followed many of its members and purchased a building at 18 West 116th Street (between Lenox and Fifth Avenues). In 1926 they moved to West 95th Street. Also in 1908, Congregation Ansche Chesed moved into a new building at 1881 Seventh Avenue at 112th Street. The congregation also moved in the 1920s. Following their congregation, in 1927 they sold their building and moved to a new synagogue at 100th Street and West End Avenue in Manhattan.[41] African Americans did live in the area between 110th and 125th, but their numbers were small and therefore did not generate the alarm before the 1920s that their greater numbers did in the area north of West 130th Street. Most of these synagogues moved out of Harlem in the 1920s when more blacks began living in the area.[42]

While St. Philip's Episcopal Church pioneered in building in Harlem, during the first decade of the 1900s other, smaller black congregations were also gaining control of real estate in Harlem. Before moving to 135th Street, Mercy Seat Baptist Church, the site of the 1904 meeting to protest evictions of African American renters in area apartments, was already in Harlem. In 1901 the church was located at 424 West 127th Street.[43] The terms of the purchase of its property at 45–47 West 134th Street, in the days following the 1904 meeting, specified that the first building to be built on the site by Mercy Seat should be a church, indicating the interest of the seller, August Ruff, in the establishment of a church. In 1912 Mercy Seat merged with Zion Baptist Church, then located at Fifth Avenue between 131st and 132nd Streets, to form Metropolitan Baptist Church. In 1916 the consolidated congregation purchased land at 120 West 138th Street for $30,000 from the executor of the estate of Mary S. Dinkney and built a large church that became known as Metropolitan Tabernacle. They occupied the building for only two years. In 1918 they purchased the large corner church building of the New York Presbyterian Church at Seventh Avenue and 128th Street (again, by way of an intermediary, Emanuel David). Metropolitan Tabernacle was acquired by Marcus Garvey's Universal Negro Improvement Association and renamed Liberty Hall. In 1920 it was the site of that organization's first convention.[44]

By 1911 "Little Zion," the mission church of Mother AME Zion, the purchaser of the Church of the Redeemer property, had become an independent congregation. In that year the congregation built a new church at 60 West 138th Street between Lenox and Fifth Avenues, purchasing land from John Gleed, an African American (possibly the J. R. Glide whose offer to purchase Church of the Redeemer was declined). In the purchase, Little Zion paid $100 and assumed a mortgage of $15,000 on the property. The new building was designed by Tandy and Foster, the architect of St. Philip's church. With the move, Little Zion changed its name to Rush Memorial AME Zion, named after Christopher Rush, the second bishop of the AME Zion denomination.[45]

Other African American congregations relocating or gaining control of Harlem real estate in the first two decades of the 1900s included:

- In 1908 Salem United Methodist Church, pastored by Rev. Frederick Cullen (the adoptive father of Harlem Renaissance poet Countee Cullen), purchased property at 102 West 133rd Street for its growing congregation, which had previously worshipped at a building on West 124th Street. The New York City Church Extension and Missionary Society of the Methodist Episcopal

Church paid $93,000 to Frederic Stimson and the trustees of the will of John Henry Bradford.

• In 1912 Bethel A.M.E. under the pastorate of social gospel minister Rev. Reverdy Ransom built a new church at 52 West 132nd Street on land purchased from Soloman Brooks and Joseph Bichler. The church paid $100 and assumed two mortgages totaling $35,000.

• Metropolitan A.M.E. Church established a congregation in a rented row house at 62 West 135th Street. In 1917 the congregation purchased a building at 132 West 134th Street from a realty company for $200 and a mortgage of $8,000.

• St. John A.M.E. moved to 132 W. 134th Street, taking over the church formerly occupied by Metropolitan A.M.E. Church

• Shiloh Baptist Church purchased 2226 Seventh Avenue in 1918 from Marion A. Daniels, assuming mortgages totaling $18,800.[46]

None of the real estate acquisitions involved transactions between the white congregations and the African American congregations. If the properties were formerly owned by predominantly white congregations, they were purchased by individuals or corporate entities who then sold to the black congregations, repeating the exit strategy employed by the Church of the Redeemer, and hopefully avoiding the disapproval of white residents who remained in Harlem (fig. 4.3).

Individual residential real estate transactions of white Harlem residents illustrated the range of responses that white residents had to the increasing residential presence of African Americans in Harlem. The restrictive covenant movement was rooted in the notion that blacks were a subordinate class whose presence would endanger both the security and the health of white Harlem residents, and therefore result in a reduction in real estate values. Many white Harlem residents believed that African Americans would not be able to afford to maintain the properties they were attempting to buy and that their limited capital would contribute to a decline in values as properties deteriorated.

But other white Harlem residents did sell or lease residential properties to African Americans. The fact that in some cases white sellers helped to fi-

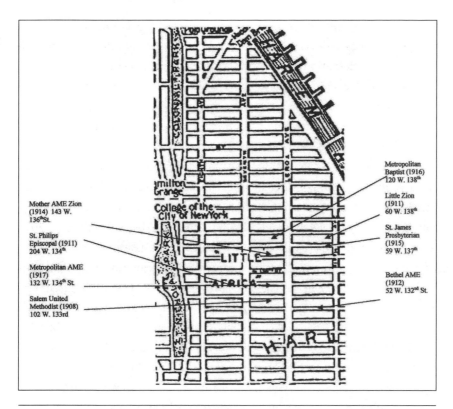

FIGURE 4.3. African American churches established in Harlem, 1908–1917.
Automobile Club of Rochester, 1920, Florida International Center
for Instructional Technology.

nance these sales suggests that they did not subscribe to the belief that the African American presence would result in a precipitous decline in property values. The security for the loans that they made to African Americans was the property that was being purchased. A reduction in the value of the property would have endangered the collateral of their loans. Others, such as Erduin v. d. H. Koch, suggested that African Americans should be able to live wherever they could afford to live.[47]

In contrast to this range of responses regarding black access to residential properties in Harlem, the white response to attempts by African Americans to acquire church properties was uniformly one of great reluctance. Some predominantly white congregations had tolerated African American members for decades by restricting their seating and taking other measures to limit their participation in worship services, illustrating the continuing belief among many whites in the subordinate status of African Americans. As the number of blacks within these congregations grew with the black population in New York after 1900, white congregations became increasingly uncomfortable with their presence. At the same time some predominantly African American congregations, located in midtown or farther south in Manhattan, began to consider moving to Harlem, either following or leading their congregants. Although by this time some white congregations were moving out of Harlem or considering it because of a decline in their congregations and the increase in the black population, no examples can be found of white congregations facilitating the moves of African American congregations to Harlem through the sale or lease of their buildings to African American congregations. Even when white congregations vacated their buildings they did not sell to African American congregations. They sold to white individuals or companies, who later sold the buildings to African American congregations. While white Harlem residents could break rank with their neighbors to engage in individual real estate transactions with blacks where residential properties were concerned (either homes or apartment buildings), Harlem churches with predominantly white congregations, did not engage as corporate bodies in such transactions, perhaps because they believed they would betray a function of the church to maintain the standards of the community, a standard that they believed was being lowered by the "invasion" of African Americans.

The movement of established congregations in Manhattan was not new. It was a function of the northern movement of the primary residential areas of the city in the nineteenth century as residential areas either fell out of favor or transitioned to commercial establishments. With limited transportation options, churches for the most part relied on the residents who lived within walking distance as their congregants. Even when improved transportation eventually made it possible to travel longer distances to church, many denominations and their congregants had grown accustomed to the church being linked with the residents nearby. The Catholic parishes with formal geographic boundaries recognized this connection, but other denominations more informally acknowledged it as well. Given these expectations regarding the role of the church in communities, as the concentration of the residents in Manhattan shifted after several decades, some churches, although remaining in the same locations, reconstituted their congregations with new residents. Others based in areas that were becoming increasingly commercial moved to new locations, and some moved because they preferred to remain near their members who were leaving rather than the newcomers. While these moves undoubtedly engendered regret and anxiety, the changes in Harlem were the first such moves precipitated almost entirely by racial changes, occurring when many of the white church buildings were still relatively new. Before 1900 the African American population in New York City had been small and the areas in which African Americans were concentrated did not result in sufficient numbers of black churchgoers attending white churches to threaten existing white congregations. The African Americans arrived in these earlier areas, such as Greenwich Village or midtown, when the areas were declining as residential communities. Departing white congregations most likely did not feel pushed out, but felt that they were following the natural evolution of the neighborhoods, leaving for more fashionable areas such as Harlem. Having to consider leaving an area that, but for the growing racial animus would still have been considered fashionable, is what made the white congregations so reluctant to leave, and when they did, it made them so reluctant to enter into transactions directly with black congregations who represented the cause of their distress. While in leaving they were conceding defeat, selling directly to African Americans seemed to have been viewed as consorting with the enemy, and hastening the loss of white control of the community that was feared.

Conversely, black congregations moving into Harlem had both pragmatic and symbolic considerations. In some cases, such as St. Philip's Episcopal, the downtown location of their church was becoming less desirable. St. James Presbyterian was in the heart of the black midtown area when it made its offer to purchase the Church of the Redeemer in 1913, recognizing that Harlem, a more attractive community, was becoming the home to an increasing number of black residents. In establishing churches in Harlem, these congregations were also sending a message to their members, the broader black community, and the white community that Harlem was becoming a community with a sufficient number of black people to require black institutions, such as churches, that would serve black people. In building a church, St. Philip's particularly conveyed the message of community formation but also permanence, and of community control. It had purchased land with its own resources and constructed a church of its own design, sending a signal that black people did not have to rely only on what white Harlem residents decided to let them have, but that they had the ability to shape this new community to which they were moving. The St. Philip's congregation's purchase of a block of apartment buildings at the same time that its church was built dramatically reinforced this point. As other black congregations negotiated with middlemen and -women to purchase churches abandoned by white congregations, they added to the momentum of black community formation. Whether they were following or leading their congregations, the presence of the churches attracted additional black residents to Harlem, and as these residents became settled, they began to seek out services for their children and other African American youth and young adults who were making Harlem their home.

5

AFRICAN AMERICAN
YOUTH IN HARLEM

❦

A s the depositions in the Morlath case, and the movement to Harlem
by black churches made clear, by 1913 African Americans had become a substantial presence in the area of Harlem bordering Lenox
Avenue and 135th Street. Philip Payton, founder of the Afro-American Realty Company, was still a resident nearby, at 15 West 131st Street. In 1908 his
company had folded following a lawsuit brought by disgruntled sharehold-
ers upset because they had not received the dividend Payton had promised
to provide, but Payton landed on his feet, and soon started another company,
Philip A. Payton Realty. By 1913, in addition to guiding his new company, he
and his wife, Maggie, were raising their niece and nephew, Bessie and Duke
Hobby. Born in North Carolina, the children, seventeen and fifteen in 1913,
had been brought north following the deaths of their parents, Julia Lee (Maggie's sister) and Greene Hobby. In Harlem, the children joined a burgeoning
population of young African Americans whose presence encouraged their
parents, guardians, and others to make the development of services for youth
a priority.[1] To meet these needs, African Americans and their allies capitalized on a web of church, professional, and personal relationships to bring resources to the black children and young adults in Harlem that approximated
those available to white children and young adults who resided in that area

and other neighborhoods in New York City. But the African American youth activities in the first two decades of the 1900s in Harlem also illustrate the boundaries of New York City's racial segregation customs. Harlem's youth service organizations for African Americans were established as accommodations to racial limitations, but the founders of these organizations continued to look for opportunities to transcend these limits wherever possible.

By the end of the 1910s, African American young adults were served by the Harlem branches of the Young Men's Christian Association and the Young Women's Christian Association. Athletic clubs provided young men with competitive opportunities to participate in sports. The Music School Settlement for Colored People provided cultural activities for young African American children and adults. There were some conflicts between the African American children and white children on Harlem's streets. African American children were the majority in two Harlem schools. In some of the schools that had fewer black students, some white teachers conveyed their prejudices against black people to their black students. But other white principals and teachers were committed to incorporating the increasing numbers of young black newcomers into the lives of the schools, and consequently incorporating their parents into the life of the community. All of these efforts illustrate African Americans' desires to strengthen the community in which they were making their homes by providing guidance outside the family to African American children and young adults.

THE YWCA AND YMCA

In the first years of the 1900s African American New Yorkers began to seek ways to provide positive social and recreational activities as well as religious guidance outside of the church for young men and women by formally affiliating with the Young Men's Christian Association (YMCA) and the Young Women's Christian Association (YWCA).

By the time Charles T. Walker arrived in New York City in 1899 to become pastor of Mt. Olivet Baptist Church, his dynamic preaching style had earned him the nickname "The Black Spurgeon," a comparison to the British Baptist minister Charles Spurgeon, who from 1854 to 1892 frequently preached to audiences of more than 10,000 people in Britain, and became known as the "Prince of Preachers." Walker's initial field of work was the black South. He was born in 1858 in Hephzibah, Georgia, and his parents died when he was young, but his scholastic talents and his family ties to the ministry (two of his uncles were pastors) soon placed him on the same road, a not-uncommon path for an educated young African American man in the post–Civil War years. In his teens Walker was pastor of the Baptist church in his hometown, and soon went on to build Tabernacle Baptist Church in Augusta, Georgia, where the congregation spared him to go on annual speaking tours to share his message with the rest of the nation. When the National Baptist Convention, Inc., was formed in 1895, uniting the autonomous black Baptist churches that had been affiliated with the Baptist Foreign Mission Convention, the National Baptist Convention, and the National Baptist Education Convention, Walker became one of its leaders. This national visibility and an earlier preaching engagement at Mt. Olivet Baptist Church in New York City undoubtedly influenced that congregation's decision to call Walker to become its pastor in 1899. Mount Olivet was founded in 1878, and its congregation grew along with the African American population of New York City in the postwar years. By the time of Walker's arrival, the church was one of the most prominent black congregations in the city, and was located on West 53rd Street between Sixth and Seventh Avenues, in the heart of African American institutional and artistic community of the late nineteenth century.[2]

In addition to preaching, C. T. Walker was also known in Georgia for developing important community programming. In New York, as he began to survey the neighborhood around his new West 53rd Street church, he "found no place for hundreds and hundreds of young colored men to spend their evenings and Sundays, except in dives, saloons, and brothels."[3]

He soon started a series of young men's Bible readings and lectures, adopting the name Colored Young Men's Christian Association. A few months later, the group decided to seek formal affiliation with the YMCA. Walker's biographer noted:

[Dr. Walker] called a public meeting at Mt. Olivet and organized a Y.M.C.A. Nearly every colored pastor in the city, regardless of denomination, became interested in the movement and gave Dr. Walker almost undivided support. Money was raised, a building at 132 West 53rd Street was leased for one year, temporary officers were elected, and on December 18, 1900, application was made to the Y.M.C.A. New York City for membership as one of the regular branches. The application was received and acted on favorably.[4]

The Young Men's Christian Association was founded in London in 1844 by George Williams, a young man who had moved to London from rural Somerset and found employment at a department store in the city. Concerned with the challenges and dangers of city life, he and a group of eleven friends began a Bible study and prayer group. With the goal of improving the spiritual and intellectual lives of men, the concept became popular in other areas of Britain as well as other countries by the 1850s. In 1851 the first YMCA in the United States was formed by Thomas Sullivan, a retired Boston sea captain whose work as a marine missionary made him aware of the needs of sailors.[5]

New York City established a YMCA in 1852, first meeting at the Mercer Street Presbyterian Church in lower Manhattan and then renting spaces at a series of Manhattan locations until 1869, when a large building was constructed at the corner of 23rd Street and Fourth Avenue, designed by noted architect James Renwick.[6] At the ceremony to lay the cornerstone for the building, William Adams, the pastor of the nearby Madison Square Presbyterian Church suggested that the building and the organization would make an important break with what had gone before: "The edifice which was to rise upon that spot was not an eleemosynary institution; it was not a church and yet it combined almost all the ideas which were represented by such buildings. It was not to be a hotel, or a clubhouse; but it was a building that would represent before the public the social element of religion."[7]

The YMCA sought to provide a consistent Christian influence on the lives of young men beyond the walls of the church. The new building's components, "a large library and reading room, rooms for games, social parlors, a gymnasium, baths, a bowling alley, classrooms, lecture rooms and an auditorium" became a template for YMCA buildings across the country.[8]

African Americans were involved in the YMCA movement almost from the very beginning, although their activities were in branches segregated from those of white YMCA participants. In 1853 Anthony Bowen, formerly enslaved, who was working in the U.S. Patent Office in Washington, D.C., organized the first YMCA for African Americans. Motivated by the same factors as their white colleagues, to provide positive religious, social, and educational opportunities for young men, African Americans also viewed the YMCA as another tool that could be used to advance the race by helping to produce responsible, productive, educated men. In the following decades, the YMCA movement became a worldwide phenomenon. Its housing component was particularly appealing to young single men who were moving to cities in greater numbers.[9]

In 1867, a generation before C. T. Walker's arrival in New York, African Americans had established a Colored Young Men's Christian Association "auxiliary unit" at 97 Wooster Street in lower Manhattan. Rev. Henry Highland Garnet, who had guided the black community to recovery following the devastating 1863 Draft Riots, was one of the speakers at the inaugural meeting, which was also attended by Robert McBurney, the trailblazing secretary of the New York YMCA. The large audience heard a discussion of the "importance of young men cultivating the spirit of Christ as the great and grand strengthening influence of all transactions in life."[10] But in spite of such an auspicious start, after four years the Colored Branch ceased operations. This past affiliation with the YMCA may account for the receptiveness of the YMCA to Rev. Walker's 1900 application to establish a Colored Branch, particularly since Robert McBurney, present at the 1867 inaugural meeting of the defunct Colored Branch, still served as secretary of the New York YMCA.[11]

New York City's YMCA branch for African Americans officially opened its doors in 1901, two years after C. T. Walker's arrival in the city. The initial location of the Colored Men's Branch of the YMCA of New York, at 132 West 53rd Street, was in the same block as Mt. Olivet, between Sixth and Seventh Avenues. In the late 1800s, West 53rd Street had become the center of the midtown Manhattan area that was known as "Black Bohemia." On the street were the Marshall and Maceo Hotels, meeting points for black musicians and other African American movers and shakers. Nearby were cabarets and "sporting houses," from which Rev. Walker hoped to redirect young African American men to the YMCA.[12] The West 53rd YMCA branch, two row houses, included "an office, reception room, reading room, a small gymnasium and dormitory quarters."[13] Cleveland G. Allen, a member at the branch, noted that "the buildings being in close proximity to the Churches, schools and other institutions, renders it an ideal location for such an institution."[14]

The staff position of executive secretary of the Colored Men's Branch of the YMCA was a unique career opportunity, considering the limited options available to educated African American men in the early 1900s. New York's Colored Men's Branch of the YMCA attracted a series of talented men to lead it. Walter Cole, a graduate of the College and Theological Institute of Biddle University in North Carolina, began work as branch secretary in January of 1901, but unfortunately the next year he died of typhoid fever. His successor, Rev. Thomas J. Bell, a graduate of Atlanta University and Hartford Seminary, came to the Colored Men's Branch after leading the Congregational Church in Selma, Alabama. In 1903 Bell moved the branch a block west to 252–254 West 53rdStreet,

> which offered larger quarters in order to meet the demands that were being made to offer proper facilities for the development of young men. . . . The Old Fifty-third Street Branch has been instrumental in starting many young men on helpful careers. In 1906 over five hundred young men were placed in helpful positions in various capacities. During the year 1906 2,110 attended lectures and educational classes at the old Fifty-third Street Branch.[15]

The YMCA continued on West 53rd Street, through most of the first two decades of the 1900s. In the late 1910s, acknowledging that the center of Manhattan's black community had shifted northward, the branch began planning a move to Harlem. By this time the branch was under new leadership. Thomas E. Taylor became executive secretary in 1916 after Rev. Bell resigned to lead the Colored YMCA in Denver. Taylor had led the Indianapolis Branch for several years, a branch that had been founded with the assistance of community leaders such as Madam C. J. Walker. Taylor's background differed from those of his predecessors. He was a native of London, Ontario,

Canada, where he had attended the Public Collegiate Institute and Business University before working as a barber with his father for eight years, and then for the Canadian Postal Service. After his arrival in Indianapolis in 1905, he was credited with building the branch's membership to 400 by 1910. He was noted for inaugurating a "Monster Meeting" mass lecture series that continued decades after his departure from the branch. Taylor applied similar skills to his work in New York, and as a result by the end of the decade the membership outgrew the West 53rd Street site.[16]

Preparing for its move, the Colored YMCA began raising funds to build a building in Harlem. With Henry Parker, partner with John Nail in Nail and Parker real estate brokerage firm, serving as the chair of its property committee, funds for the new building eventually included a $25,000 contribution from philanthropist Julius Rosenwald. In spite of some resistance from the YMCA City Association (the central decision-making body) because the location was on a predominantly white block, the Colored Men's Branch of the YMCA bought lots on West 135th Street, a main thoroughfare in Harlem, near Seventh Avenue. A six-story building was constructed at 181 West 135th Street at a total cost of $375,000 (the City Association had recommended a two-story building). The new building, "the most modern and largest YMCA building for Negroes in the Country," opened on Armistice Day, November 11, 1919. Its facilities included a swimming pool, a lecture hall, and a gymnasium.[17]

Ten blocks away, at 5 West 125th Street, the Harlem Branch YMCA served Harlem's white residents. The YMCA's presence in Harlem dated to 1868, when it was founded by members of Harlem's Old Dutch Reformed and Congregational churches. In 1880 it opened the 125th Street building, where it provided reading rooms and other amenities common to YMCA branches. The two branches coexisted until the 1930s, when the Harlem Branch was folded into the Washington Heights Branch, and the 135th Street branch became known as the Harlem Branch.[18]

By 1919, when the 135th Street YMCA branch opened, young African American women had been served by a YWCA branch in Harlem for more than five years, but their journey to Harlem had included several unique challenges. As with the men, their entry into the Y network began at Mt. Olivet

Baptist Church. In 1905, six years after the meeting at that church led to the formation of the Colored Men's Branch of the YMCA, Carrie King, Lucy Robinson, and eighty-three other African American women, some of whom had assisted in the YMCA's formation, met to form a Young Women's Christian Association (YWCA) to serve African American women in New York City. King, a member of St. James Presbyterian Church, then on West 51st Street, and Robinson, a member of Mt. Olivet, undoubtedly noticed the increasing numbers of single young African American women moving to New York City at the turn of the century. In the African American community there was a great concern that, without proper support and guidance, these women would be exploited while they looked for lodging and employment. Tales were common of naive women who arrived from the South and were sexually assaulted, lured into lives of prostitution, or otherwise exploited. Housing and guidance for women became a priority. In 1897 Victoria Earle Matthews created the White Rose and Industrial Association to provide housing for these women. But the number of women moving to New York far exceeded the capacity of the association's rooms. In addition to lodging, the women forming the Colored YWCA hoped to provide a continuing Christian influence on young African American women whether they lodged at their branch or lived elsewhere.[19]

The women at the 1905 meeting at Mt. Olivet represented some of the best-educated reformers that black New York had to offer. Soon after the founding meeting, the women negotiated an agreement with the 15th Street branch of the YWCA to become an affiliate of the branch. The national YWCA had recently required that all new branches establish affiliations with existing branches. During the negotiations regarding affiliation, the African American women successfully denied the request of the 15th Street branch to assist with the drafting of the new group's constitution and bylaws, which they drafted independently of the branch with which they were to be affiliated.[20]

In its initial years, Lucy Robinson served as the president of the branch's board of management. She was born in North Carolina in 1855, and in 1859 her father was killed in John Brown's raid of the Harpers Ferry army arsenal. She studied at Hampton Institute in Virginia, and afterward taught school in

North Carolina. After her marriage in 1878, she moved to New York, where she supplemented her teacher's income by dressmaking. In New York she became a member of Mt. Olivet and was in attendance at the 1899 meeting that led to the formation of the YMCA.[21] Under her leadership, the Colored Women's Branch of the YWCA first secured rented space at 169 West 63rd Street, within the San Juan Hill black neighborhood of Manhattan. But when the building was sold they soon moved to 143 West 53rd Street, down the street from the Colored Men's Branch of the YMCA. By the spring of 1907 they were regularly hosting Bible study groups, prayer meetings, lectures, and other social and educational activities for young women.[22] In 1907, the branch hired its first paid staff person, Eva Bowles, also a teacher from the South, as the branch's general secretary. She remained in the position for less than a year, leaving in 1908 due to illness. Over the next few years, a series of educated young women held the staff position for short periods of time.

In contrast to the frequent staff changes at the Colored Women's Branch of the YWCA, the board of management of the branch had stable leadership. Following the death of branch president Lucy Robinson in 1908, Carrie King, who had been present at the initial meeting, served as president in 1908. In January 1909 Emma Ransom was elected president. She was new to New York, having arrived in 1907 when her husband, Rev. Reverdy Ransom, an innovative Progressive minister, was assigned as pastor of Bethel African Methodist Episcopalian (AME) Church on West 25th Street after serving as pastor of Charles Street AME Church in Boston. A native of Selma, Ohio, she had taught school before her marriage. As a pastor's wife she co-edited a missionary journal, *Women's Light and Love for Heathen Africa*, and was active in the African American women's club movement that was beginning to provide a national network for black women to address social and civil rights issues. At the New York Colored Women's Branch of the YWCA, Ransom initially focused on the branch's financial stability. The Central YWCA, created in a reorganization of New York City's branches, was also concerned about the finances of the Colored Women's Branch, and in 1911 announced its desire to "secure a white woman to act as General Secretary at the Colored Women's Branch for six months." Louise Goodrich was hired in April and paid $35 per month more than the previous African American branch secretary. When she left the position in October, she noted that she had "decided that a white secretary is not acceptable to the colored women."[23]

The history of the Young Women's Christian Association (YWCA) parallels that of the YMCA. Begun as a women's prayer group in London by Emma Roberts and Lady Mary Jane Kinnaird in 1855, more than a decade after the YMCA had formed (also in Britain), the group adopted the name Young Women's Christian Association and sought ways to offer tangible assistance to women by providing housing for single women, a library, an employment bureau, and Bible classes. The YWCA in the United States grew out of a series of Protestant revivals in New York City in 1857 and 1858 that led to the formation of the Ladies' Christian Union, which developed into a YWCA affiliate. Their target group was "young white working women who did not attend any church." In 1893 African American women in Dayton, Ohio, received permission to form the first black affiliate branch of the YWCA in the United States.[24]

The West 53rd Street lease for the Colored Branch of the YWCA expired on May 1, 1913, and the members of the branch saw an opportunity to move to Harlem in recognition of the earlier moves of other black institutions and former residents to that neighborhood. Similar to the YMCA, a Harlem Branch of the YWCA had existed since 1891, established by Dutch women; in 1913 it was located at 72 West 124th Street. As with the men's branches, racial segregation and cultural customs dictated that African American women would need to identify their own site for a building to serve their own. By 1913, Emma Ransom's husband had become editor of *The A.M.E. Church Review*, but during his pastorate at Bethel the family had lived in a parsonage on West 129th Street in Harlem, which would have acquainted Emma Ransom with the needs and possibilities in the community. The women of the Colored YWCA identified a building at 118 West 131st Street that they planned to lease, but they were discouraged from moving forward when the Metropolitan Board of the YWCA, the governing body of all branches in the city, was approached by "a portion of the Harlem community" who opposed the move. The 100 block of West 131st was a restrictive covenant block, and undoubtedly signers of the covenant or their sympathizers had made their feelings known to the board.[25] Similar to YWCAs across the country, while the Metropolitan YWCA provided some support to the Colored Branch, its leadership was drawn from the local power structure and therefore its branches were usually required to work within the confines of that structure, such as acceding on matters of racial segregation. But the women of the Colored YMCA had strong ties to Harlem's African American real estate investors. The chair of the YWCA's finance committee was Ella Thomas, wife of undertaker James C. Thomas, who had been president of Philip Payton's Afro-American Realty Company. A member of the Colored YWCA's Board of Management, Maybelle McAdoo, had been the chief stenographer for the Afro-American Realty Company. Later in the spring of 1913, the branch announced that it had leased two adjoining houses at 121 and 123 West 132nd. After renovations to join the two houses and their backyards, the new headquarters for the Colored Branch of the YWCA opened in Harlem in July 1913.[26]

The services of the YWCA were quickly in great demand as Harlem's African American population increased dramatically during the early years of the Great Migration. Thousands of single young African American women and men moved to New York and other northern cities from southern towns, seeking better employment opportunities and an escape from racial segregation and violence. Harlem's Colored Women's Branch of the YWCA provided connections to potential employers as well as limited housing, with nineteen beds.[27] Soon the Colored Branch also screened and enrolled Harlem residents to provide housing for young women in area homes and apartments. World War I exacerbated the demand for the Y's services, and this demand coincided with a 1913 $4 million capital campaign of the Metropolitan YMCA and YWCA. With an understanding that the Metropolitan YWCA would receive $3 million of the campaign proceeds, Emma Ransom played a pivotal role in obtaining a fair share for the Harlem Y. She eventually extracted a commitment from the Metropolitan Y to increase its financial support of capital campaign funds to the Colored Women's Branch from $10,000 to $100,000. Using these funds as seed money, the women of the Colored Branch raised more than $200,000 in additional funds to acquire land and build a multi-service five-story building at 179 West 137th Street. When the building opened in January 1920, a few months after the YMCA's new 135th Street building opened, it included "a cafeteria with a capacity of one hundred, an information desk, reception rooms, offices, meeting rooms, classrooms, a gymnasium, a pool and shower and locker rooms, this YWCA became the best-equipped African American YWCA in the country."[28]

By 1920, from their new buildings on 135th and 137th Streets, the African American branches of the YMCA and the YWCA provided clear symbols of the commitment of the members of these institutions to Harlem as a future base of black New Yorkers, while also symbolizing African Americans' determination to provide ongoing support to the young adults in their community as they entered the world of work.

ATHLETIC CLUBS

When the YMCA moved from 53rd Street to Harlem in 1919, it provided an additional recreational option for some young African American men in Harlem who had already been participating in sports through small private athletic clubs. Conrad Norman was nine years old in 1893 when he arrived in New York City from the Spanish Town section of Jamaica with his parents and his two brothers and two sisters. The family soon found an apartment on West 16th Street just north of the old Greenwich Village black enclave. Their father, who had worked as a printer for the *Daily Gleaner* newspaper in Jamaica, found work in New York. By the time Conrad reached his teens, he and his brothers, Gerald and Clifton, were swept up into the national obsession with physical culture. Across the country debates raged regarding whether the American man was becoming soft with the disappearance of the western frontier and the continuing movement from the farm to urban areas, where men spent their days indoors. A parallel debate had begun among African Americans, who, as they moved to cities in increasing numbers, were often consigned to crowded areas where they suffered disproportionately from diseases such as tuberculosis. For both groups, athletics was one proposed solution. Young African American men, however, faced considerable obstacles to participating in this effort. Later reflecting on his motivation for forming an athletic club, Conrad Norman noted that in turn-of-the-century New York, "although there were seventy thousand colored people in New York at the time, and the big city fairly teemed with athletic clubs of all kinds, recreation centers, playgrounds, settlements, schools, Turn Verein halls, and colleges, each provided with a gymnasium, there was not a single one devoted to colored people."[29]

Conrad Norman, along with his brothers and other West Indians, formed the Alpha Physical Culture Club in 1904 in Harlem to begin addressing this lack of athletic facilities. They initially operated out of a room in a "church house" on West 134th Street. With a commitment to education, as well as to the growing trend of physical education to counter health problems that troubled African Americans, the Norman brothers all attended City College of New York, and all became standouts in the Alpha Physical Club. By 1906 the thirty-five dues-paying members of the club were able to lease a brownstone at 79 West 134th Street, in the heart of the growing African American enclave, for their headquarters. The club soon became a pioneer in the new sport of basketball and began competing against other local athletic clubs, among them the Salem Crescent Athletic Club of Salem United Methodist Church.

The African American congregation of Salem United Methodist Church was established in Harlem in 1902, by Rev. Frederick Cullen. In 1911, Rev. Cullen started the club by persuading boys who gathered on West 133rd Street in the vicinity of the church to use the church for their meetings and eventually to work within the church through the Salem Crescent Athletic Club. The club fielded athletes in several sports, including track and field, boxing, and basketball, which was in its infancy. The club was particularly respected for its track and field athletes and sent athletes to compete in the 1915 San Francisco International Exposition as well as other international competitions.[30]

St. Christopher's Athletic Club was another competitor among African American athletic clubs in Manhattan. It operated under the auspices of St. Christopher's Guild for young men which was organized in 1895 by St. Philip's Episcopal Church on 25th Street. In addition to boxing, track, and basketball teams, the guild sponsored a glee club and amateur dramatics. In 1911 when St. Philip's moved into its newly constructed church in Harlem, the gymnasium of the adjacent parish house on West 134th Street became the base for the athletic club. New York's athletic clubs participated in fierce rivalries that extended across the city and included African American clubs such as the Smart Set Athletic Club in Brooklyn, and eventually clubs in other cities, such as Washington, D.C. The athletic clubs laid the foundation for black participation in professional basketball in the 1920s.[31]

The athletic clubs came into existence because the color line prohibited black men from participating in white YMCA teams (or even attending games as spectators). Although African Americans had established YMCA branches in many cities across the nation by the 1910s, most did not have gymnasiums, which were essential for learning the techniques of the new game of basketball. In 1906 the *New York Age,* speaking of New York City's Colored Branch of the YMCA, noted: "The little play room, called a 'gymnasium,' will soon be thoroughly fitted up for use of the Athletic Club." St. Philip's new parish house on West 133rd Street included a gymnasium, and the St. Christopher Club became a competitive team. The purpose of these athletic activities was more than just casual play. Salem United Methodist and St. Philip's Episcopal both became noted for their wide range of community programs, of which athletics were just a small part. The Social Gospel movement of the late nineteenth and early twentieth centuries challenged churches to improve the communities in which they were located. In the same way that African Americans sought YMCA and YWCA branches as a way to productively direct the energy of young men and women, athletic clubs offered athletic opportunities where African American YMCA branches with sufficient athletic facilities were not available. The clubs also provided African American young men with leadership and management opportunities. The Salem and St. Christopher clubs operated under the auspices of churches, but the young participants had considerable latitude in decision making. Members of the Alpha Physical Club ran the club themselves, which provided excellent training for other activities that they would pursue later in life.[32]

PUBLIC SCHOOL ATHLETIC LEAGUE

Opportunities for African American women to participate in athletics were not as numerous as those available to young men, but the 1910s were a time when women were advocating for wider access in many areas, such as the vote and educational opportunities. Participation in sports complemented their demands on other issues. The YWCA provided women with an opportunity to participate in organized recreation, and the Public School Athletic League (PSAL) included girls in its offerings of scholastic sports. In 1905, when the Girls' Branch of the PSAL was formed, its vision included the following ideas about sports for girls:

1. Athletics for all girls
2. Athletics within the school and no inter-school athletics
3. Athletic events in which teams (not individual girls) compete
4. Athletics chosen and practiced with regard to their suitability for girls and not merely in imitation of boys' athletics.[33]

This list illustrates the perceptions of what was appropriate for young women. Individual competition was promoted among boys and men, but clearly not desirable for women. The desire to maintain the image of femininity within the context of athletics was also important. African American girls in Harlem schools could participate in sports that met these criteria, including walking, swimming, ice skating, and rope skipping.[34] By the early 1900s the color line in the New York City schools had been removed, and in contrast to New York's YMCAs, YWCAs, and local athletic clubs, black and white children participated on the same PSAL teams.

PSAL athletics for boys had a more ambitious vision compared to that for girls:

1. No boy is eligible who has ever taken part in professional athletics
2. No boy may represent his school unless he has been a member of the school for a certain length of time ...
3. No boy is admitted into any contest who has not received a passing mark for the month previous in effort, proficiency and deportment
4. No entry is accepted unless approved by the principal of the school.[35]

The sports offerings for boys were much greater and more rigorous than those for girls. For instance, the high school section of the league offered the following: indoor track and field games, outdoor track and field games, soccer, cross-country, lacrosse, indoor rifle shooting, tennis, indoor swimming, hockey, outdoor rifle shooting, basketball, baseball, and football.[36]

PSAL athletics provided one of the few venues where black and white children in New York City participated as teammates.

HARLEM PUBLIC SCHOOLS

The absence of the color line in the Public School Athletic League reflected the broader policy of the New York City public school system, which in the first decades of the 1900s was one of the few New York institutions in which the color line was barred by law, and in which, despite segregation in almost every other aspect of daily life, some efforts were made to provide African American children with the same opportunities as their white classmates enjoyed.

In the 1910s integrated schooling was a relatively new idea in the city. New York's public schooling for African American children began in 1787 when the New York Manumission Society established the first nonreligious free school for African American children. In 1794 it was incorporated as the African Free School.[37] By the early 1800s there were three schools, all with black teachers, reporting to a committee appointed by the Manumission Society. The schools were known for their rigor. In 1827, when the French general Lafayette visited New York City, he was impressed by the recitation of a ten-year-old African American student, James McCune Smith, who would later go on to attend medical school in Glasgow and become a physician and leader in the African American community of New York. Many mid-nineteenth-century African American leaders were products of the African Free School system, including pastor and activist Henry Highland Garnet and priest and missionary Alexander Crummell. By 1853 all African Free Schools were subsumed under the New York City Board of Education, with black students remaining segregated in separate "colored" schools.[38]

In 1870 seven colored schools were operating, but when the system came to its end in Manhattan in 1884, only two remained, serving a total of 500 students. It was estimated that another 800 African American students were already attending Ward schools with white students closer to their homes than the colored schools. The impetus for ending the separate system was not community protest but cost. When the Board of Education's 1883 appropriation of city funds was reduced, the board voted as a cost-saving measure to close the colored schools and reassign the students to existing schools. The board seems to have initially planned to fire the black teachers and administrators, but after strong protests from the black community, and an extension on the school closures, at the end of 1884, the African American students, teachers, and principals were reassigned to Ward schools. Going forward, placement of African American students would be based on their place of residency rather than their race.

In 1898, when the borough of Manhattan was consolidated with the boroughs of Brooklyn, Queens, Staten Island, and the Bronx to form Greater New York City, the color line customs in schooling still existed in Queens. The area had not been subject to the 1880s decision of the Board of Education, which had then covered only Manhattan. In 1900 the racial restrictions in schooling in Queens and in other areas of the state were eradicated with a bill passed by the state legislature prohibiting schools based on race.[39]

Jacob Theobald began his teaching career during this time of transition. Born in Germany in 1878, he had arrived in New York at the age of three with his father, who was a painter. During his childhood, his family, which included two brothers and a sister, lived on 11th Street between Sixth and Seventh Avenues. A graduate of City College of New York, Theobald had become an elementary school teacher in 1898. He became principal of P.S. 89 at Lenox Avenue and 134th Street in 1906, just as the African American presence in the area was expanding dramatically beyond its small enclave one block away at 135th Street. Six years later, in 1913, Theobald was leading a biracial school of more than 1,800 students.[40] In *Colored School Children in New York*, settlement worker Frances Blascoer reported on schools she had studied in 1913:

Public School 89 on Lenox Avenue, running from 134th to 135th Streets, had the largest registration of colored pupils—1277 out of a total of 1841, the next largest being Public School 119, a girls' school on 133rd Street near Eighth Avenue, which had 774 colored girls out of a total of 2080 pupils. Public School 100, at 135th Street and Fifth Avenue had a large proportion of colored pupils. . . . Public School 68, at 112 West 128th Street, with 241 colored boys and girls, is the only other Harlem school showing any large number of colored pupils.[41]

The locations of the schools identified in Frances Blascoer's report provide a sense of the settlement patterns of African Americans in New York City (see tables 5.1 and 5.2 for a full list of Manhattan schools), and particularly highlight the dramatic increase and concentration of the black population in Harlem. Out of approximately sixty Manhattan public schools, the three schools with more than 35 percent black students were in Harlem: P.S. 119, at 133rd Street and Eighth Avenue; P.S. 89, at 135th Street and Lenox Avenue; and P.S. 100, at 135th Street and Fifth Avenue. In addition to these schools, four other schools had student populations that were more than 10 percent African American.

P.S. 68, on West 128th Street, represented the southward expansion of Harlem's African American enclave. P.S. 69 was located within the older Black Bohemia community, while P.S. 141 was located in the San Juan Hill neighborhood and P.S. 28 was located in the heart of the Tenderloin community. The population of black students in most of the other schools ranged from one percent to 3 percent, with a few having 5 percent to 9 percent.[42]

TABLE 5.1 Harlem Schools with More Than 35 Percent
African American Student Populations, 1913

School		Colored			White				
Number	Location	Boys	Girls	Subtotal	Boys	Girls	Subtotal	Total	% Black Students
119	8th Ave. & W. 133rd St.	56	718	774	289	1,017	1,306	2,080	37
100	5th Ave. & 135th St.	55	298	353	50	157	207	560	63
89	Lenox Ave. & 135th St.	923	354	1,277	482	82	564	1,841	69

TABLE 5.2 Harlem Schools with 10–34 Percent
African American Student Populations, 1913

| School | | Colored | | | White | | | | % Black |
Number	Location	Boys	Girls	Subtotal	Boys	Girls	Subtotal	Total	Students
68	116 W. 128th St.	78	163	241	366	954	1,320	1,561	15
141	464 W. 58th St.	41	125	166	383	571	954	1,120	15
69	125 W. 54th St.	77	108	185	686	509	1,195	1,380	13
28	257 W. 40th St.	38	104	142	167	861	1,028	1,170	12

A closer look at the three schools with high concentrations of black students provides a window on the fairly dramatic impact that black students had on Harlem's schools. P.S. 89, on Lenox Avenue, spanned the block from West 134th to West 135th Streets, across the avenue from the African American enclave that had been the setting for the 1904 showdown between the Afro-American Realty Company and the Hudson Realty Company. The four-story building of Gothic and Roman styles had a redbrick facade with stone trim bordering its tall windows and accenting parts of the lower and upper floors. The building was constructed in two stages, with the first section along West 134th Street and Lenox Avenue opening in September 1890. In the January 1891 issue of *School,* the weekly magazine for New York City educators, it was noted that

> in the past twenty-five years the centre of public school interests of the city has moved from 13th Street to Harlem. Among the public schools of Harlem Mr. Elijah A. Howland's Grammar No. 89, Lenox Avenue and 134th Street is easily with the first. . . . [The Grammar and Primary Departments] are nearly filled to their limit and it is expected that the vacant lots to the north of the school will be purchased for 89.[43]

By 1891, No. 89's principal, Elijah Howland, had served as a principal of Harlem schools for more than twenty-five years. In 1865 he had become principal of the No. 43 school in Manhattanville at Amsterdam Avenue and 129th Street; in 1875 he moved to become principal of Grammar School

No. 68 on 128th Street. He had become principal of No. 89 in 1889 and continued as principal at its new location. The school established a reputation both for scholarship and for athletic achievement during his tenure. As predicted by the *School* writer, to meet the growing population in the surrounding neighborhood, the second part of the school was built a few years after the initial opening of the Lenox building, extending the school along Lenox Avenue to 135th Street. The offspring of residents of the African American enclave on 133rd, 134th, and 135th Streets would have attended school in the spacious new No. 89, only blocks from their homes.[44]

This was the legacy that Jacob Theobald inherited when he became principal of Grammar School No. 89 in 1906. In spite of hostile responses from some residents to the increased African American presence in Harlem after 1904, as principal, Theobald was an advocate for his students regardless of race. He was an advocate for their parents as well. In 1920 he observed:

> Perhaps the most hopeful aspect of the school situation . . . is the enthusiastic desire on the part of parent, parents, or guardian to give the boy [girls also were students] all the opportunity . . . along educational lines. I can recall not a single instance in over five and a half years where a parent wished deliberately to sacrifice educational opportunities in order to have the benefit of a few dollars, the boy might be able to earn. I am convinced as the result of 22 years of service in the schools of New York that there is not another section where so much is sacrificed and even want is endured in order to keep the boy in school.[45]

The parental sacrifices described by Jacob Theobald were familiar to black New Yorkers of the 1910s. For generations they had been required to be particularly diligent to ensure the adequate schooling of their children.

As Harlem's population grew, the increases in the number of schools and the student population, described in the 1891 issue of *School*, were evident as Harlem schools made their mark academically and athletically. Jacob Theobald's school reflected these gains even as its racial composition was transformed. The changes in the student body at P.S. 89 also led to changes in the teaching staff, and. by 1920 twelve of fifty-seven teachers (21 percent) at P.S. 89 were black.

Adam Clayton Powell, Jr., who attended P.S. 89 in the 1910s, had fond memories of the school: "In those days the old brick school on 134th Street seemed to have such huge rooms and oversized windows—windows with sunlight pouring in over potted plants into the room that had all sorts of pretty cutouts pasted on the wall. And I loved school . . . all the teachers were beautiful angels."[46]

Musician Thomas "Fats" Waller, five years older than Powell, also attended P.S. 89 in the 1910s. He played music for school assemblies, and at these events he began to entertain his classmates by inserting improvisational phrases, "Wallerisms," into the marches and classical selections. As a result, "attendance at the classical sessions [was] no longer an obligation but a 'must.'"[47]

While life in some Harlem classrooms seemed pleasant for white and black students, at a meeting discussing Blascoer's study she reported that some students had "complained to her that they had been called 'nigger' by both teachers and students in the public schools."[48] Outside of school, away from the gaze of strict principals and teachers, childhood animosities that led to confrontations between children who were different were also a part of Harlem life in the 1910s, at least in the 130s neighborhoods where African American children were increasing in number. After living on West 134th Street, Adam Clayton Powell, Jr.'s family briefly relocated to 40th Street to live in an apartment building next door to the church his father led, the Abyssinian Baptist Church. The son did not like the downtown school experience, and he was pleased when the family soon returned to Harlem, this time living on West 136th Street between Seventh and Eighth Avenues, where Powell Junior attended P.S. 5 on Edgecombe Avenue near 140th Street (2 percent black in 1913). Race was definitely an issue for the children in the neighborhood, as the fair-skinned boy soon discovered.[49]

The first night that my father sent me out to buy the evening paper in our new neighborhood on 136th Street, a gang of Negro boys grabbed me and asked, "What are you, white or colored?" I had never thought of color. I looked at my skin and said, "White!" Whereupon I was promptly and thoroughly beaten.

The very next night I had to go to Eighth Avenue to get something from the store for Mother, and a gang of white boys grabbed me and demanded, "What are you?" Remembering my answer, and my beating of the preceding night, I answered, "Colored!" Whereupon I was again bloodied.[50]

Samuel Battle, the first African American policeman to be appointed in Manhattan, had similar memories:

All of Eighth Avenue was Irish, and Seventh Avenue was a mixture of Irish and Jewish. One hundred and thirty-seventh Street to 140th Street, any place below 133rd St., was Irish, German, and Italian. One thing I shall never forget. The Irish boys on Eighth Avenue wouldn't let the other races come on Eighth Avenue at all. It was forbidden ground to them.[51]

Although there were childhood skirmishes in the street, some of the school buildings welcomed not only African American children but their parents also. P.S. 89 did this in the 1910s through the creation of the Lenox Community Center, whose stated purpose was to "establish in P.S. 89, Manhattan, a civic, social, and recreational center, to develop social life and the spirit of cooperation through clubs, classes, public meetings and any other activity which may broaden and enrich the lives of its members, and the community in which it is located."[52]

In 1915 the center announced:

Henceforth Community Center 89 will be called the Lenox Community Center. The Lenox Community Center at 135th Street and Lenox Avenue invites all clubs to hold their meetings in its quarters at the nominal charge of 50 cents a meeting. Clubs chartered by the center will be charged only 25 cents. The Lenox Community Center will begin a course of lectures Friday night, November 5. This is an educational opportunity.[53]

The lectures described in the announcement were part of an ambitious national, progressive initiative toward adult education, both formal and informal. Some of the impetus for the evening programs came from criticism that public schools, which represented substantial capital investments, were underutilized since they were empty at the end of the school day as well as in the summer when most were closed. Across the nation, many schools developed adult lecture programs as well as summer programs for children and adults. The New York Public School System had a Bureau of Lectures, which organized weekly events at a number of public schools on evenings and weekends. The Lenox Community Center was not part of this initiative, but it was established independently in an environment in which adult educational enrichment was promoted, and this belief extended to the African American adults who were a part of the center's audience. In 1915 Afro-Caribbean activist Hubert Harrison was among the speakers who presented weekly lectures.[54]

Formal education for adults was also promoted at the Lenox Community Center. By 1920, *The Crisis*, the magazine of the National Association for the Advancement of Colored People, regularly ran advertisements for the Lenox Community Center's classes in stenography, typing, and bookkeeping. Many community centers were self-governed by committees, with group rental fees being used to cover their operations costs. The Lenox center seemed to be in this category. The director of the Lenox Community Center was Fitz Mottley, a native of the British West Indies.[55]

The school with the next largest population of African American students in 1913 was P.S. 119 (37 percent), at Eighth Avenue and West 133rd Street. By the time Frances Blascoer's study took place in 1913 (it was published in 1915), the school was on the edge of the western boundary of the black population's settlement in Harlem. Lenox Avenue, the previous implicit western boundary for black Harlem residents, had been breached in 1910 when Hutchens Bishop led St. Philip's Episcopal Church in acquiring land and then building a church and community house on 134th Street between Seventh and Eighth Avenues. P.S. 119, built in 1899 as the James Russell Lowell School, was at the western end of the block.

P.S. 119's five-story building had cornices and towers that led a later writer to describe it as "medieval in appearance."[56] In the 1910s P.S. 119 was a school for girls. Gertrude Ayers, an African American principal, reflected decades later that in the 1910s the principal, Mrs. Harriet Tupper, had made her school popular. This was due to the fact that the girls were given a full program of academic work. In addition, everyone of them had a try at dressmaking, millinery, flower-making, novelty and tea-room work. The outstanding success of the last was due to the enthusiasm of Mrs. Maude B. Richardson, one of the early Negro graduates of Pratt Institute.[57]

Mrs. Tupper even wore the dresses her students made for her, a practice that undoubtedly served to motivate them. P.S. 119 had an active parent-teachers association, which by the 1920s was led by Fred R. Moore. A man who had fathered eighteen children would seem well suited to be president of a parent-teacher association, but Moore had many other equally important qualifications for the position. He was publisher of the *New York Age*, as well as the New York agent for Booker T. Washington's National Negro Business League. Unfortunately only six of his eighteen children lived to adulthood, but his youngest daughter, Marian, most likely attended P.S. 119 after Moore moved the family from Brooklyn to Harlem. There he purchased adjacent brick townhouses at 228 and 230 West 135th Street. One townhouse became the office of the *New York Age*, while the other housed the twelve members of the extended Moore family, which included Moore; his wife, Ida; his youngest daughter, Marian (17); sons Gilbert (26) and Eugene (34) and their wives; a nephew (20); three grandchildren; and a domestic, who undoubtedly had her hands full in helping to maintain such a large household. Moore used his extensive national African American contacts to bring before P.S. 119 leaders such as Robert Russa Moton, head of Tuskegee Institute, and Harlem physician Dr. E. P. Roberts.[58]

Five blocks away from P.S. 89, at West 138th Street, P.S. 100 was also a magnet for black students in the 1910s. Opened in 1909, the four-story brick and stone building was approximately 100 feet west of Fifth Avenue. By 1913, when Frances Blascoer's study on black children in the public schools was made, P.S. 100's principal, Dr. Charles J. Pickett, recommended that the school be renamed the Vocational School for Boys to reflect its focus. High schools were still a relatively new phenomenon in Manhattan. While several had existed in Brooklyn when it was a separate city (before 1898), the first three high schools in Manhattan were established at later dates: Stuyvesant High School was established in 1904 on 15th Street as a "manual training school for boys." Wadleigh High School for Girls, founded in 1897, moved from 36 East 12th Street to a new $900,000 showcase building on West 114th Street and Seventh Avenue in Harlem in 1902. DeWitt Clinton High School was also established in 1897 on 13th Street. These schools had a negligible number of black students in 1913.[59]

With its location, at 135th Street near Fifth Avenue, in the heart of the growing African American neighborhood, P.S. 100 had a large number of African American students. The school had been established as an elementary school, but in 1911 its emphasis shifted to vocational training at the high school level, while continuing to maintain some elementary school classes in the building. Before the establishment of these high schools, many students ended their scholastic careers in the eighth or ninth grades. Those interested in continuing their education attended DeWitt Clinton High School at 174 West 102nd Street or Peter Cooper High School for Boys and Girls (also established in 1897) at 157th Street and Third Avenue in the Bronx. Students from more prosperous families went away to high school. City College's move to Harlem in 1907 provided less-wealthy male students with a third option, Townsend Harris High School on the City College campus, which offered classes in preparation for college work.[60]

Principal Charles J. Pickett described P.S. 100's purpose in a 1911 *New York Times* article, saying: "Vocational schools aim to send out their graduates with trained skilled hands, guided by minds trained to quick, adequate thinking of the work to be accomplished. We do not want any rule-of-thumb boys in our school: we want boys to receive a training which will enable them to be thinkers."[61]

At a time when very few high school students continued on to college, Pickett viewed high schools such as the Vocational School for Boys as essential to providing skills that would prevent boys from being trapped in dead-end thought-numbing jobs or, even worse, ending up without employment and becoming derelicts. Pickett's views about the school were directed to a predominantly white student body, but they echoed the educational philosophy that Booker T. Washington had been promoting to African Americans for more than two decades.

Graduates of P.S. 89 grammar school who continued their schooling in all likelihood attended the Vocational School for Boys. It is possible that Philip Payton's nephew Duke Hobby was among them. In 1913 Duke would have been fifteen years old, and while he may have attended P.S. 89 for grammar school, P.S. 100, three blocks from his home on West 131st Street, would have been an ideal choice for high school if he was not academically inclined. Frances Blascoer indicated that by 1913 more than 60 percent of the school's student population was black, and Charles Pickett despaired over the challenge of finding jobs for African American graduates in the racially discriminatory New York skilled trade market. The school was featured in several articles during the 1910s, many with accompanying photographs. Whether by chance or design, however, none of the black students were included in the images of P.S. 100 students diligently at work in various workshops.[62]

MUSIC SCHOOL SETTLEMENT FOR COLORED PEOPLE

Athletics addressed the physical fitness and competitive spirit of Harlem's youth, and engaging schools provided thriving scholastic environments for young people, but there were also concerns regarding their cultural development. In 1911 a group of interested benefactors sought ways to provide cultural activities for New York's African American children and adults through the Music School Settlement for Colored People. They included philanthropist George Foster Peabody; Felix Adler, founder of the Ethical Culture Society; Natalie Curtis, a well-to-do white New Yorker with an interest in African American traditional music; and New York Philharmonic violinist David Mannes, who had previously helped to establish a music school in the Third Street Music Settlement on the Lower East Side. The purpose of the Music School Settlement for Colored People was "the educational appeal to the negro through music . . . ; the foundation of a social centre which shall produce a healthy moral environment for adults and provide instructive recreation; and . . . the preservation, encouragement and development, along natural lines of the music of the negro."[63]

Many of those in the founding group believed that music education could bring down the barriers between the races by demonstrating the skills of African American musicians while also exposing African Americans to a broader range of cultural experiences, including drawing on traditional African American music rather than minstrel songs and other popular entertainments. Violinist David Mannes described his interest in teaching young students by saying: "I promised myself that someday I would send out such a call, based on the desire to extend to poor children the means of learning music through the instrument of their choice in surroundings that were beautiful and in an environment that would be stimulating. I would discourage mediocre professionalism and teach music as a means to spiritual enlightenment."[64]

As implied by the word "settlement" in its name, the school was established in the tradition of the settlement house movement that by the 1910s was serving poor urban residents in cities across the nation. Even so, like the Colored Men's Branch of the YMCA and the Colored Women's Branch of the YWCA, the Music School Settlement for Colored People reflected the racial mores of New York City in the 1910s. Although some of the founders hoped the school for African Americans would bring down the barriers between the races, the precise name of the institution was required to distinguish it from the existing Music School Settlement on East Third Street, in which African American students were not welcome as students.

The first location for the Music School Settlement for Colored People was on West 34th Street, in the heart of the old African American midtown neighborhood. African American violinist David Irwin Martin was hired as the school's director. When the Music School Settlement for Colored People was incorporated in 1912, its board of directors included white philanthropists such as Mrs. Charles Sprague-Smith and Lyman Beecher Stowe (grandson of Harriet Beecher Stowe), as well as black leaders such as W. E. B. Du Bois, musician Harry Burleigh, and Rev. Hutchens Bishop, rector of St. Philip's Episcopal Church.[65]

In 1912 African American bandleader James Reese Europe organized a fund-raising concert drawing from his Clef Club musicians, who regularly provided entertainment at the parties of wealthy New Yorkers across the city. For the concert at Carnegie Hall, Europe assembled an orchestra of fifty-five musicians, performing on standard orchestral instruments in unusual quantities, such as ten pianos, as well as on instruments unique to the Carnegie Hall concert stage such as mandolins, ukuleles, guitars, and banjos. When ticket sales lagged, the Music School Settlement's board of directors published an editorial appeal in the *New York Evening Journal*. The concert was sold out, and so well received that similar concerts were presented in the following three years.[66]

Acknowledging the shift of the African American population center to Harlem, in 1914 the Music School Settlement moved to Harlem, occupying twin row houses at 6 and 8 West 131st Street, across the street from real estate broker Philip Payton's home, and began offering a range of activities extending well beyond musical training:

> Recreational activities included folk dancing, basketball, baseball, track, and tennis. The buildings also provided space for concerts, lectures, social gatherings, and other forms of "wholesome recreation." A weekly lecture series on various topics in music, originally intended for the African American community, began attracting white audiences as well. The lectures featured well-known musicians, writers, and scholars.[67]

J. Rosamond Johnson, well known for the Broadway compositions he had written with his brother, James Weldon Johnson, was appointed the Music School Settlement's second director. "My wishes finally came true," was how Johnson described the appointment. After years of traveling and performing, with a new baby at home, he was ready to leave the road. In Harlem, the Music School Settlement provided a variety of music lessons on the piano and other instruments, as well as recitals and other performance opportunities for students in glee clubs, string quartets, and orchestras. The range of musical offerings and the goals of the school attracted well-known musicians such as composer and conductor Kurt Schindler and other public figures such as Madam C. J. Walker, who provided lectures.[68] The Music School Settlement continued its programming until 1919 when, upon the resignation of J. Rosamond Johnson, its operations were folded into those of the Martin-Smith School, also in Harlem, founded by the Settlement's first director, David Irwin Martin, and pianist Helen Elise Smith.[69]

The color line was firmly drawn for the African American YMCA and YWCA branches that eventually moved to Harlem, for the athletic clubs that served the area's young people, and for the Music School Settlement for Colored People. At a time when northerners were expressing increasing concerns regarding the "social equality" of the races, the formal and informal opportunities to socialize, even in the same-gender settings of the YMCA and YWCA, would have suggested that the races were interacting on an equal basis, which most northerners were no more ready to do than were southerners. The 1908 Springfield, Illinois, riots, in which two black people were killed and blocks of blacks' homes were burned to the ground by a white mob, exposed northern racism and eventually became the impetus for the founding of the National Association for the Advancement of Colored People in 1909. In this context of tenuous racial interactions, there was no suggestion, even by the white benefactors of the Music Settlement School for Colored People, that black children desiring music education might attend classes with white children at existing schools. While the Music School Settlement for Colored People provided a wide range of rich cultural opportunities, it existed as an accommodation to the racial limitations that black New Yorkers faced in this field as well as in most others.[70]

Figure 5.1 illustrates that by 1919 there was a network of organizations in Harlem providing services to African American youth in the vicinity of Lenox Avenue and 135th Street. These organizations, ranging from public schools with programs beyond the classroom to churches and athletic clubs that provided weekday recreational activities to the YMCA and YWCA, which linked young adults in Harlem with a national network of service providers, all facilitated the development of relationships between youth and young adults, as well as between the adults who advocated for the institutions to be formed and in many cases played substantial roles in providing the services. Some of these institutions traced their beginnings to Manhattan's midtown African American community. Once in Harlem, most of the private institutions

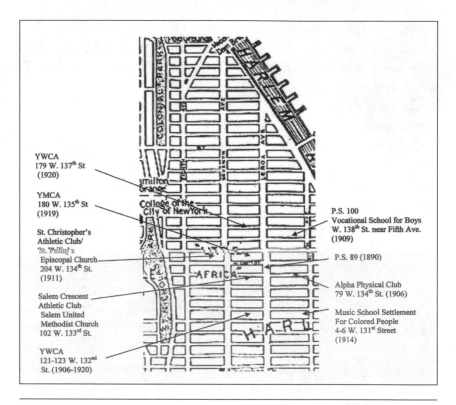

YWCA
179 W. 137th St
(1920)

YMCA
180 W. 135th St
(1919)

St. Christopher's
Athletic Club/
St. Philip's
Episcopal Church
204 W. 134th St.
(1911)

Salem Crescent
Athletic Club
Salem United
Methodist Church
102 W. 133rd St.

YWCA
121-123 W. 132nd
St. (1906-1920)

P.S. 100
Vocational School for Boys
W. 138th St. near Fifth Ave.
(1909)

P.S. 89 (1890)

Alpha Physical Club
79 W. 134th St. (1906)

Music School Settlement
For Colored People
4-6 W. 131st Street
(1914)

FIGURE 5.1. Some organizations serving African American
youth in Harlem, 1890–1919. Automobile Club of Rochester, 1920,
Florida International Center for Instructional Technology.

began as renters, but some of them eventually purchased or built properties. These properties were evidence of the ability of the African Americans to obtain sufficient funds to accomplish the goal of ownership, but even more importantly, they were signs of the advocates' confidence in their future in Harlem, a future in which they wanted to be sure that the young people in their community could fully participate.

While African American youth and young adults were finding their places in Harlem's educational and recreational institutions, their elders began to position themselves to have a direct voice in the allocation of resources to the community by seeking elective office.

6

REAL ESTATE
AND POLITICS

L
ike thousands of other black Virginians at the turn of the twentieth century, John Mabery Royall traveled from his home state to New York City looking for better opportunities. The fourth of five children born to carpenter Pinkney Royall and his wife, Lucy, John Royall had attended the Virginia Normal and Industrial Institute, but by the time he turned thirty, in 1902, he was working in a blue-collar job, with H. J. Heinz Company in New York. When he became a Pullman porter, however, his income likely increased, and his new job gave him access to a national network of other similarly ambitious black men. Because of the exposure to a wider world through their travel, and their good incomes compared to the wages of other employment available to black men, Pullman porters were admired in the African American community. Using the resources of savings and contacts, by 1907 Royall had begun to establish himself as a real estate and insurance broker in New York City. In 1913, he mounted a campaign for alderman representing Harlem in the Twenty-First District.[1]

As black voters' numbers increased in Harlem in the 1910s, they became a more important factor in the political calculations of both the Democrats and the Republicans. Initially, African Americans in Harlem traded votes for

patronage, such as better access to jobs, both menial and government positions. That a real estate agent would be the first black candidate for elective
office in Harlem illustrates the important role that the profession played in
both the physical and the political formation of the black community there.
The association between real estate and politics had a long history for African Americans in the state of New York. The state's first constitution, in
1777, linked all men's voting rights to real estate ownership, as did the constitutions of most other states at that time: "A freehold [ownership of land
or a lease for life on land] [shall] be the basic standard for determining the
right to vote." Color was not a criterion for voting in New York. Anyone who
owned land valued at twenty pounds ($50) or leased property at an annual
rate of at least forty shillings ($5) was eligible to vote. Few black residents
of New York State met this requirement, but those who did could vote in the
same manner as white citizens. This standard changed with the writing of
a new constitution in 1821. While the new constitution dispensed with land
ownership requirements for white men, it retained a property qualification
for men "of colour" and increased the property requirement value to $250. As
a result, all but a small number of black New Yorkers were disenfranchised.
Ownership of real estate became a significant goal for black New Yorkers in
the following decades, since it was their only way to participate fully in the
electoral process.[2]

In 1846, landowner and abolitionist Gerrit Smith attempted to provide
black New Yorkers with the opportunity both to become yeomen farmers and
to gain access to the vote when he offered to give away thousands of acres of
upstate property in forty- and sixty-acre parcels to blacks willing to establish farms. The venture was not successful because of the inexperience of the
new farmers, the challenges of cultivating the hilly terrain, and the remote
location of the land.[3] In New York City the Seneca Village settlement, located
between the current 81st and 89th Streets on the western side of what is
now Manhattan's Central Park, became a refuge for blacks starting in 1825
when they began purchasing land from its white owners, John and Elizabeth
Whitehead.[4] By the middle of the nineteenth century it was also attractive to
African Americans as a means of gaining the franchise: "In 1855 half of all the
black families in Seneca Village owned land, a rate 500 percent that for the

city. Seneca's men met New York State's property qualification on Negro voters more often than black men in other sections of Manhattan."[5]

Black New Yorkers and their allies unsuccessfully challenged the state's
voting restrictions several times in the nineteenth century. Statewide votes
proposing to end the restrictions were held in 1846, 1860, and 1869. Each
time the electorate voted against the measure. Thus the Fifteenth Amendment, ratified in 1870, giving black men the vote was not significant only for
southern states. It also gave black men in New York State unrestricted voting
rights for the first time. In New York City this access to the vote came just as
the black population was beginning a period of dramatic growth. In the three
final decades of the nineteenth century, the black population in New York
City grew from 13,000 to 36,000.[6]

While the Reconstruction period in the South, from 1865 to 1877, led to
substantial black voting for the first time, as well as scores of black office-
holders and the unheard-of participation of black men in the writing of state
constitutions, the impact of the Fifteenth Amendment in the North was less
dramatic. Black men could vote, but their numbers were not large enough to
elect their own candidates. Still, successful black candidates sometimes were
elected with white support. In Chicago schoolteacher John W. E. Thomas
was able to gain the support of white voters, and in 1876 he was elected to the
Illinois State Senate even though African Americans accounted for only one
percent of Chicago's population.[7]

In New York City it would be several decades before a black person gained
elective office, but by the 1880s blacks were included in the network of political organizations that were the foundation of local patronage jobs and the fo-
cal point for organizing working-class voters. New York City had long been a
Democratic stronghold symbolized by Tammany Hall, once the Canal Street
headquarters of the party in New York. In the late nineteenth and early twentieth centuries, African Americans voted mostly Republican, recognizing the
"party of Lincoln" that had facilitated emancipation, but locally and nationally there were suggestions among some blacks that they should divide their
vote between the parties and not become beholden to either. Disenchantment with the Republican Party's failure to continue to support Reconstruction efforts in the 1870s helped fuel this line of thinking.[8]

With the entry of African American men into the voting population of New York City following the passage of the Fifteenth Amendment, the Democratic and Republican parties began to include black voters in their political calculations. Unlike Chicago, where black support of the dominant Republican Party resulted in a black elected official in the 1870s, black New Yorkers' allegiance primarily to the Republican Party, the minority party, did not have such an effect. Conversely, in New York City, black involvement with the dominant Democratic Party was so minimal that there was no reason for that party to consider providing black voters with the gift of a black candidate. Eventually, New York City's political leaders in both parties devised strategies to use the new group of black voters to their advantage. As in many other northern cities, New York's local political clubs did not welcome African American participants, but encouraged them to establish "colored" clubs. In 1870, black New Yorkers interested in "furthering the interests of the Republican Party in the coming campaign" formed a political club to carry out these activities. Black New Yorkers' participation in the Democratic Party lagged, but by the mid-1880s at least three black Democratic clubs had been formed in New York. In the 1890s the *Harlem Local Reporter*, a newspaper with white and black readership, regularly advertised the meetings of the Colored Democratic Club and the Colored Republican Club. The black clubs gave white political leaders a means of communicating with black potential voters while maintaining racially separate meetings and organizational structures, and they also created an efficient mechanism through which white political leaders often selected African American leaders to dispense patronage, and to organize black voters and deliver them to white candidates. But the vote of blacks was not needed for success by candidates from either party.[9]

An early black political leader who was a product of this process was John B. Nail, father of real estate broker John E. Nail. The owner of a saloon and hotel on Seventh Avenue in the midtown Tenderloin district, Nail was approached in 1886 by a Democratic Party leader who asked him to organize African Americans. Nail was told that he was not to deal with white voters. The fact that Democrats asked him was significant, given the black population's Republican leanings. Nail was not particularly interested in politics, but he recognized the potential for his business to be affected negatively if he declined the request. As he later recalled, "Now what was I to do? I had been Republican. But there were too many ways these Fellows could make it hard for you, like licenses, taxes, assessments, etc."[10] But the Democratic association also had the potential to affect his business positively by the increased visibility he would have among potential customers. Nail's career as a political leader was launched and his business continued to flourish as well.[11]

The principal political reward for black political leaders in New York and elsewhere in the late nineteenth century was patronage jobs. Most were unskilled service jobs, but through patronage jobs some blacks got their first opportunities to move into white-collar work. At a time when most African Americans were relegated to menial service positions, an opportunity to become a clerk in a government office was significant for a black man. Charles W. Anderson was a high-profile example of a black man who obtained a clerical position and used it and later positions to build a career in club politics. Born in Oxford, Ohio, in 1866, Anderson arrived in New York City in 1886 and immediately became active in Republican politics. In 1890 he was elected president of the Young Men's Colored Republican Club of New York County and awarded a position as a duty inspector with the federal Internal Revenue Service. Anderson's education at a business college in Cleveland and at the Berlitz School of Languages in Worcester, Massachusetts, gave him the foundation to be an able administrator. In the 1890s as Booker T. Washington rose to national power, Anderson aligned himself with Washington and became the Tuskegee leader's eyes and ears in New York City, a city of significance for Washington because of its philanthropic base and also because it was the home to many of Washington's opponents.[12]

As Washington's ally, Anderson perfected skills of behind-the-scenes political maneuvering that supported Washington's own political goals. Anderson was able to craft a career out of a succession of state and federal appointments that continued long after Washington's death in 1915. Few other black New Yorkers received similar white-collar patronage jobs. The Republican Party was a minority party in New York City and its access to patronage was limited. Most blacks who did receive work obtained jobs as unskilled laborers, but these jobs provided them with the same important foothold in the New York City economy that the Irish and Italians were receiving. Saloon owner John Nail was so successful at dispensing this type of patronage for the Democrats that "Negro preachers became alarmed because they had been distributing Republican patronage in this form." White Democrats also complained "on more than one occasion . . . that he was giving Negroes too much."[13]

Black political influence in New York City did not grow in the late nineteenth century because even though the African American population of the city increased, the growth of the city's general population diluted the voting power of blacks. By 1880 the black population was 20,433, and by 1890 it had increased by 26 percent, to 25,674. Because the overall population of New York increased at the same rate, spurred by European immigration, the black population still remained less than 2 percent of the total New York population. In addition to total numbers, residential dispersion of this population prevented African Americans from leveraging the vote once they did get it. In 1890 there was only one ward (the Fifteenth, between Houston and Fourteenth Streets) where African Americans constituted more than 5 percent of the population; in this ward they were almost 9 percent of the population.[14]

In Philadelphia, another Republican stronghold, blacks had earlier success in politics, electing their first candidate, Jacob Purnell, to the Common Council (the lower of two city legislative bodies) in 1884, a time when Philadelphia's black population of more than 31,000 people exceeded New York's by more than 10,000 people and represented almost 4 percent of Philadelphia's population. In Chicago, which, like New York, had a black population below 2 percent in the 1890s, blacks also had more success in electoral politics. In 1894 African American Edward H. Wright was elected as a Republican commissioner for Cook County, and in 1895 he was elected as town clerk for South Chicago. Although smaller in numbers, when compared to New York's, Chicago's African American population (14,852 in 1890 vs. 25,674 in New York) was concentrated in a Black Belt whose votes were sought after by white politicians and was instrumental in the rise of black politicians in Chicago in the late nineteenth century. The Republican Party's strength in Chicago made the black vote there more vital to Republican success. In New York the Republican Party was already weak, and therefore the relatively small number of black Republicans added little of value to the voting power

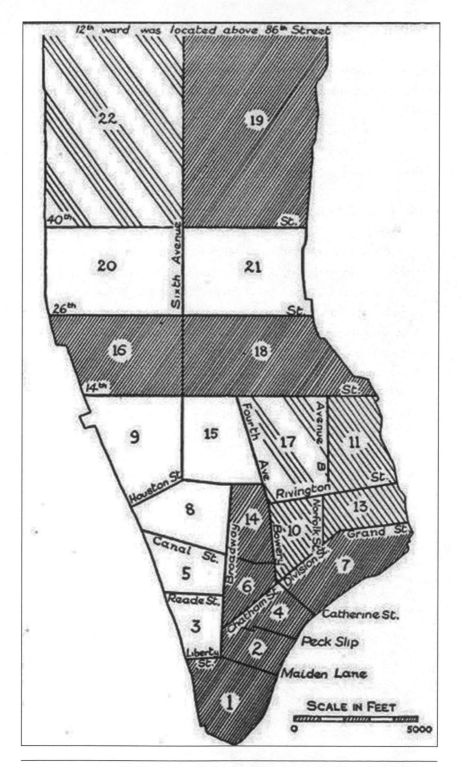

12th ward was located above 86th Street

22

19

40th

Sixth Avenue

St.

20

21

26th

St.

16

18

14th

St.

9

15

Fourth Ave

17

Avenue B

11

St.

Rivington

13

Houston St.

8

Norfolk St.

10

Grand St.

Canal St.

Broadway

14

Bowery

Division

7

5

Reade St.

6

Chatham St.

4

Catherine St.

3

Peck Slip

Liberty St.

2

Maiden Lane

1

SCALE IN FEET

0   5000

FIGURE 6.1.   Manhattan wards, ca. 1900. http://www.demographia.com/
db-nyc-ward1800.htm.

of the party that was already in the minority.[15] Similarly, by the 1890s blacks in Philadelphia, allied with the Republican Party, had also experienced electoral success. In *The Philadelphia Negro* (1899), W. E. B. Du Bois noted: "In spite of the fact that unworthy officials could easily get into office by the political methods pursued by the Negroes [allying with "the better elements" of the electorate], the average of those who have obtained office has been good. Of the three colored councilmen one has received the endorsement of the Municipal League, while others seem to be up to the average of the councilmen."[16]

By 1900 African Americans in Manhattan constituted approximately 8 percent or more of the population in four assembly districts (the political divisions then used by the Census Bureau) (table 6.1). While 8 percent of the population might have been enough to use for political leverage in seeking patronage from politicians, the numbers were not sufficient for African Americans to seek to elect their own candidates.

Given their political weakness, blacks formed voluntary organizations to address their grievances. In 1911 some of New York City's African American residents joined forces to form the Equity Congress, designed to push for African American access to then-closed opportunities on the police force, in the fire department, and in the National Guard. James C. Thomas, Sr., the first president of Philip Payton's Afro-American Realty Company, was one of

TABLE 6.1   Manhattan Wards in 1900 with Approximately
8 Percent or More African American Population

Assembly district	Location	Total district population	Negro district population	Negro population as a % of total district population
11	West Side- 14th–34th	41,247	3,756	9.11
19	West Side 59th–72nd	65,025	4,982	7.66
25	Midtown 34th–14th	36,800	2,950	8.02
27	West Side 42nd–34th	36,984	3,318	8.97

SOURCE: "POPULATION OF INCORPORATED PLACES," TABLE 26,
CENSUS OF POPULATION, NEW YORK CITY, 1900, LXXVII.

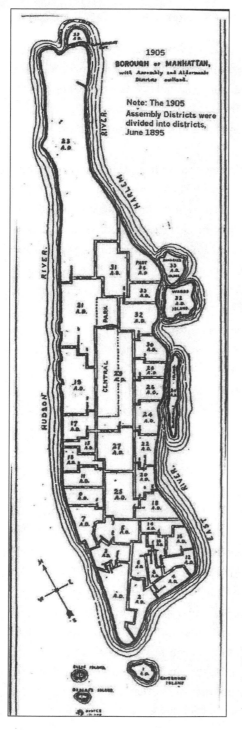

FIGURE 6.2. Manhattan assembly district map, 1905. http://bklyn-genealogy-info.stevemorse.org/Ward/1905.NYC.AD.html.

the founders of the Equity Congress, along with entertainer Bert Williams and lawyer J. Frank Wheaton. In 1898, before moving to New York, Wheaton had been Minnesota's first black state legislator. He was a prominent criminal defense attorney, but was also involved in civil rights litigation. The Equity Congress met on Sundays at Thomas's midtown undertaking establishment to discuss community issues.

The Equity Congress also raised funds to challenge Harlem's restrictive covenants. In 1911 it formed a "provisional" black regiment as a means of pressuring state legislators to establish an official black National Guard unit. Equity members (including real estate broker Philip Payton) signed up for the regiment, but legislation making the unit official was stalled by Governor John Dix. In 1913 legislation was finally passed to establish the unit. Also in 1911, Samuel Battle became New York's first black policeman, although not specifically through the efforts of the Equity Congress, but through a high Civil Service exam score and the intervention of Booker T. Washington's New York assistant Charles W. Anderson and of Fred Moore, publisher of the black newspaper the *New York Age*.[17]

By 1910 the black population in Manhattan had increased to 60,525 (a 67 percent increase since 1900), which far outstripped the growth in Manhattan's overall population (26 percent). For the first time, the concentration of the black population in some Manhattan political districts exceeded 10 percent. In the Thirteenth Assembly District, between 52nd and 67th Streets on the west side, the black population approached 18 percent, and in the Twenty-First Assembly District in Harlem, between 127th and 141st Streets, the black population was almost 15 percent (table 6.2).

The growth in Harlem's black population did not go unnoticed by Republicans. In the gubernatorial election of 1910, on the night before the election, former president Theodore Roosevelt made a number of campaign appearances before Hungarians, Italians, and other groups throughout New York City on behalf of the Republican candidate, Henry L. Stimson. In Harlem, Roosevelt spoke at Mercy Seat Baptist Church, still located on 134th Street, where it had been the site of successful African American organizing against the 1904 attempt to evict them from the area. President Roosevelt ended his remarks before more than five hundred black residents with an appeal

TABLE 6.2 Assembly Districts in 1910 with Substantial Black Populations

Assembly district	Location	Total	Negro	Negro % of total assembly district population	% of city Negro population
13	Hudson River, 52nd, 67th, Columbus Ave.	52,290	9,273	17.73	15.32
21	Hudson River, 127th, 141st, 5th Ave.	73,446	10,912	14.86	18.03

SOURCE: THIRTEENTH CENSUS, BULLETIN, "POPULATION: NEW YORK," "COMPOSITION AND CHARACTERISTICS OF THE POPULATION FOR WARDS (OR ASSEMBLY DISTRICTS) OF CITIES OF 50,000 OR MORE" (WASHINGTON, DC: U.S. DEPARTMENT OF COMMERCE AND LABOR, 1910), 43–46.

reminding the audience of the links between the Democratic Party and the institution of slavery:

> I only have this moment to say how well I wish you, and to ask you in your in-
> terest, for the sake of your good name, and the sake of the State of New York, to
> stand against your ancient oppressors, the men who wronged you and sought
> to degrade your race—Tammany Hall—and to vote solidly for the ticket headed
> by Henry Stimson.[18]

In spite of Roosevelt's energetic campaigning, John A. Dix was elected the first Democratic governor in New York State in sixteen years. Democrats also gained control of both legislative houses.[19]

In the 1913 election for alderman in Harlem, African American real estate broker John Royall, a native of Virginia, ran as an independent for the office in Harlem's Twenty-First District (during this period this district served also as the Twenty-First Assembly District), the Manhattan district with the second highest concentration of black residents.[20] In 1907 Royall started a real estate brokerage business, and by 1913 his real estate office was at 21 West 134th Street. He was also the president of the New York City chapter of the National Negro Business League (NNBL), Booker T. Washington's network of black entrepreneurs. The annual meetings of the NNBL provided opportunities for members to cultivate business relationships and promote African

American achievement. For Washington, who established the organization in 1900, the NNBL served as an important mechanism to consolidate
his power through his relationships with prominent and obscure entrepreneurs who were eager to be near the most powerful black man in the country
and to remain in his good graces. Royall's leadership in the local chapter of
the NNBL placed him within the orbit of Booker T. Washington's national
power base.[21]

John Royall was not simply a realtor but a very active participant in the
racial transition of Harlem. He provided a deposition on behalf of Caroline
Morlath, the defendant in the *Raphael Greenbaum against Caroline Morlath*
restrictive covenant case. The *New York Age* suggested that Royall was the
broker who had facilitated the rental of Caroline Morlath's West 137th Street
apartments to African Americans, the act that precipitated the legal challenge.[22] Royall had most recently worked on behalf of Theodore Roosevelt's
1912 presidential campaign under the Progressive Party and had sought the
Republican nomination for alderman in 1913. When the party nominated attorney Oscar Igstaedter, the incumbent, Royall decided to defy the party and
mount an independent campaign.[23] His candidacy for alderman emerged
from the formation of the Negro Civic League in September 1913. The league
was formed in Harlem by some of the same people who led the Equity Congress, with the stated belief that

> our political and civic welfare can best be advanced by the organization of a
> league along non-partisan lines with a membership made up solely from a ra-
> cial standpoint without regard to party affiliation. . . . One of our main objec-
> tives will be the placing of strong, representative Negro men in nomination for
> various elective offices in our municipal and state campaigns without regard
> to party lines.[24]

Royall was elected president of the league at its first meeting. At the same
meeting the nomination of a candidate for alderman in the Twenty-First
District in Harlem was discussed. A nominating committee was assembled
that evening and after caucusing they reconvened and presented the names
of John Royall and Louis Leavelle, an attorney, as candidates on which the
league members were to vote.[25] Before the vote could be taken, Leavelle "at-

tacked the integrity of the meeting, asserting that he would not be bound by it" and would run for the office regardless of the outcome. Leavelle had strong ties to the Democratic Party and at the meeting was supported by Charles Stinson, the Democratic leader for the Twenty-First District. When Leavelle was unable to substantiate his claim that he had already received four hundred signatures on previously circulated nominating petitions, the league members unanimously voted for John Royall for candidate for alderman in the Twenty-First District. Leavelle was in a position similar to Royall's. Having been denied a nomination by the Democratic Party, he understood that the league represented an opportunity to get on the ballot, a choice that no black candidate in New York City had yet experienced. In spite of his threat, he did not run against Royall.[26]

Harlem's Twenty-First District, which Royall sought to lead, ran from the Hudson River on the west to Lenox Avenue on the east and from 127th Street on the south to 141st Street on the north (table 6.3).[27] Within this district it was estimated that there were 3,000 registered African American voters (or 77 percent of the blacks eligible to vote). African American men, women, and children were 15 percent of the total population in the district. Supporters of Royall organized a voter registration campaign with the goal of adding another 3,000 voters to the rolls by the October 18 registration

TABLE 6.3 Twenty-First Assembly/Aldermanic District, 1910

Males of voting age	23,312	% of total males of voting age
Native white—Native parentage	5,718	24.5
Native white— Foreign or mixed parentage	6,205	26.6
Foreign-born white	7,522	32.3
Naturalized	4,149	27.8
Negro	3,867	16.6

SOURCE: NINETEENTH CENSUS, 1910 BULLETIN, "POPULATION: NEW YORK," "COMPOSITION AND CHARACTERISTICS OF THE POPULATION," TABLE 5, NEW YORK CITY, 45.

Note: The census table indicates the sum of males of voting age as 23,376, but the sum of the numbers presented, counting only naturalized foreign-born white males, is 23,312.

deadline. With only 867 unregistered African American men in the district, the registration campaign would have had to focus on white as well as black unregistered men.[28]

As the Negro Civic League hoped, John Royall's candidacy received bipartisan support among African Americans who responded to the call to lay down their political differences for the cause of racial unity. While some black ministers were reluctant to provide outright endorsements, many strongly supported the concept of an African American seeking elective office. Dr. W. R. Lawton, pastor of St. James Presbyterian Church, then on West 51st Street, noted: "The candidacy of a colored man for alderman in New York City at this time when the race is celebrating the fiftieth anniversary of its emancipation is a most fitting aspiration, and his success would be a most unique exhibit in its achievement of a half century of freedom."[29]

When Royall spoke in October 1913 at a meeting of black ministers of the Inter-Denominational Conference, he noted that African American voters had been "tied to the tail end of the Democratic party, the Republican party and the Progressive party," and suggested that they vote according to their racial interests rather than party affiliation.[30]

Fund-raising for Royall extended beyond New York City. Booker T. Washington in Tuskegee, Alabama, was contacted for a contribution. Royall's Finance Committee included *New York Age* publisher (and Washington ally) Fred Moore, journalist Lester Walton, nightclub owner Barron Wilkins, and physician H. Malachi Griffin.[31] Royall also spent a large amount of his own money in the campaign. To raise visibility, mass rallies were held at the Palace Casino at 116th and Madison on Sunday afternoons.[32] In addition to business leaders, Royall's candidacy also attracted more radical black leaders. A. Philip Randolph, then taking classes at City College of New York while also sharing his socialist philosophies with classmates and coworkers, was excited by Royall's candidacy, a first for a black New Yorker. Randolph distributed literature for Royall and also encouraged his colleagues in the Independent Political Council, a current affairs discussion group that he founded, to work on the campaign.[33]

In the fall of 1913 another African American, James Anderson, the editor of the black newspaper *Amsterdam News* announced his candidacy for alderman in the Thirty-First District of Harlem. The district was bound by Lexington Avenue on the east, Lenox Avenue on the west, and the Harlem River on the north. The district's southern boundary moved diagonally north and west from East 119th at Lexington to West 135th Street and Lenox Avenue. Whereas John Royall's Twenty-First Aldermanic District had the same boundaries as the Twenty-First Assembly District, Anderson's Thirty-First Aldermanic District was slightly more than half of the Thirtieth Assembly District, with the Thirty-Second Aldermanic District occupying the other half of the Thirtieth Assembly District.

An estimate of the district's composition from the demographics of portions of the two contributing assembly districts suggests that it had fewer African American residents than John Royall's Twenty-First District, both numerically and as a percentage of the district (table 6.4). The foreign-born population in the Thirty-First District was almost twice that of the Twenty-First District, reflecting the continued settlement of immigrants from Italy and Eastern Europe.

The *Harlem Home News*, a newspaper with a predominantly white readership, ridiculed Anderson's candidacy: "It is whispered in the negro belt that Anderson has been endorsed by a negro Republican, a negro Fusionist, a negro Progressive, and a negro whatnot. They are all for Anderson the whole

TABLE 6.4 Estimated Population, Thirty-First Aldermanic District, 1910

Males of voting age	15,849	%
Native white—Native parentage	1,697	10.7
Native white—Foreign or mixed parentage	3,363	21.2
Foreign-born white	9,246	58.3
Naturalized	3,280	21.2
Negro	1,508	9.5

SOURCE: NINETEENTH CENSUS, 1910 BULLETIN, "POPULATION: NEW YORK," "COMPOSITION AND CHARACTERISTICS OF THE POPULATION," TABLE 5, NEW YORK CITY, 45.

Note: Assuming that the Thirty-First Aldermanic District was approximately 55 percent of the Thirtieth Assembly District, the numbers presented represent information for the Thirtieth Assembly District multiplied by 55 percent.

four of them."[34] The newspaper article then alluded to the key to the past abilities of white candidates to attract the black vote:

> In the 31st Aldermanic district there are about 5,000 enrolled voters. Of this number 4,000 it is estimated are negroes and most of them usually cast their ballot for the Republican Party. They always have relied upon white men for patronage and never have complained. . . . It is predicted that the usual negro vote will be cast for a white man for it is said they have confidence in his ability to deliver the goods to them. Anderson's case is a comical one.[35]

The statistics presented in the *Harlem Home News* article are so far from census record statistics that it appears that the paper was stretching the facts to make its point that even when blacks constituted a substantial majority of the vote, they would continue to see the benefit of voting for a white candidate. Some basic assumptions regarding the black population in Harlem suggest that the *Harlem Home News* estimates were unrealistic. The *Harlem Home News* indicated that the total number of voters in the district was 5,000, and then estimated black registered voters in the district to be 4,000. At a time when political districts in Manhattan had less than 20 percent African American population, to suggest that African American's represented 80 percent of the registered voters in any district was an extreme exaggeration. The large differences between the estimates of the white and black voters in the Thirty-First District and the numbers of actual voters could be the result of a typographical error, but it could also be the result of the writer's effort to make a larger point. To suggest that 80 percent (4,000 African Americans of a total voting population of 5,000) of the voters in the district were African American could reflect the perceptions of white Harlem residents to the "invasion" of their community by African Americans. The numbers of blacks moving to Harlem had increased dramatically, but in comparison to the white population, it was still a small percentage of the entire population. But many white residents may have viewed the black presence in Harlem as becoming dominant, even though in reality it was still quite small. In response to this perception, which the *Harlem Home News* writer seems to have shared, the article predicting the voting behavior of African Americans could have had the goal of encouraging white residents to conclude that Af-

rican American voters would not become politically independent or dominant even as their numbers increased. The writer's analysis revealed a para-
doxical perspective. He acknowledged the presence of blacks in Harlem, and
even exaggerated their numbers, but then he suggested that whites need not
worry about these numbers in regard to the political arena, since black voters
would continue to rely on the white community to serve their interests even
if the black community was in an extreme majority.

Another explanation for the discrepancy between the writer's perception
of the black voting population and the data for the neighborhood could be
that the population may have actually been largely Caribbean immigrants or
newcomers from the South who were not yet able to vote. United States naturalization laws required a residency of five years before immigrants could
become naturalized citizens. New York State required voters to have become
citizens at least ninety days before the election and to have lived in New York
State for one year before they could become qualified to vote. With the continued arrival of black newcomers to Harlem in 1913, these requirements
could have disqualified a substantial portion of black residents from voting.[36]

The *Harlem News* writer's perspective suggesting that even when they
made up a substantial majority of the vote, African Americans would continue to see the benefit of voting for white candidates, was a perspective
shared by many white New Yorkers who were unaccustomed to blacks' seeking elective office. They assumed that the goal of the participation of blacks,
an economically marginalized group in New York City, in electoral politics
was to elect officials who would provide them with jobs and other forms of
patronage. White New Yorkers knew that white elected officials were more
likely to be positioned to provide such patronage, since their contacts politically and economically were more extensive than those of almost all African
Americans. Black New Yorkers did want jobs and other economic opportunities from their politicians, but New York City had experienced a large race
riot in 1900 in midtown, and a smaller riot in 1905 in the same area, after
which the African American victims came away disappointed when their
grievances and requests for damages were politely heard and then ignored.
John Royall's campaign slogan, "The black man first, the black man last, the
black man all the time," left no doubt as to his priority. A more detailed record

of Royall's campaign platform has not survived. While his campaign slogan was undoubtedly a rallying cry before black audiences, in a district with a potential black voting base of slightly more than 16 percent, a race-neutral or multiracial appeal would have been more pragmatic.[37]

When votes were tallied in the 1913 campaign for alderman in the Twenty-First District, the incumbent, Oscar Igstaedter, was reelected with 5,780 votes. Another attorney, Edward S. Brogan, received 3,651 votes, and John Royall received 1,242 votes. A Socialist Party candidate, Estelle Feigenbaum, received 303 votes, and Peter M. Johnson received 26 votes as a Progressive Party candidate. The balance of the 405 votes were either blank or void. Of the 23,312 men eligible to vote in the district, 11,407 (49 percent) voted in this election. To win, John Royall would have needed the votes of all of the 3,867 African American men eligible to vote as well as the votes of some of the white men in the district. Assuming that the majority of the votes he received were from African Americans, they represented 32 percent of the African Americans who were eligible to vote. Since the racial breakdown of voting data of the election is unavailable, an assessment of whether this level of support was typical cannot be made. In the Thirty-First District, newspaper editor James H. Anderson also came in third, receiving 467 votes, while the victor, Hyman Pouker, received 1,681. In the mayoral election, fusion candidate John Purroy Mitchel won. The 1913 election was the end of neither the Negro Civic League nor John Royall's political career. In the aftermath of the election the league held a banquet under its new name, the United Civic League, with Royall retaining his position as president. While the banquet was not the victory celebration that Royall and the league would have preferred, it was still an opportunity to acknowledge a first step by blacks into electoral politics in Harlem, and to debrief in preparation for future battles.[38]

Royall's 1913 candidacy indicates that in Harlem in the 1910s some real estate brokers had attained a profile in the community that had previously been reserved for the black minister. As agents facilitating the movement of African Americans into Harlem and thereby the formation of the black community there, in the 1910s, the brokers, in the candidacy of Royall, sought to lead it politically. Some black residents recognized this significant role, and acknowledged it by viewing real estate brokers as community-minded businessmen capable of providing broader leadership as elected officials. But this view was not universal. The fact that Royall did not even receive a majority of black votes in the district suggests that some blacks did not believe that he should be their leader or, conversely, that incumbent Oscar Igstaedter and the Republican Party could do more for blacks than a novice like Royall. In addition to providing a voice to black residents, Royall was most likely also seeking ways to create conditions that would benefit his and other black businesses in Harlem. Royall's candidacy for elective office indicates that in this regard, he may have surpassed the African American minister, whose political activities at the time in New York City were restricted to acting as a conduit of patronage by supplying food and wood to congregants, encouraging congregations to vote, and supporting candidates, but not actually running for office.[39]

Subsequent events furthered Royall's political aspirations. World War I had a lasting impact on the formation of Harlem's African American community. As fighting proceeded in Europe in 1914, U.S. industries, primarily based in the North, expanded to meet the needs of the combatants. With European immigration to the United States greatly restricted because of the war, a labor shortage resulted, creating opportunities for African American workers who in the past had not been considered for such jobs. New York became one of several northern cities that attracted blacks from the South, and Harlem's black population grew dramatically. By the 1910s Harlem had been identified nationally as an up-and-coming community for African Americans. Their arrival in Harlem during the period after 1914 strengthened the potential voting base for African Americans seeking elective office.[40]

John Royall returned to the political arena in 1915, running again for alderman (they served for two-year terms), but this time in the Thirty-First District, in which James Anderson had run in 1913. Royall's 1915 campaign did not receive the prominence in the *New York Age* that his first campaign did, nor did it generate the same unanimity within the black community. Royall, once the New York president of Booker T. Washington's National Negro Business League, had broken with Washington by 1915, and according to one critic "he criticized and abused the Doctor [Washington] almost nightly in his public speeches." By 1915, the last year of his life, Washington

had positioned himself as the conduit for most white philanthropists interested in contributing to black causes. Royall noted that his shift regarding
Washington was inspired by his concern about "the financial forces back-
ing Washington's program." Royall's reservations about Washington could
have contributed to the limited coverage he received in the *New York Age*, a
newspaper that had long had close ties to Washington (and was rumored to
have been owned by him). After meeting with Royall in 1915, Afro-Caribbean
radical Hubert Harrison noted that "Royall has a firmer and finer grip on the
financial, economic, and political factors of the Negro situation and of their
inter-relations than any other Negro American with whom I have spoken." In
the 1915 election Royall received 880 votes, which outpaced the 760 votes of
the incumbent Hyman Pouker, but the victor was John McKee, who received
1,520 votes. He was the first Democrat ever elected to the seat.[41]

While John Royall was not successful in his 1915 campaign, in Chicago
another African American real estate man was. Oscar DePriest became the
first black candidate elected to the Chicago City Council, representing the
Republican Party in the city's Second Ward. He had moved from Alabama to
Chicago in 1889 and had begun work as a house painter before becoming a
successful real estate investor.[42]

In 1915, while John Royall was again running for office, another Harlem resident with real estate ties was entering the political field. James C.
Thomas, Jr., the son of the black undertaker, was elected as a delegate for the
state constitutional convention. James C. Thomas, Sr., had been one of the
initial investors in Philip Payton's Afro-American Realty Company in 1903.
Thomas Senior's purchases of property in the area helped to provide an anchor for the African American community. In 1910 Thomas moved his undertaking business and residence from the midtown Tenderloin district to West
134th Street in Harlem, acknowledging that the center of the black community in Manhattan had shifted northward. His son, the child of a prosperous
businessman, graduated from City College of New York at a time when few
African Americans attended college. Thomas Junior then went on to Cornell
University, where he received a law degree and was admitted to the New York
Bar in 1912. He lived at 2229 Fifth Avenue near 135th Street and was elected

as a delegate at large to the Constitutional Convention, receiving more than 67,000 votes statewide.[43]

Two years later, in 1917, Thomas Junior built on this foray into elective politics when he ran for alderman in Harlem's Twenty-Sixth District, which was bound by the Harlem River on the north and east, Edgecombe Avenue on the west, and 135th and 141st on the south.[44] Thomas's campaign was linked to that of another African American from Harlem, attorney Edward A. Johnson, who ran for state assemblyman in the Nineteenth Assembly District. A native of North Carolina, where he had been an alderman in Raleigh, Johnson had also been an assistant U.S. district attorney for the eastern district of North Carolina. He moved to New York in 1907 and established a law practice there. The Nineteenth Assembly District ran from 118th Street on the south to 136th Street on the north, with a western boundary running from Manhattan to Eighth to Seventh Avenues, and an eastern boundary running from Park to Madison to Fifth Avenues.[45]

Both Thomas and Johnson were Republican Party candidates in 1917, and also received support from the United Civic League, still led by John Royall. When they both won the primaries over white candidates, the black newspaper *Chicago Defender* observed that the "entire Race in Harlem has been rejoicing since the recent primary victories of Thomas and Johnson." Both campaigns capitalized on the continuing increase in Harlem's black population due to the war. For Thomas and Johnson some of these migrants helped create a voting base that made the possibility of elective office a reasonable goal. The Republican Party also recognized the strength of the candidacies of Thomas and Johnson, who became the first black candidates endorsed by the party.[46]

For African Americans who were Democrats, the candidacies of the Republicans Thomas and Johnson presented a dilemma of choosing racial allegiance over party loyalty. They reached a compromise. The *New York Age* reported that "Colored Tammany workers were active in asking Negroes to remain neutral in the aldermanic fight and not vote for anyone." The article suggested that white residents were given a different appeal that was also motivated by racial allegiance in circulars distributed by Tammany that read:

"Do you want your alderman to be a Negro? James C. Thomas, Jr., is a colored man. Vote for Frank Mullen, who has been your alderman for four years."[47]

In its weekly edition following the November election, the front page of the *New York Age* announced "Thomas and Johnson Elected in Harlem" and concluded "The election of Thomas and Johnson gives to the Negro race its first representatives in the Aldermanic Board of New York City and the Assembly of New York." The report noted that Johnson had been elected by 100 votes over his Democratic opponent, while Thomas led his Democrat opponent, Frank Mullen, by 1,962 votes to 1,754 votes.[48]

In the days following the election, the Johnson results held, but the results of the Thomas election shifted as absentee ballots from soldiers were counted. The most dramatic change in the number of votes from the Thursday, November 8, result reported in the *Age* occurred when it was discovered that the ballots for six election districts of the area were missing. When these ballots were found and counted, the result shifted to 2,394 votes for Thomas and 2,782 votes for Mullen. On November 20 Thomas petitioned the court for a recount of the ballots and accused his opponent of securing a plurality by fraud, noting that witnesses had seen individuals who were not voters and were believed to be associated with Mullen, placing ballots in the ballot boxes. Thomas also alleged that his voting results were purposely underreported at the police station where the ballots were impounded.[49]

As a result of Thomas's petition the court mandated a recount of the votes, but Mullen appealed this decision. In early December the recount was stopped while the appeal was considered. Mullen's appeal argued that Thomas's allegations of fraud were based on hearsay and conjecture and should not be considered by the court as grounds for an appeal. The court considered Mullen's argument and ruled that the recount should be halted permanently and Mullen was certified the winner.[50]

Thomas ran for alderman again in 1919 in the Twenty-Sixth District, but was removed from the ballot on a technicality. He failed to file a certificate of character for two men who were circulating petitions for him. The challenge was prompted by John Royall's United Civic League. By this time the league was headquartered in its own three-story building at 184 West 134th Street and was known as the National United Civic League, a name that reflected its national aspirations. James Thomas claimed that the challenge to his campaign was prompted by his refusal to pay the league to be nominated. In spite of this intraracial squabbling, the election of 1919 did result in two more black Republican elected officials to complement Edward Johnson's state assembly position. In that year the first African American aldermen in New York City, Dr. Charles Roberts, a dentist and native of North Carolina, and George W. Harris, editor of the black newspaper *New York News* were both elected. In office Roberts advocated for the establishment of milk stations for low-income Harlem children and for a bathhouse for residents of the Twenty-Seventh Aldermanic District. Roberts provided a more concrete platform to black residents than John Royall's "black man first" pledges, and he also benefited from the growth in Harlem's black population, which continued even after the war was over. In 1917, Roberts's brother Eugene, a physician, became the first black man appointed to serve on the consolidated New York City Board of Education. Similarly, in the Twenty-Sixth Aldermanic District in George Harris's first year in office he was able to bring a food and produce market and a bathhouse to his constituents.[51]

For black New Yorkers living on the economic margins, patronage jobs, whether menial or clerical, and access to resources such as food and wood were the principal attractions to supporting both Republican and Democratic candidates in the late nineteenth and early twentieth centuries. The 1910s critics of white accommodation to blacks in Harlem had anticipated that the black residential presence in Harlem could eventually translate into political power, but even they had not expected that these residents would want more than jobs and would seek to elect their own candidates. But the increase in numbers and the advancement of some black professionals created the conditions that led to the shift in their roles from beneficiaries to actors in the electoral process. Real estate broker John Royall, the first black candidate for elective office in Harlem, was a product of this advancement. He played a critical role in the formation of the black community in Harlem through facilitating access to housing and his business provided him with both the economic independence and the community stature to seriously consider running for elective office. As he prospered, his successes allowed him a measure of economic independence that enabled him to consider challenging the existing political power structure without being daunted by the possibility of retribution from opponents. That elective office would bring increased visibility, access to information, and the potential to cultivate relationships with power brokers would certainly benefit Royall's business as well. Although the profession of James C. Thomas, another African American candidate, was law, real estate investments by his namesake father had provided him similarly with both a public profile and a measure of financial independence, which enabled him to step out and take the risk of running for office even if it meant creating political enemies. But Royall and Thomas were not successful. The dentist, lawyer, and editor won the first elective offices.

The background of early black candidates from Harlem was not markedly different from that of white candidates for office: attorneys and entrepreneurs dominated the political field. The distinct characteristic for Harlem was that real estate professionals were among the first candidates to run for office. Real estate was an important field of entrepreneurial activity in the white and black communities, but also in Harlem new black residents were aware of the 1904 pronouncements of broker Philip Payton that Harlem housing should be made available to blacks, and many also knew of the work of other brokers, such as John Royall and John E. Nail, that had been important to the formation of the African American community.

At the end of August 1917, a few weeks before the September primary, the news reached Harlem that Philip Payton, Jr., founder of the Afro-American Realty Company, had died at his summer home in Allenhurst, New Jersey. In the following days the encomiums conveyed the importance of his individual role, and that of real estate professionals in the eyes of African American residents of Harlem. Several years before, Payton had begun to be called the "Father of Negro Harlem," an acknowledgment that even though his initial company had not thrived, the notion that he had conveyed, that blacks had a right to live in the quality housing of Harlem, had been essential to the realization of Harlem as an African American community, an area that at the time of his death was continuing to grow.[52] Those real estate brokers who followed Payton were acknowledged by Harlem residents and national observers of black life for their roles in solidifying the African American presence in Harlem.

John Royall's candidacy, although unsuccessful, demonstrated the ambition of these new entrepreneurs.[53]

During the 1910s the black population in some Manhattan political districts rose above 10 percent for the first time, partly because of the movement of African Americans within New York, but much more because of the arrival of migrants from the South and the Caribbean who were drawn by the potential to obtain factory jobs in the wartime economy. But the black population was still too slight to elect black candidates until 1917, when Edward A. Johnson was elected to the state assembly, and 1919, when Charles Roberts and George W. Harris became the first blacks elected to New York City's Board of Aldermen. In the closing years of the decade the presence of blacks in Harlem would be further solidified by movements promoting black ownership of apartment buildings and houses.

7

THE GROWTH IN PROPERTY OWNERSHIP BY AFRICAN AMERICANS IN HARLEM

—◆◇◆—

A s early as 1915, it was clear that real estate broker John E. Nail had been wrong in 1913 when he predicted to the Harlem Board of Commerce that blacks had sufficient housing in Harlem for the foreseeable future. His firm, Nail and Parker, would play an important role in addressing the needs of blacks seeking housing there during a period of extreme housing shortages.[1]

From 1910 to 1920 the African American residential presence in Harlem continued to grow, pushed both by the movement of black New Yorkers from the midtown Manhattan neighborhoods and by the dramatic increase in blacks moving to New York after 1914. Racial restrictions on housing in Manhattan meant that many of these new residents came to Harlem, where they exacerbated a housing shortage that was being felt citywide.[2] Although Harlem in the 1910s is often characterized as a community of African American renters and white landlords, the latter years of the decade saw a significant increase in black property ownership. African American investors continued to purchase apartment buildings, and middle-class black residents obtained the anchor of homeownership in the community with the purchase of townhouses. The close proximity of the apartment buildings purchased by blacks in Harlem, the acquisition of two full blocks of townhouses by African

Americans in the late 1910s, and the publicity about these purchases in the *New York Age* solidified the perception among African Americans that Harlem was a community in which the African American residents owned a significant amount of property. This perception was consistent with increases in the black population in Harlem. By the end of the decade, almost two-thirds of the blacks in Manhattan lived within the four assembly districts that spanned Harlem. Within these districts, African Americans accounted for approximately 22 percent of the population.[3]

Black purchases of real estate in the later years of the decade resulted in black ownership of buildings containing approximately 2 percent of the apartment units in Harlem and approximately one percent of the owner-occupied homes in Manhattan. These numbers were modest, but Harlem blacks owned substantially more property in that community than in other previous black neighborhoods in Manhattan (other than the short-lived Seneca Village settlement of the 1820s–1850s). The significant black population increases, combined with the modest but visible increase in black property ownership, contributed to the perceptions, expressed by the *New York Age* and by some black public figures, that blacks in Harlem were residing in their own community rather than in a settlement or quarter that was owned and controlled by others.[4]

In the 1910s, the movement toward elective office by black candidates such as John Royall, James C. Thomas, Jr., and Edward Johnson provided one example that black Harlem residents viewed the community as theirs and expected to have a voice in it. The movement and construction of churches, a significant long-term investment that had not occurred with the move to midtown a generation earlier, was another indicator of the expectation that Harlem would be the center of New York's black community for a long time. In contrast to previous locations in lower Manhattan that had been occupied by blacks when those areas had already been long established and had fallen into decline, Harlem offered a significantly higher quality of housing that was either new or relatively new. Most of the apartments into which black residents were moving had been built after the 1901 Tenement House Act went into effect, and therefore reflected the much higher standard for light and air in apartment units that was dictated by that legislation. With all of these advantages available for the first time, in the 1910s black residents of Harlem prepared to make the community a permanent center of African Americans in New York.[5]

World War I had a dramatic impact on the African American population of Harlem, triggering the Great Migration, the largest movement to that time of African Americans from the South to northern states. They were drawn by expectations of jobs in factories as European immigrants returned to their home countries and industry expanded production even before the United States entered the war in 1917. Blacks in the South were targeted by employment agents who traveled south on behalf of northern industries, encouraging blacks to leave the South and even financing their travel to the North. The black press, particularly newspapers such as the *Chicago Defender*, urged African Americans northward as well, encouraging them to take advantage of the employment opportunities that were becoming available in cities such as Chicago, Cleveland, Detroit, and New York. Upon arrival in New York most of these low-income migrants became renters, often lodgers in the apartments of others, and Harlem was their primary destination. Very soon the community experienced a housing shortage.[6]

The late 1910s housing crisis in Harlem was part of the citywide crisis related to World War I. Though the ramping up of wartime production attracted large numbers of job seekers to New York and other northern cities, concomitant restrictions on the production of nonessential goods had resulted in a virtual halt in housing construction. Consequently many cities experienced housing shortages during the war years.[7]

Black real estate investors used Harlem's housing crisis to their advantage. Local and southern black investors met the continuing African American demand for housing in the area by purchasing buildings occupied by white tenants, evicting them, and "opening" the buildings to African Americans. Some white owners of rental properties adopted a similar policy, using African American managing agents to facilitate the opening of formerly all-white buildings to African Americans. While some black property owners characterized their actions as being for the good of the race, there was clearly a strong economic motive. Because blacks had limited housing choices in

New York, landlords could charge them higher rents. This policy had been the case even in the absence of a housing crisis, but the wartime scarcity of housing for all New Yorkers, and the price increases of certain commodities such as fuel and maintenance supplies, made it easier for landlords to justify the higher rents.[8]

In the fall of 1916 African American tenants in Harlem organized to protest rent increases of "from $4 to $14 per month for apartments recently opened to colored tenants" on West 143rd Street between Seventh and Eighth Avenues. The tenants targeted African American real estate agents Charles A. Knowles, A. G. Thompson, and John Royall, as well as a white agency, the Growham Brothers, all of them managers of the buildings on West 143rd Street. The protesting tenants complained that the agents were summarily evicting white tenants in order to replace them with black tenants who would be charged higher rents. The former white tenants cooperated with the new black tenants by providing their rent receipts to the new tenants. These records demonstrated that the whites had paid substantially lower rents than the new African American tenants were charged. White tenants who still remained on the block protested what they believed were their imminent evictions, indicating that they preferred to remain in their buildings as African Americans became tenants in neighboring buildings.[9]

With assistance from a staff member of the National League on Urban Conditions Among Negroes (soon to become the National Urban League), three residents of the block circulated a petition, signed by 109 African American residents on West 143rd Street, criticizing other African American residents who

> rush into these apartments, accept and even offer unreasonable terms to obtain accommodations. . . . We shall take this opportunity to warn owners of this property [that] the vast majority of Negro families are unable to pay such rents without "commercializing" their apartments. This means in most cases, many lodgers, "socials," loud and offensive language, and too often, prostitution.[10]

The claims of the petitioners were not exaggerated. While wartime labor shortages had created job opportunities, most of these jobs were low-wage positions. The rents demanded for Harlem apartments did strain the budgets of tenants, resulting in many of them using a range of options to supplement their income and pay their rent.

The fight against the rent increases in Harlem continued with a mass meeting in early October under the auspices of the Negro Civic Improvement League, an organization established a few years earlier as an umbrella of New York City neighborhood associations "to educate Negroes in their civic responsibilities."[11] At the mass meeting, with 1,500 in attendance, anger was directed at the real estate agents who were present. One of them, John Royall, attempted to align himself with the tenants, expressing his concern regarding the high rents. But he did not offer to lower the rents in the buildings he managed. In the following weeks the *New York Age* continued its support of the protest movement by criticizing a December purchase of a row of buildings on Seventh Avenue between 136th and 137th Streets by African American attorney J. Frank Wheaton (one of the founders in 1911 of the Equity Congress that had advocated for black policemen and a National Guard unit). When Wheaton increased the rents on the properties, the *Age* reported that the purchase was a lost opportunity for lower rents. The *Age* also criticized Wheaton for using a white agency, Aldhouse & Co., for the transaction. The reporter stated that that agency had been a supporter of the restrictive covenant movement to contain black residency in Harlem. In highlighting Wheaton's purchase, the *Age* implied that Wheaton was betraying African Americans and complained that the substantially higher rents would be used as a precedent by "the white landlord and agent . . . in making increases in rents where property is made available to colored tenants."[12]

At another tenant meeting held in late December 1916 to protest the higher rents in Harlem, broker John Royall was unapologetic. With a hardnosed businessman's perspective, he declared that he

> had no solution for the matter under consideration and that he did not believe that there was any. For twenty years, he said[,] he had never heard of such a thing as bettering the condition of the renting class by providing lower rents for them. Characterizing the whole thing as a foolish idea, he demanded to know why a movement was not started to lower the high cost of living instead

of rents, saying that when the cost of living is reduced the rent problem would be solved.[13]

While African American managers and owners may have been instrumental in "opening" certain buildings to African American tenants, as the protests indicated, they were also seeking to generate the substantial revenue from increased rents that African American tenants were typically charged. Philip Payton's Afro-American Realty Company had been criticized for this tactic ten years earlier.[14] Black tenants in New York City had limited choices, and the real estate brokers, black and white, were able to exploit their situation (and perpetuate it) by charging as much as people would pay. In some cases landlords even divided individual apartments to obtain greater rents. As the 143rd Street rent protesters predicted, the new tenants often had to take in lodgers to meet the rents. In many cases new tenants were targeted with the higher rent scale while longer-term tenants remained at old rent levels, resulting in a rent structure that did not reflect the size or condition of the apartments. While the blacks replaced some of the white Harlem apartment owners, the structure of the real estate market remained the same, with black owners benefiting from the limited choices available to black renters in the same manner that their white predecessors had benefited.

In December 1916 the *Age* offered Harlem real estate brokers an opportunity to explain the rent increases in letters to the paper. Broker John Nail "said he could not adequately or justly explain the various [reasons] for increased rents in a letter." Philip Payton's letter noted: "[If] 'misery likes company' the colored people get plenty of it" because the rent increases were part of a citywide phenomenon spurred by increased taxes, cost of materials, and cost of coal.[15]

A review of the rent increases from 1910 to 1920 in eleven tenement houses on 133rd and 134th Streets between Lenox and Fifth Avenues (the focus of the 1904 eviction attempts) indicated building-by-building rents (table 7.1).

The apartments at the upper rent ranges showed the most dramatic increases in the eleven buildings over the decade. This review did not take into account the annual inflation rate, which rose from 1.35 percent in 1914

TABLE 7.1 Rents in Tenement Buildings on 133rd and 134th Streets*

Building	Type of building Five stories (old law)	1910 rent range	1920 rent range	What the range should have been to keep pace with 7.29% average annual inflation over the decade[†]
1.	5 apartments	$30–$33	$80–$100	$65–$72
2.	11 apartments	23–26	15–28	50–56
3.	10 apartments	17–20	18–25	37–43
4.	10 apartments (divided into 20)	18–20	15–24	39–43
5.	11 apartments	23–26	25–40	50–56
6.	11 apartments	21–23	20–27	46–50
7.	9 apartments	16–18	12–19	35–39
8.	10 apartments	17–20	10–35	37–43
9.	11 apartments	20–22	10–40	43–48
	Six stories (new law)	**1910 rent range**	**1920 rent range**	
10.	28 apartments	$19–$22	$16–$32	$41–$48
11.	33 apartments	14–21	15–50	30–46

Notes:

*Woofter, *Negro Problems in Cities*, 129; "old law" and "new law" refer to the New York City laws governing tenement house construction; in 1901 the law was changed to require that all living spaces have windows and other elements to provide sufficient light and air to residents; apartment built that were governed by this change are referred to as "new law" buildings while buildings constructed before this law are referred to as "old law" buildings.

[†]The decade average inflation rate was computed from monthly and annual average inflation rates available from 1914 to 1920 from http://inflationdata.com/inflation/Inflation_Rate/HistoricalInflation.aspx?dsInflation_currentPage=7. Inflation information before 1914 was not available, so an assumption was made that the annual rate during the years 1910–1913 was 1%; this rate was then added to the annual inflation rates for the period 1914–1920 (1914: 1.35%, 1915: 0.92%, 1916: 7.64%, 1917: 17.80%, 1918: 17.26%, 1919:15.31%, 1920: 15.9%) resulting in an average annual inflation rate of 7.29%, i.e., to keep pace with inflation, from 1910 to 1920 rents would have had to increase by 7.29% each year.

to 17.26 percent by 1918. When the rate of inflation is considered, the rent increases being charged did not keep pace with inflation except in Building 1, where the increases exceeded the rate of inflation. Though the Harlem building owners and managers may have used the limited choices available to black tenants as a way to obtain rent increases from these new tenants, the resulting seemingly high rents still did not allow the owners to keep pace with inflation. While some owners and managers struggled to satisfactorily explain the increases to the public, their assessment that the increases were needed because of higher costs for a range of products was accurate. Because the apartment data did not include the number of rooms in each apartment, comparisons with rents of apartments in other parts of Manhattan cannot be made.[16]

The citywide housing crisis received attention from lawmakers after the end of the war in 1918. Although military demobilization led to a return of industrial production to civilian uses, the pent-up demand for housing could not be met. Across the country governmental agencies began investigating the causes of the continued housing shortage and exploring ways to solve it. There were suspicions that building contractors, real estate brokers, and others who benefited from the crisis were colluding to keep prices high even after the wartime conditions that had precipitated the crisis had ended. In New York City, housing officials estimated that an additional 30,000 units were needed in 1919 to meet the demand. Apartments were almost impossible to find, and when they could be found, landlords, not just in Harlem but throughout the city, recognizing an opportunity for increased profits, charged substantially higher rates than they had before the war. Officials warned that if drastic action was not taken the result could be families living on the streets. As it was, families doubled up with other families, while some separated and rented rooms at different locations.

In the postwar years the provision of sufficient housing became a high priority for New York lawmakers.[17] The public outcry regarding the housing shortage eventually led the New York State Assembly in 1919 to form the Joint Legislative Committee on Housing "to investigate all possible causes of the post–World War I housing shortage." Chaired by Charles Lockwood, an assemblyman from Brooklyn, the Lockwood Committee, as it became known, had a broad investigative purview. The committee sought evidence of collusion to artificially raise prices on housing-related products among general contractors, plumbers, concrete suppliers, real estate brokers, real estate investors, and lenders. To investigate what had become the common practice of landlords demanding substantial rent increases from existing tenants on short notice, New York City mayor John Hylan created the Mayor's Office on Rent Profiteering to determine whether building owners were engaged in unfair business practices. During much of 1919 the Lockwood Committee and the Mayor's Committee on Rent Profiteering heard testimony from witnesses across the spectrum of the real estate industry. Before the committee disbanded in 1922, 416 individuals and 250 corporations and trade organizations were indicted for price-fixing activities, but the many convictions that were secured resulted primarily in small fines or jail terms of less than ninety days.[18]

In the war years, the *Messenger*, a monthly magazine edited by black Socialists Chandler Owen and A. Philip Randolph, added its voice to the criticism of Harlem landlords. In 1918 the *Messenger* encouraged the formation of a tenants' and consumers' cooperative league, noting that for blacks, "their only salvation lies in organizing themselves against their exploiters." The following year the magazine began advocating a policy first made popular by Henry George in the 1880s: taxation on vacant land at high rates to prevent speculation and to encourage the development of housing.[19]

The aggressive legislative response to the citywide housing crisis provides perspective on the earlier tenant protests of "rent profiteering" in Harlem. What was already an extreme housing shortage in New York was exacerbated by the fact that blacks did not have access to all neighborhoods even if they could pay the rent. While Harlem tenants demanded lower rents, black ownership of apartment buildings continued to be advocated by the *New York Age* as part of the solution to high rents in spite of the evidence that black-owned and -managed buildings were not likely to provide rent breaks to blacks. By the latter years of the 1910s the *New York Age* front page regularly highlighted purchases of multi-family buildings by African Americans.

The paper's publisher, Fred R. Moore, had been a colleague of Booker T. Washington and was a key member of Washington's National Negro Business League. The messages from Moore's newspaper announced real estate purchases by African Americans but also served to celebrate African American progress in Harlem and to reaffirm the messages, initiated more than ten years earlier by Philip Payton's Afro-American Realty Company, that Harlem was a community where blacks could expect to live and succeed. Having taken this stance, Moore felt a responsibility to pressure the brokers whose work he was championing to moderate the rents they charged African Americans. The National League on Urban Conditions Among Negroes assisted with organizing the Harlem rent protests. Moore was an active member of the league, and perhaps this affiliation led him to advocate for a moderation in rents while continuing to promote black capitalism.[20]

During the same period, Robert Abbott, editor of the *Chicago Defender*, played a similar role. After encouraging blacks to move to the North, he then encouraged them to buy property and regularly reported on high-profile purchases and leases made by African Americans. In 1914 the *Defender* noted: "It probably will startle the world when it realizes that the race has acquired over one billion dollars in real estate in the United States. The colored people of Chicago now own $5,000,000 worth of property."[21]

Some black real estate brokers and investors in Harlem framed their work in the context of the race leadership promoted by Moore, even if it did not result in lower rents. In July and August 1917 Philip Payton ran a half-page advertisement for six apartment houses on 141st and 142nd Streets in Harlem in the *Age*. The properties were well north of the previous 136th Street northern boundary for black residency in Harlem. The advertisement noted that the buildings were for "Refined Colored Tenants." To make very clear that African Americans were targeted as potential tenants, each of the six "Deluxe Elevator Apartment Houses" was named after a black icon: Wheatley Court for the Revolutionary-era poet Phillis Wheatley; Toussaint Court for Haitian liberator Toussaint L'Ouverture; Washington Court for Booker T. Washington; Dunbar Court for writer Paul Laurence Dunbar; Douglass Court for abolitionist Frederick Douglass. A portrait of each person was to be placed in the foyer of the building that bore his or her name. In addition to the cultural appeal, Payton used the notion of exclusivity to attract the class of African Americans that he was seeking:

Only People Able to Furnish Satisfactory Reference as to Character and Standing are Invited to Inspect these Houses as it is Intended that a Tenancy in these
Houses shall be Almost Equivalent to a Certificate of Character and a Recom-
mendation as to Responsibility.[22]

Payton's appeal to middle-class blacks as potential renters was a strategy
aimed to prevent complaints about the rents to be charged. The aura of exclusivity created by the advertising copy could be used to justify the rents. If
black tenants viewed their residency in the buildings as a status symbol, they
would be unlikely to challenge the rents and bring attention to the fact that
their economic conditions were more tenuous than those of their middle-
class black neighbors.

After Payton's death in late August 1917, Watt Terry, an African American
businessman from Brockton, Massachusetts, took over the properties and
continued to market them to African Americans. With headlines of "Only a
Few More Left!" and "Rents Reduced," his advertisements appealed to potential tenants' concerns regarding rents while continuing to suggest that
an apartment in the "Finest and Most Modern Apartment" buildings was
a scarce commodity.[23] Early in 1918 Terry, who continued to live in Brockton, announced the formation of the "largest business enterprise to be organized and promoted solely by Negroes," the Terry Holding Company. The
company's directors included leading Harlem residents such as business-
woman Madam C. J. Walker; Adam C. Powell, Sr., pastor of the Abyssinian
Baptist Church; and W. H. Brooks, pastor of Harlem Congregational Church.
Advertisements with Madam Walker's photograph appeared in issues of
the *New York Age*. The Terry Holding Company had the ability to raise up to
$750,000 in capital in $10 shares, and the article announcing the company's
formation noted that the interest of prospective tenants in the buildings on
141st and 142nd Streets had been the impetus for the formation of the company. The article implied that other investments would follow: "Mr. Terry
says the Harlem section offers more magnificent opportunities for successful investments than is true of any other section in Manhattan, where reasonable profits may be made as well as comfortable housing conditions obtained at reasonable rental."[24]

Although the advertisements by both Payton and Terry suggested that they had purchased the buildings, during the time from 1917 into 1918, when their advertisements were promoting the buildings for African Americans, the buildings were actually owned by 135 Broadway Holding Corporation, a company formed in 1915. The principals of the corporation were five white men—Cyril H. Burdett, Frank L. Cooke, Gerhard Kuehne, Floyd W. Davis, and Leo Schloss—who lived in Manhattan, Brooklyn, and New Jersey. The company had been capitalized with $1,000. Three of the men were senior officials with New York Title and Mortgage Company. Burdett was the general manager, Cooke the secretary, and Kuehne the treasurer. Burdett owned forty shares of the company, while the other principals each owned fifteen shares.[25]

Neither Payton nor Terry had an ownership interest in 135 Broadway Holding Corporation or in the properties on West 141st and West 142nd Streets that they were promoting. Payton and Terry had sought renters for the buildings as managers rather than owners. Payton's name was well known among African Americans in Harlem, and in spite of the failure of his Afro-American Realty Company in 1908, he was still well regarded by black New Yorkers for his brokerage and management activities undertaken through his next business venture, the Philip A. Payton, Jr. Company. This "brand" recognition would have been important to the 135 Broadway Holding Corporation in leasing the six buildings to blacks at relatively high rents (Payton's advertisements listed apartments of three rooms to six rooms with monthly rents from $26 to $52). While 135 Broadway Holding Corporation would likely have been viewed by many potential African American tenants as white exploiters, Payton's advertisements emphasized the opening of deluxe housing for the first time to blacks who had previously been deprived of these accommodations.[26]

Watt Terry, who took over promotion for the properties after Payton's death, was developing a reputation similar to Payton's. He was known for his humble beginnings as a custodian at the YMCA in his hometown of Brockton, Massachusetts. Through diligent savings he was able to accumulate sufficient funds to begin buying property, and in the 1910s he had expanded his real estate investment activities to Harlem. Terry altered Payton's marketing message slightly by reducing rents, but maintained the characterization of his work as providing a desired good to potential tenants.[27]

By March 1918 a new company, Payton Apartments Corporation, had been formed to "take title to the valuable properties" on 141st and 142nd Streets. The principals of the company were two African Americans, Edward C. Brown and Andrew F. Stevens. Brown had been mentioned as a partner to Watt Terry after Terry took over the properties. Based in Philadelphia, both Brown and Stevens were natives of Virginia. In Norfolk they had formed a bank, Brown and Stevens, and had expanded their investments to include New York real estate. Brown and Stevens each owned 12,350 shares of Payton Apartments Corporation stock. Three others had small ownership interests of 100 shares: Edward P. Butler, secretary of the Universal Carpet and Rug Company; John A. Burns, a white private detective; and Daniel Getz, secretary of the Foreign Language Newspaper Delivery and Circulation Company. Assuming that Butler and Getz were also white, the roles these associates played in the company are unclear. The Payton Apartments Corporation was characterized by its principals as a "race enterprise." The company's shares were initially valued at $10, and the company began with capital of $250,000 on hand.[28]

Regarding the formation of the Payton Apartments Corporation, E. C. Brown said that "the possession of these apartments marks the largest real estate proposition in the world undertaken by Negroes." He noted that the apartments "constructed at a cost of $1,500,000 are being offered at moderate rentals to respectable colored people." The article also stated that the company's secretary would be Emmett Scott, who, having been passed over to succeed Booker T. Washington as leader of Tuskegee, had served as assistant to the secretary of war during World War I. Another director was Heman Perry, an African American who had founded the Standard Life Insurance Company of Atlanta and other business enterprises.[29]

When the *Age* publicized the formation of the Payton Apartments Corporation, no mention was made of Terry Holding Company. The transfer of the ownership of the apartments to Payton Apartments Corporation was announced in March 1918 but did not actually happen until October 1918 when the purchase was finalized. The Payton name was then formally attached to the 141st and 142nd Street properties and the Payton Apartments Corporation assumed the payments on mortgages on the properties totaling $964,000. It is probable that in the preceding months E. C. Brown's company had taken over the management of the buildings from Terry Holding Company until the actual purchase was made.[30]

E. C. Brown's assessment of the importance of the transaction for the Payton Apartments was accurate. It was a large undertaking with symbolic significance in the promotion of Harlem as a community controlled by African Americans as illustrated by the front-page coverage in the *Age*. In 1910 the black congregation of St. Philip's Episcopal Church had purchased ten apartment buildings on 135th Street for more than $600,000. Quite possibly St. Philip's successful management of the apartments it had purchased had benefited the Payton Apartments Corporation. Allowing this black-led company to assume the payments on more than $900,000 of loans originally made to the white businessmen who had previously owned the 141st and 142nd Street properties was not typical. While the actual ownership of the Payton Apartments was somewhat murky, the photographs of the buildings on 141st and 142nd Streets accompanying stories about them, and the laudatory tone used when speaking of the African Americans associated with the buildings, reinforced the significance of the development as a symbol of African American ownership of property in Harlem.[31]

Philip Payton and Watt Terry used the influence of their names among African Americans to facilitate the leasing to black renters of properties initially owned by white investors. This strategy suggests an awareness that black ownership of real estate was an important element in the minds of black residents as the community expanded, and could have also made it more acceptable to charge relatively high rents. The appeal of the perception of black ownership of properties was also used by a group of white investors in marketing buildings to black Harlem residents. In the late 1910s brief notices in the *New York Age* periodically announced real estate purchases and sales made by the Moton Realty Company. A front-page article in the *Age* reported that Moton purchased six houses in the 300 block of West 139th Street that would "soon be occupied by colored families." The newspaper stated that the corporation was controlled by J. Douglass Wetmore, and "the company is organized of course as a commercial proposition to secure a profit on its investments, but its officials also are anxious to aid members of the race by relieving to some extent the congested housing situation."[32]

The Moton name was well known among Harlem's middle class. When Booker T. Washington died in 1915, Robert Russa Moton was appointed to succeed him as head of Tuskegee Institute in Alabama. In this role he continued the Washington tradition of traveling across the country frequently to generate funds, but also to speak on issues of importance to African Americans. He also continued Washington's mission of promoting black business. While this promotion did not involve Moton's personal visible and direct ownership and operation of businesses, the name Moton Realty Company suggested homage to the new Tuskegee leader. J. Douglas Wetmore, who the *Age* indicated "controlled" the company, was the attorney for Moton Realty. A native of Jacksonville, Florida, and a friend of NAACP official James Weldon Johnson, Wetmore was a fair-complexioned African American. He was later suggested to have been the model for Johnson's fictional work *The Autobiography of an Ex-Colored Man*. Wetmore had an almost exclusively white clientele in his law practice, which had its offices on Park Row in lower Manhattan.[33] The five principals of Moton Realty, which was formed in October 1918 in New York City, were from two white families. Ida and Augustus Schmidt lived at 510 West 140th Street near Broadway, far west of the area of Central Harlem to which African Americans were moving. The other principals were Elizabeth Webster and her daughters, Madge Webster and Mabel Bundiak, who lived on Quincy Street in Brooklyn. The company had convinced the *New York Age* that it was sympathetic to the needs of African American tenants, and maybe it was. [34]

At the end of 1919 the *Age* provided a progress report regarding African American real estate activity in Harlem:

> Within the last year Negroes have acquired a dozen elevator apartment buildings in Harlem, many of them tenanted by white people, the most recent being a seven-story building at the northwest corner of Seventh avenue and 137th. As a result of the shortage of living accommodations the southerly limit of the so-called "black belt" has gradually been extended. Several months ago a number

of Negro home seekers crossed the "line" at 130th Street and purchased private dwellings occupied by whites in the streets to the south.[35]

In 1919 white New Yorkers also recognized the extent to which Harlem was a black community. Lawson Purdy, an official with New York City's Tenement House Department (and also the former senior vestryman of the Church of the Redeemer, which had unsuccessfully resisted the sale of its church to African Americans in 1914) observed that "the colored people residing in the Harlem district are good tenants, they preserve property as well as white tenants of similar standing, they are prompt in their payments and the houses tenanted by them are as good investments as similar houses tenanted by white people."[36]

Purdy's statement could have been meant to reassure white investors who were familiar with the notorious reputation of the midtown black neighborhoods, or possibly to encourage the black investors that Fred Moore sought to attract to Harlem. The front-page placement of Purdy's statement in the *Age* would have facilitated this latter goal. Five years after the Harlem Board of Commerce had sought input from black real estate broker John Nail regarding the future of blacks in Harlem, Lawson Purdy's statement suggests that the presence of blacks in Harlem had not destabilized the community. His acknowledgment that black tenants were comparable to white tenants suggested that while they might not live in the same buildings, black and white residents could coexist in different parts of Harlem. Although their tenants might resent them, according to Lawson Purdy, white and black real estate investors could prosper regardless of the race of their tenants.[37]

African American investments in Harlem in 1919 also moved beyond residential properties. In June of that year, the *Age* reported that the "first definite move on the part of Negroes to conduct big business in Harlem" had been made by a group of African Americans with their purchase of the Lafayette Theater on Seventh Avenue between 131st and 132nd Streets. Built in 1910, the Lafayette had been one of the first New York City theaters to desegregate, in 1912, and while it was white-owned (it had been constructed by Meyer Jarmulowsky, the Lower East Side banker who had attempted to continue the restrictive covenant movement after John G. Taylor's death), it had its own company of black actors and welcomed black audiences. The head of the group of investors that purchased the Lafayette Theater was E. C. Brown, also the principal of the Payton Apartments Corporation.[38] In March 1920 the purchase of a large corner lot at 135th Street and Seventh Avenue by Wage Earners Savings Bank of Savannah, Georgia, was also announced in the *Age*. "The transaction represents an investment close to $200,000, and so takes ranks among the largest single real estate transactions of recent days." L. E. Williams, president of Wage Earners, was also an owner of the Lafayette Theater organization.[39]

In 1920 regular reports of African American apartment building purchases continued, with the *Age* noting that an African American woman from North Carolina had invested $50,000 and that a group of black men from Jacksonville, Florida, had created an investment fund of $110,000 for Harlem properties. These purchases were framed in the context of uplift: "The real estate men are being commended for encouraging good, sound property investments as a means not only to financial independence but also to racial self-respect and progress. They unite in declaring that they will frown upon out-and-out property speculation."[40]

During this period two large black churches also decided to move from midtown to Harlem. Rather than take over the buildings of white congregations, they made plans to construct new buildings. In April 1920 the Abyssinian Baptist Church, then located on West 40th Street, announced that it would move to Harlem and build a "modern church plant" for $200,000 on West 138th Street between Lenox and Seventh Avenues. At the end of the year St. Mark's Methodist Episcopal Church, then located on West 53rd Street, announced that it had purchased property at West 137th Street and St. Nicholas Avenue and would construct a new building there.[41]

The African American investors who purchased the apartment buildings, theaters, and land in Harlem were a new generation of black businesspeople. They used the opportunities provided by the increased concentration of black population in many U.S. cities to build businesses targeting this market. Their business successes provided them with the capital to invest in Harlem real estate and take advantage of the opportunities afforded by the explosive growth in New York's black population. The steady reports of these purchases and plans in the *New York Age* reinforced the perception that in Harlem, African Americans would have an unprecedented level of ownership of the properties in their community.[42]

By 1920 large areas of Harlem had significant black populations. Almost two-thirds of Manhattan's black population of 109,133 lived in the four assembly districts that included Harlem (table 7.2).

In the 1910s black investors purchased more than thirty apartment buildings containing over eight hundred apartment units (fig. 7.1). While these units accounted for approximately 2 percent of the 46,000 apartment units in the area from 130th Street to 155th Street, the close proximity of the buildings, in the heart of Harlem's black community, made the acquisitions significant for black residents. The *New York Age* framed these purchases as the signs of increasing black control of the community, and this message was shared by blacks across the country.

In the final years of the 1910s black real estate ownership in Harlem would extend beyond apartment buildings to individual homeownership through the activities of the Equitable Life Assurance Society at King Model Houses, a townhouse development on West 138th and 139th Streets. These actions would dramatically increase the African American homeownership base in Harlem, solidifying the element of community control for individual homeowners in the same way that apartment building ownership had done for black investor groups.

Insurance companies played a significant role in real estate through their investments of millions of dollars of premium payments. Some of these funds were invested in stocks and bonds, but some were used to provide loans for large and small borrowers to purchase real estate. Because of the role of insurance companies in the industry, the Lockwood Committee during its investigations questioned insurance executives about their failure to maintain high levels of investment in New York real estate. The Equitable Life Assurance Society, headquartered in New York, was one of the companies called before the commission in June 1919. Founded in 1859, Equitable was one of the largest insurance companies in the country. In his testimony, the company's president, William Day, told the commission that the company reduced its real estate lending because the purchase of wartime bonds

TABLE 7.2 1920 Populations in Harlem Assembly Districts

Street locations	Assembly district	Total assembly district population	Total whites in assembly district	Total blacks in assembly district	Other	Black assembly district population as a % of total district population	Black assembly district population as a % of Manhattan black population (109,133)
118th–136th/5th to 7th Ave.	19	78,052	50,805	27,136	109	34.77	24.87
E. 115th to E. 133rd/E. River to Park Ave.	20	83,156	80,101	3,012	43	3.62	2.76
136th. to 155th/Convent Ave to Hudson River	21	78,982	39,402	37,436	144	47.40	34.30
144th–161st/Lenox Ave. to Broadway	22	74,895	72,253	2,531	111	3.38	2.32
Total		315,085	242,561	70,117	407		64.25

SOURCE: FOURTEENTH CENSUS, VOL. 3, POPULATION 1920, "COMPOSITION AND CHARACTERISTICS OF THE POPULATION BY STATES," TABLE 13. COMPOSITION AND CHARACTERISTICS OF THE POPULATION FOR WARDS (OR ASSEMBLY DISTRICTS) OF CITIES OF 50,000 OR MORE) (WASHINGTON, D.C.: BUREAU OF THE CENSUS, 1920), 714–715.

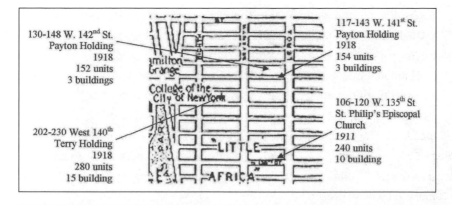

FIGURE 7.1. Harlem apartment building purchases by black investors, 1911–1918. Automobile Club of Rochester, 1920, Florida International Center for Instructional Technology.

had reduced its available funds. After Charles Lockwood, the committee chairman, pressed Day to make a definite lending commitment, Day indicated that "he would recommend to his finance committee that Equitable set aside $500,000" for additional real estate loans. An amount close to this figure would soon be used for loans in Harlem.[43]

In addition to real estate lending, Equitable also owned and managed real estate, some of it acquired through foreclosure proceedings against borrowers and some purchased as investment property. Most of this property was held and managed by Equitable for short periods, usually less than five years, after which the state insurance board required a company to request permission to continue holding a property. The 1919 Lockwood Committee's criticism of insurance companies' real estate activities did not extend to property ownership, but in approximately twelve months, from the fall of 1919 through the fall of 1920, Equitable sold to African Americans more than eighty properties in Harlem that it had owned since 1895.[44] Some insight into Equitable's rationale for selling the King Model Houses buildings during that year can be gleaned from a statement in a February 1921 report by Equitable president William Day to the company's board of directors: "Real estate is not regarded as a suitable investment except to such extent as may be necessary to provide working quarters for the Society's home office staff. It is the policy of the Finance Committee, therefore, to dispose of all other real estate owned whenever adequate prices can be obtained, but not to force properties on the market."[45]

Equitable may have believed that if it had attempted to sell King Model Houses townhouses during the early years of white flight from Harlem it would not have been able to obtain adequate prices. Ironically, as blacks became the principal market for the homes, the real estate market stabilized and because of their limited choices, the strength of blacks' demand for housing enabled Equitable to obtain a better price in 1919 and 1920 than it might have received earlier.[46]

The properties sold, on West 138th and West 139th Streets between Seventh and Eighth Avenues, constituted a unique residential development of 138 homes known as the King Model Houses (fig. 7.2). Named after the developer David H. King, Jr., and completed in 1891, they represented innovative residential design and gracious living.[47] By the time King began work on the project, he was well known as a builder of significant sites in New York City. In 1886 he had completed the construction of the pedestal and the installa-

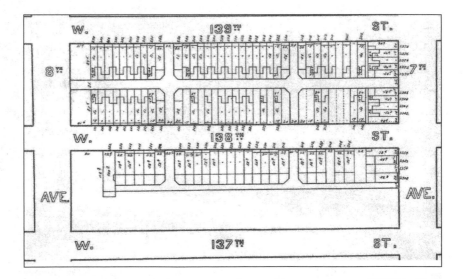

FIGURE 7.2. King Model Houses. Archives of AXA Equitable Insurance Company.

tion of the Statue of Liberty. Other projects included the Washington Arch in New York's Washington Square Park and the New York Times Building on Park Row. King had acquired the land for the project from several owners over a two-year period from 1890 to 1891. To design the buildings, he selected three prominent architectural firms: Bruce Price and Clarence S. Luce; James Brown Lord; and McKim, Mead, and White. Stanford White, of McKim, Mead, and White, had designed many of the buildings previously constructed by King, including Madison Square Garden (the second Garden, at Madison Avenue and 26th Street), and the Statue of Liberty pedestal.[48]

Each architectural firm focused on designing a blockfront in the development. James Brown Lord designed the south side of West 138th Street with buildings "from the Georgian tradition . . . constructed of red brick with brownstone trim, in exceedingly good taste." Price and Luce designed the north side of West 138th Street and the south side of West 139th Street "in the Georgian style of the Eclectic Period . . . of buff-colored brick with Indiana limestone detail." The north side of West 139th, by McKim, Mead, and White, was designed in "the Italian Renaissance style . . . of handsome dark brown mottled brick."[49]

A unique aspect of the development was the alleys running behind the homes through the middle of the blocks so that service activities such as trash removal would be unseen from the streets. The alleys also provided access to individual garages at the rear of each home, a particularly unusual feature for New York homeowners. The entrances to the alleys were placed on Seventh and Eighth Avenues. The blockfronts were also periodically interrupted by gated gardens that allowed access to the alley from the front of the blocks. The development was completed in 1891, and advertisements for the homes highlighted the unique character.

Despite the advertising campaign, most of the units were not sold. The blocks to the immediate south, east, and west were vacant, and perhaps the King Model Houses seemed too remote for potential buyers. The economic downturn following the Panic of 1893 undoubtedly made purchase of the homes even less attractive or feasible. In 1895, only four years after completion, David King transferred the complex to the Equitable Life Assurance Society. The transaction seems to have been a gentlemen's agreement.

Creating A Neighborhood By controlling a large area of land and carefully restricting it against nuisance, every purchaser of one of the King Model houses will be secured against injury both now and in the future. For terms apply on premises.[12]	**The King Model Houses** ...If we had a Society for Improving the Condition for the Rich it would educate people to Live in ideal homes such as the King Model Buildings, 138th to 139th Sts., 7th to 8th Avs. Two entire blocks.[13]

FIGURE 7.3. King Model Houses advertisement, *New York Times*, May 16, 1892, 8.

Equitable had provided financing for the development, and King, who had built Equitable's New York headquarters building, was a close friend of its president, Henry Hyde. They were both members of the Jekyll Island Club, a cottage resort off the coast of Georgia. This personal relationship and the high quality of the housing seemed to have enabled King to convey the properties to Equitable in lieu of payment of the debt he had incurred to build the development. Another sign of the close relationship between King and Equitable was the construction of a uniquely designed local office building for Equitable at the western end of the 138th Street block of King Model Houses "to sell life insurance to residents of this newly opened 'suburb' of Harlem."[50]

After acquiring King Model Houses, Equitable sold a few of the homes in the 1890s and thirty-one of them from 1904 to 1905. The buyers were middle-class whites. Equitable also rented the unsold townhouses to white residents. During the period from 1904 to 1914, when white Harlem residents were concerned about the westward expansion of the African American settlement near West 135th Street and Lenox Avenue, King Model Houses, although in close proximity, was unaffected by the racial tension: the 1910 federal census indicated that only white residents lived on the West 138th Street and West 139th Street blocks.[51] Equitable retained control of the unsold King Model Houses properties for more than twenty years, possibly attempting to ensure that these symbols of gracious living would remain with white owners. By 1913 many of the 138th Street King Model Houses were "leased to natives of South and Central American countries having business interests in the United States." At the end of the decade Equitable adopted a different strategy.[52]

While individual sales of King Model properties to African Americans were noted in the *New York Age* and the broader press, the scale of the transfers being made by Equitable was not recognized. Between September 1919 and November 1920, Equitable sold more than ninety single-family townhouse properties in the King Model Houses development. The majority of the buyers were African Americans who purchased the homes for their primary residences. A few buyers were real estate companies that then resold the homes to blacks. The facts that insurance companies were required to file requests for extensions to continue holding property for more than five years, and that Equitable had retained the King Model Houses properties for more than twenty, suggest that the buildings were important to the company and that Equitable had concluded that the proper conditions, either racial or economic, had not previously existed for selling the properties. For Equitable, the transfer to African Americans of properties that had been rented to whites for decades was an acknowledgment that the black presence in Central Harlem could not be reversed, as some had hoped for earlier in the decade.[53]

As it had with the apartment building purchases by African Americans, the *Age* framed the purchases in the context of community control. A February 1920 article noted the buyers of several properties sold by Equitable on West 138th Street. Although the article did not emphasize that these were significant sales, the placement of this information on the front page of the newspaper suggests that the sales were seen as important information.[54]

New York City's African American homeownership rate was so low that the purchases of the ninety-four King Model Houses made a significant impact on the level of black homeownership not just in Harlem but in New York City as a whole. In 1920, 12.7 percent of New York City households owned their own homes, well below the rate in other major American cities, many of which had rates two to three times that figure. The low rate in New York was a reflection of the predominance of multi-family housing (the cooperative form of individual apartment ownership had not yet become popular in the city), the relatively high cost of the single-family houses that did exist, and the limited ability to finance purchases. Financing for home purchasing was extremely conservative in the early 1900s. A study of national homeownership rates from 1911 to 1914 found "that the average down payment for single-family houses in 22 cities was almost 68 percent of the purchase price, and that 46 percent of homes were acquired debt free." Few black New Yorkers were in a position to meet such terms. In 1920 only 3.2 percent of African American households in New York City owned their homes.[55]

What made the King Model Houses purchases possible, and is an indication of Equitable's interest in facilitating the purchases rather than making a quick profit (after twenty years of holding the properties), was the fact that Equitable provided the black buyers with mortgage financing, which was essential to the transfer of so many properties to African Americans. For black New Yorkers the obstacles to homeownership that all New Yorkers faced were compounded by limited economic opportunities, limits on access to housing in most areas of the city, and obstacles to obtaining home loans (table 7.3).[56]

The 3.2 percent of African American homeowners in 1920 New York City owned 1,163 homes. The King Model Houses sold in 1919 and 1920 by Equitable represented approximately 8 percent of all of the black homeowners

TABLE 7.3 Negro Home Ownership in Five Boroughs, New York City, 1920

Borough	Total [Negro] homes	Negro-owned homes	Percent owned	Black population
Brooklyn	7,791	477	6.1	31,912
Bronx	975	76	7.8	4,803
Manhattan	26,156	184	.7	109,133
Queens	1,173	370	31.5	5,120
Richmond (Staten Island)	317	56	17.9	905
Total city	36,412	1,163	3.2	151,873

SOURCE: WOOFTER, *NEGRO PROBLEMS IN CITIES*, 141; FOURTEENTH CENSUS, POPULATION, "COMPOSITION AND CHARACTERISTICS OF THE POPULATION," 712–716.

in New York City in 1920. The purchases were even more significant when placed in the context of homeownership rates in each of New York City's five boroughs. In Manhattan African Americans owned only 184 homes. More than half of these dwellings were represented by the King Model Houses purchases. Even with these homeowners, the Manhattan homeownership rate for African Americans was below one percent. The black homeownership rate was much higher in other cities, ranging from 7 percent in Chicago to 32 percent in Lynchburg, Virginia. The higher rates were attributed to lower home costs in those areas.[57]

Equitable worked with several real estate brokers to sell the properties, but the most prominent African American agency that participated was Nail and Parker. Founded in 1907 by John E. Nail and Henry Parker, the company drew on a wide range of familial and social relationships among New York's black elite to build a thriving business. John E. Nail was a second-generation entrepreneur. His father was John B. Nail, the saloon owner who in the 1880s had been tapped for leadership by the Democratic Party representing the United Colored Democracy. Part of the early wave of African Americans moving to Harlem after 1900, the senior Nail sold his midtown building and relocated to Harlem, where he lived the life of a retired gentleman, occasionally attending the theater and supervising his Harlem real estate investments.[58]

John E. Nail, the son, entered the real estate business as an employee of Philip Payton's Afro-American Realty Company. When that company began to flounder in 1907, Nail joined forces with a coworker, North Carolinian Henry Parker, to form Nail and Parker. In 1919 Nail and Parker played an important role in the expansion of African American homeownership in Harlem by brokering many of the purchases of townhouses in the King Model Houses development.[59]

Many of the buyers were key figures in the African American community. The *Age* had noted the purchase of 260 West 138th by NAACP deputy field secretary William Pickens thus:

Among the latest investors in Harlem realty is William Pickens, the recently appointed associate field secretary of the N.A.A.C.P. Through Nail & Parker,

Mr. Pickens has purchased from the Equitable Life Assurance Co., the three-story and basement brick dwelling with garage, at 260 West 139th street, and there he and Mrs. Pickens will make their New York residence.[60]

Pickens, a 1902 graduate of Yale, had been a vice president at Morgan State College, a black institution in Baltimore, before joining the staff of the NAACP. Across the street from Pickens's new home, Harry Pace had purchased 257 West 138th Street in December 1919 for $18,756.25. Pace was a partner in the music publishing firm Pace and Handy. His partner, William C. Handy, a native of Memphis, as was Pace, had transcribed blues songs, as well as created new compositions. One of his most famous, "St. Louis Blues," was published in 1914. W. C. Handy purchased 232 West 139th Street on the same day as Pace's purchase. Physician Wiley Wilson purchased 2354 Seventh Avenue in August 1920. Wilson had been a doctor at Freedman's Hospital in Washington, D.C., but he and partners had recently purchased the Edgecombe Sanitarium, on Seventh Avenue one block from his new home. He had also recently married black hair care products heiress A'lelia Walker, daughter of Madam C. J. Walker.[61]

Equitable facilitated the successful sale of the properties to black buyers by financing all of the purchases in 1919 and 1920. Buyers were able to purchase their properties with mortgage loans from Equitable in amounts ranging from $4,500 on the West 138th Street block to $14,000 for homes on the West 139th Street block. The terms of the loans varied. William Pickens, the NAACP official, received a loan of $4,500 from Equitable to purchase his home. Since other buyers on the same block received loans of up to $8,700 for similar homes, Pickens may have made a substantial down payment as part of his purchase. The terms of the Pickens loan called for interest-only payments at the rate of 5 percent to be made biannually, with principal due on May 20, 1925. The terms of the loan made to musician W. C. Handy for his home at 232 West 139th Street were different. His loan of $8,700 from Equitable called for monthly payments of $100, with a portion of this payment applied to reduce the principal, pay taxes and insurance on the property, and cover interest (at 6 percent).The principal balance would be due after five years, but the terms included an option for Equitable to extend the payment of principal for another five years if the payment terms for the initial five years were met. These terms were much more conservative than home purchase loans that Equitable was making in other places across the country. Such loans were made at the comparable interest rate of 6 percent, but for terms of ten years. The King Model Houses loans, with shorter terms but options to extend, reflected Equitable's interest in mitigating its risk to black borrowers, who although they were middle class were more susceptible to economic reversals. The shorter terms allowed Equitable to evaluate the payment history of the borrowers and if it was not satisfactory terminate the loan at the end of five years.[62]

The King Model Houses purchases were important symbols for African Americans in Harlem. By the time of the 1920 census, 90 percent of the residents on the King Model Houses blocks West 138th and West 139th Street were black. The acquisition of these homes by black businessmen, doctors, lawyers, and entertainers was celebrated by the *New York Age,* but some in the African American community, not so interested in promoting the goals of the black middle class, ridiculed the purchases as empty attempts to impress by striving for things beyond their means. In the 1920s some began to refer to the two blocks pejoratively as "Strivers' Row."[63]

As early as 1907 white Harlem residents, such as restrictive covenant leader John G. Taylor, had attempted to contain the African American settlement in Harlem to an area south of West 135th Street and east of Lenox Avenue. Even with the collective organizing that the covenants represented, movement of blacks into previously all-white areas of Harlem continued to occur. Restrictive covenants with fifteen-year terms were not effective, and by the 1910s white residents had conceded to the northern expansion of the African American settlement. The King Model Houses blocks were not part of this collective movement. No restrictive covenants were filed by residents on those two blocks. With Equitable as the owner of most of the property, a covenant between neighbors was not needed. Equitable's corporate policy was sufficient to determine who would be able to rent or purchase Equitable's homes. During the period from 1895 until 1918 Equitable implemented a policy that did not include selling or renting to African Americans. In 1919, when Equitable began selling to African Americans, the properties that it did not own on the King Model Houses blocks were occupied by white renters or owners who had not been long-term residents of the block. Even more than in the neighborhoods in which the covenants failed, the white residents of the King Model Houses were of diverse backgrounds and therefore, while they may not have been happy with Equitable's actions from 1919 to 1920 in selling to African Americans, they were not unified longtime residents and therefore were not so passionate about remaining that they would have selected the Chicago strategy of attacking African American homes to retain control of their neighborhood. After 1919, King Model Houses would serve as symbols of community control, stability, and middle-class prosperity to some black Harlem residents, while others viewed the development as symbols of materialistic excess.[64]

Harlem of the 1910s and 1920s is often depicted as a community of renters exploited by white outsiders. The reality is more complex. As the rent protests of 1916 indicated, there were some black tenants who believed they were being exploited, but an additional source of their frustration was the fact that they believed black property owners and managers were their exploiters. While the rent increases they experienced were relatively large, they still were not sufficient to keep pace with the inflationary climate of the war years. African American property ownership in Harlem did grow dramatically in the second half of the 1910s. This black ownership, of apartment buildings, of theaters, and of the King Model Houses, was publicized by the *New York Age* and viewed by its publisher, Harlem residents, and blacks in other parts of the country as a sign that in Harlem African Americans had attained an unprecedented level of control of their own community.

This perspective was shared by one of Harlem's most talented leaders. At the beginning of 1920, James Weldon Johnson, then field secretary with the NAACP, wrote an editorial titled "The Future of Harlem" for the *New York Age*. Johnson was well suited to provide a broad perspective on both the past and the future of African Americans in New York. He had first begun to visit New York at the turn of the century with his musician brother, Rosamond, when they frequented the midtown artists' hotel on 53rd Street while writing for the musical theater. A lawyer, writer, and lyricist, he was appointed U.S. consul to Venezuela and Nicaragua during the administration of Theodore Roosevelt. In 1916 he became field secretary to the NAACP. He was married to the sister of real estate broker John E. Nail, which gave him particular insight and most likely a financial interest in Harlem real estate.[65] In his editorial Johnson noted the importance of property ownership by African Americans and concluded that Harlem was different from the other areas of New York in which African Americans had lived previously: "In the older sections they owned only their churches. In Harlem they own not only their churches, but are fast buying homes; and not only homes, but large apartment houses."[66]

In light of this broader ownership and no remaining undeveloped area of Manhattan to which blacks could be pushed, Johnson concluded: "I feel confident that the Negro is in Harlem to stay. And what a fine part of New York City he has come into possession of! High and dry, wide and beautiful streets, no alleys, no dilapidated buildings, a section of handsome private houses and of modern apartment and flat houses, a section right in the heart of the empire city of the world."[67]

As a lawyer and former educator, Johnson presented his prediction from a firmly middle-class perspective. Socialist A. Philip Randolph may have shared some elements of Johnson's prediction regarding the black presence in Harlem, but in criticizing "rent profiteering" and advocating the formation of tenants' leagues, Randolph acknowledged that lower-income black Harlem residents faced challenges: "The remedy is not prayer; for as the prayers have ascended the rents have ascended also. It is not denunciations of landlords in mass meetings; we have too often met, resolved and adjourned. It is not race loyalty—a black landlord or agent will dispossess a Negro as quickly as a white landlord or agent."

Randolph suggested that the remedy was the taxation of land to spur owners to develop their vacant land in order to generate revenue from it to pay the tax. In the course of seeking ways to pay the taxes, the landowners would build apartments that would address the housing shortage.[68]

Their acquisition of an increasing number of apartment buildings and homes in Harlem in the 1910s gave African Americans a significant ownership interest in the community. The publicity of these acquisitions provided black New Yorkers with the impression that Harlem was not only the future primary area of settlement for them, but in contrast to other previous areas of settlement in the city, it was a community that they would control. Which blacks would control it, however, was not yet clear.

CONCLUSION

———◆◇◆———

F rom 1890 to 1920, the northern Manhattan community of Harlem changed from a village dominated by white middle-class merchants and professionals, with a small community of black residents, to a densely built urban community that was called the Black Capital of America. Although the period of dramatic change in Harlem is often described as one of "invasion" by black newcomers and "resistance" by white Harlem residents, details of the real estate transactions of the period indicate a more complex reality that challenges some elements of the "ghetto formation" model used by many historians to describe similar changes taking place in many northern cities in the first decades of the 1900s.

A small number of blacks had resided in Harlem for decades before 1890 when most blacks in New York lived in areas of lower and midtown Manhattan. In the decades after the Civil War, as the midtown areas became overcrowded with the continued arrival of black migrants from the South and the Caribbean, the need to find other areas of settlement became increasingly important. Eventually Harlem became one of those areas.[1] Before 1900, when the numbers of blacks in Harlem were modest, some white property owners saw black renters as revenue generators. White real estate investors willingly rented apartments to blacks in certain locations in Harlem.

An incentive for these investors was the fact that blacks' limited housing choices meant that they could be charged premium rents for average housing, providing the owners with an attractive return on their investments. After 1900, hostility to blacks in Harlem began to grow for two reasons. The value of the land on which the small apartment buildings of the 135th Street black community stood increased dramatically with the completion of New York's first subway system, which included a stop at Lenox Avenue and 135th Street in the center of the then-small black enclave. Also, the midtown enclave became overcrowded due to continually increasing numbers of black migrants. Some of the owners of properties near the 135th Street subway stop, along with some of Manhattan's largest real estate investors, attempted to evict the same black residents who had been welcomed a decade earlier. The growth in hostility toward blacks in Harlem that followed emanated from an even larger number of white property owners, many of whom lived in Harlem. Their defensive efforts were motivated by the larger numbers of blacks attempting to move beyond Harlem's black enclave into areas that had previously been off-limits to them.[2]

The presence of black residents in Harlem became known as "an invasion" only when their numbers rose dramatically after 1900, but the real estate transactions of Harlemites in the period after 1900 reveal that relations between white Harlem residents and black newcomers were more complex than the uniform accounts of white resistance to blacks in Harlem that are recounted in studies of Harlem such as Gilbert Osofsky's *Harlem: The Making of a Ghetto* or Irma Watkins-Owens's *Blood Relations*. White residents and investors in Harlem were a diverse group whose actions regarding race were influenced by length of residency, social class, ethnicity, and personal worldview. The inferior status of blacks in Harlem had been assumed by many whites. African Americans in Harlem had previously been consigned to the black enclave because it was not thinkable that they would be integrated into the white community, even if they could afford to live there. When the location became desirable, whites tried to evict black residents in 1904, and the renters were characterized with a broad brush as troublemakers. The eviction attempts in Harlem were thwarted in large measure by the assistance of another group of white residents, German Americans, who sold property to black investors and provided mortgage financing for the purchases. This group, and the assistance they provided, has not been previously recognized. They were not opportunists seeking to buy properties at a discount from panicked fleeing whites or to sell at a premium to blacks anxious to obtain decent housing. The financing offered by the white sellers was for moderate-length terms, and it exposed the sellers to some financial risk. These were not the actions of people interested in making a quick dollar. The whites, such as August Ruff and Louis Partzschefeld, who assisted black purchasers were middle-class, self-employed German Americans. The large German American community that existed in New York in 1904 gave the white sellers the confidence to maintain different perspectives on interactions with blacks than those of some of their white neighbors, and to take actions that contradicted the desires of some of those neighbors. As active participants in the rich social life available to German American New Yorkers, they were not dependent on Harlem's non-German white residents for social acceptance.[3]

The German Americans' involvement was the most dramatic example of efforts made by white Harlem residents to accommodate blacks in Harlem. The unseen, white, small-business owners who provided this financing prioritized class above race in entering into transactions with blacks who were also entrepreneurs. The actions of the white business owners enabled blacks to acquire property in Harlem at a time when local newspapers were declaring that they should be ousted even from Harlem's existing modest black enclave. Without these sales to black buyers, the black "invasion" could have been turned back, if not permanently, at least until some later date. These actions indicate that some white Harlem residents did not subscribe to the notion of black inferiority that could have been used to justify either the removal of blacks or their restriction from residency in Harlem. The group of whites who facilitated this black real estate ownership in Harlem has been unrecognized in the historiography of Harlem, and similar groups have not been noted in accounts of neighborhood change during the same period in other northern cities. It is possible that in other cities whites played similar roles, but historians' focus on the dominant anti-black racial ideologies of the era prevented them from looking for or seeing the varied racial ideologies of those whites who attempted to assist new black residents. The presence of the group of white "facilitators" in Harlem indicates that access to Harlem real estate by blacks, particularly in the earlier cases, happened as a result of white and black agency rather than solely because of white panic. The efforts by some whites to coexist with blacks have been obscured by the much more visible actions of the whites who resisted black access to Harlem and then left Harlem in panic when their efforts failed. Understanding the actions of both of these groups of whites in Harlem, and possibly in other cities, provides a more accurate picture of interactions between blacks and whites and of community formation during that period.[4]

The existence of business relationships between whites and blacks in Harlem, while modest in number, is significant, both symbolically and practically. The properties purchased by blacks provided them with anchors in the community. To hostile whites, the purchases represented flaws in their armor of resistance against black expansion in Harlem. The broader significance of the transactions is that they challenge several elements of the "ghetto formation" model used by authors ranging from Gilbert Osofsky in *Harlem: The Making of a Ghetto*, to Allan Spear in *Black Chicago: The Making of a Negro Ghetto*, to Kenneth Kusmer in *A Ghetto Takes Shape: Black Cleveland, 1870–1930*, to describe the entry of increasing numbers of blacks to these communities. These works focused on the resistance to black entry into predominantly white neighborhoods and the panicked selling that occurred once a few blacks arrived. They also described the social problems that quickly overwhelmed communities that became overcrowded when racial discrimination caused more and more blacks migrating to cities to be steered to these neighborhoods. An understanding that in Harlem there were cooperative business transactions between whites and blacks, establishing long-term financial relations that facilitated expanded black entry into these neighborhoods leads one to consider in more detail the characteristics of the black buyers and the white sellers in Harlem, as well as the nature of the communities that were being created by the new black residents in Harlem and in other cities.[5]

Harlem: The Making of a Ghetto is a landmark study of the community, but while Gilbert Osofsky provided a full picture of black real estate investor Philip Payton as a Harlem pioneer business operator, he quickly passed over Payton's actual business deals, and also the more broad transitional period of the 1910s, focusing instead on a description of Harlem as a slum in the 1920s and 1930s. The transactions of Philip Payton and one of his partners, James C. Thomas, in which both purchased properties from white sellers who provided the men with mortgages of five to six years, challenge the notions that the black purchases resulted from a panic of selling or that the transactions represented sales by white real estate investors intent on making a quick dollar on the way to precipitating a panic of selling among the remaining white residents.[6]

While panics did occur in Harlem and other cities, that result was not the intent of either the buyers or the sellers in these transactions. Initially both groups envisioned a biracial residential community. In 1913, nine years after the purchases of the first key properties by blacks, as the debate regarding the black presence heated up among white residents, Erduin von der Horst Koch, heir to Koch's Department Store on 125th Street and president of the Harlem Chamber of Commerce (and a person of German ancestry), stated at a public meeting that blacks should be able to live wherever they could afford to live. Most white residents did not agree with him, and as the black presence in Harlem grew in the 1910s, the well-publicized notion that such an outcome would be calamitous for white Harlem generated fear and panic. Block by block, real estate values dropped dramatically as blacks began to move into previously all-white areas. Because of the ethnic, religious, and class diversity of Harlem's white community, and the fairly recent arrival of some white residents, a unified resistance to black entry to the community could not be sustained even through racial restrictive covenants or legal challenges to those who violated the covenants. A self-fulfilling prophecy was set in motion as many white residents rushed to leave before the value of their properties declined further, thus creating possibilities for blacks (and some whites) to purchase properties at bargain prices. The scenario repeated itself on a series of Harlem blocks during the first decades of the twentieth century. As blacks entered areas, prices dropped, only to rise again as blacks' demand for housing pushed prices higher than what they had been before. In many cases these new owners, blacks and whites, when renting properties to African

Americans were able to charge premium rents because of the demand by blacks to live in Harlem and the limited choices available to them to live elsewhere in New York. As whites left Harlem in the 1910s, blacks' vision of the community shifted: they began to promote Harlem as a black community.[7]

The *New York Age* newspaper was a leading advocate of the new black property owners' vision of Harlem as a black community that would be different from the "black settlements" previously occupied by African Americans in New York. The *Age* suggested that in Harlem blacks would be able to purchase quality properties and to participate in the management of the community. An understanding of the social class of the black purchasers of the townhouses and apartment buildings in Harlem in the 1910s leads one to consider the nature of the newly forming northern black neighborhoods as black *communities* before they were categorized as ghettos. The black people making the substantial investments in real estate in Harlem expected to obtain homes for themselves or a reasonable return on their investments. Many of them also sought to protect these investments by strengthening the community around them. The establishment of black churches, the founding of organizations to serve the community's youth, the quest for elective office by black community leaders, and the promotion of more black property ownership were components of this process of community formation that some historians have underemphasized in analyses of the racial transition in northern cities, focusing instead on the problems that eventually emanated from these communities. Considering the transitional period of Harlem in the 1910s in detail through the lens of real estate transactions provides a better understanding of the basic elements of the community before it was overwhelmed by continuing population increases.[8]

In addition to residential properties, during the 1910s black churches became important vehicles in establishing a black presence in Harlem. The resistance of departing white congregations to selling their buildings to black congregations, even though many of the white congregations were unable to sustain themselves as their congregants moved away, illustrates the depth of their reluctance to relinquish control of properties that were viewed by both blacks and whites as symbols of white claims to the community. The purchase of churches by blacks was another element of the ownership movement that served to anchor blacks in Harlem.[9]

The establishment of youth-serving organizations in Harlem made clear the commitment of African American parents and others to a future for the black children and young adults in that community. Many of these organizations, such as the YMCA and the YWCA, migrated from the black community in midtown and eventually built headquarters in Harlem that were much more extensive than their midtown locations had been. In some cases the young adults themselves established organizations, such as the Alpha Physical Athletic Club, or maintained substantial control of them, such as the Salem Crescent Club and the St. Christopher Athletic Club.

In the 1910s, the substantial black population in several Harlem districts became the political base for New York City's first black candidates. This population, through its patronage of black businesses, provided the business owners who became candidates with a measure of economic independence that allowed them to consider running for office. The first black candidates for the Board of Aldermen from Harlem in 1913 were John Royall, a real estate broker, and James H. Anderson, publisher of the *Amsterdam News*, a black newspaper. Although neither was successful, they viewed the political offices as opportunities to improve the economic interests of their constituents and themselves. In 1917, black attorney Edward Johnson was elected to represent Harlem in the New York State Assembly, and in 1919 two other African American businessmen, dentist Charles Roberts and *New York News* editor George W. Harris, were elected to the Board of Aldermen as Republican candidates.[10]

The role of black property ownership as an indicator of community formation has not been explored in detail. Descriptions of many neighborhood transitions in northern cities suggest that the new black residents were primarily renters. This was true of Harlem, but what has not been recognized in earlier accounts is the significant number of black investors who owned the multi-family buildings in Harlem that were then rented to black tenants. To solidify the community, by the mid-1910s a real estate ownership campaign was undertaken in which a number of large properties were purchased by blacks and publicized in the *New York Age*. By the end of the decade black investors owned more than thirty apartment buildings containing more than 1,000 units. While these units constituted approximately 2 percent of the 46,000 apartment units in the area from 130th Street to 155th Street, the close proximity of the buildings, in the heart of Harlem's black community, made the acquisitions significant for black residents. The buildings reinforced the vision of Harlem as a black-controlled community. As blacks became more of a presence in Harlem during the 1910s, details of their real estate transactions illustrate the variety of ways in which some black investors appealed to race to their benefit. In some cases while managing or leasing properties owned by whites, they gave the impression that they owned the properties and that their business activities, such as charging premium rents, were furthering racial progress.[11]

In the closing years of the decade, the ownership movement expanded beyond apartment buildings to individual townhouses when Equitable Life Assurance Society sold more than ninety King Model Houses townhouses to black middle-class buyers. The sales, and Equitable's provision of mortgage financing for these purchases, had a dramatic impact on Harlem's minuscule homeownership ranks. The entertainers and professionals who purchased the homes helped to inspire the nickname "Strivers' Row" for the enclave, a term that was used to express derision, envy, and eventually admiration.[12]

At the root of the changes that occurred in Harlem from 1890 to 1920 were population shifts, most notably an increase in the number of African Americans and Afro-Caribbeans moving to New York. Although high rents caused overcrowding in some parts of Harlem by the 1910s, before 1920 Harlem was viewed by many blacks as a place of possibilities. James Weldon Johnson optimistically suggested in his "The Future of Harlem" editorial in 1920 that those moving to Harlem did so with an air of anticipation. Johnson's vision was grounded in his firmly middle-class perspective as an official of the NAACP whose brother-in-law, John Nail, was one of the leading real estate brokers in Harlem. But alternative black visions for Harlem existed as well. Black tenants who organized against rent increases did not admire the black investors who owned their buildings and who they believed were exploiting them. A. Philip Randolph and Chandler Owen used their *Messen-*

ger to criticize the actions of black real estate investors for rent profiteering. Their vision for Harlem was imbued with the concepts of cooperative housing and other interventions that would allow poor black people to live with dignity, something that had been denied to them in their previous New York settlements.[13]

By 1920, for the first time, many black New Yorkers in Harlem occupied quality housing. They expected Harlem to become a well-functioning city within a city. Although black Harlem existed because of segregation customs, within the community this second-class citizenship could often be forgotten. It is important to consider Harlem before the overcrowding of the 1920s and 1930s happened, because one finds that the basic elements of the formation of Harlem as a black community with churches, newspapers, political aspirants, youth organizations, and property owners become clearly evident. These positive developments persisted even though they are often obscured by a focus on the problems in Harlem and other communities in the 1920s and succeeding decades.[14]

The year 1920 was the beginning of another phase in Harlem's formation as a black community. Although the area from 135th to 145th Streets between Lenox and Eighth Avenues had a predominantly black population by 1920, and some blacks also owned businesses there, many of the businesses continued to be owned by whites. The "Don't Buy Where You Can't Work" campaign on 125th Street in the 1930s, in which blacks picketed and boycotted stores that would not hire blacks, would attest to the stubbornness of the racial hierarchy in employment in area businesses. Other residential areas of Harlem also remained predominantly white. The Hamilton Heights area, in the 140s west of St. Nicholas Avenue and the Mt. Morris Park area in the 120s near Lenox Avenue maintained a predominantly white presence into the 1930s.[15]

Many of the principals in the racial battle for Harlem did not live to see the positive and negative changes. Philip Payton, founder of the Afro-American Realty Company, died in 1917 before his biggest real estate deal, the purchase of six buildings on 141st and 142nd Streets, could be completed. John G. Taylor died in 1914 in the middle of the challenges to the restrictive covenant, but his widow, Agnes, remained true to the cause. Although she remarried, she adhered to the restrictive covenant that she had signed in 1910. By the 1920s, the 136th Street block that included the home John G. Taylor had purchased in 1903 was almost 100 percent black, but Taylor's widow did not sell 213 West 136th Street until 1925, when the term of the covenant expired.[16]

Erduin Koch, whose father had moved H. C. F. Koch & Company dry goods store to 125th Street in 1891, died in 1928. At the time of his death he was no longer living in Harlem, but on East Ninety-Second Street near Fifth Avenue. In 1913 he had disagreed with his business colleagues and suggested that blacks should be able to live anywhere in Harlem that they could afford. By the 1920s his store had adopted a policy that was much more restrictive toward blacks than that philosophy would suggest. Koch's obituary in the *New York Herald Tribune* mentioned his business as well as his hobby of horse racing. The *New York Amsterdam News* was more direct. In describing the store a few years later, it noted that as a business, "Koch's paid scant attention to the Negro trade. Due to a feeling that they were not wanted as patrons, many persons living in Harlem patronized smaller stores and downtown companies. . . . At no time did the Koch store advertise with Negro newspapers."[17] The store was sold in 1930 to clothing wholesaler A. Schaap & Sons and reopened in 1934 as a desegregated store.[18]

Some Harlem investors experienced business challenges. In the mid-1920s E. C. Brown, who had purchased the Payton Apartments on 141st and 142nd Streets after Philip Payton's death, experienced a number of reversals. In 1921 he had to sell the Dunbar Theater that he had built in Philadelphia, and then a 1925 run on his Brown and Stevens Bank pushed him close to financial ruin. He retreated to Harlem, but his Philadelphia creditors followed, complaining about the lavishness of his new office. He died in 1928 still trying to reorganize his financial affairs for a business comeback.[19]

Hutchens Bishop, whose intrepid purchase of properties west of Lenox Avenue on behalf of his congregation, St. Philip's Episcopal Church, broke the "deadline" for black settlement in Harlem, became a pivotal neighborhood leader. His congregation continued to prosper, in the church edifice that they had designed and built. The row of apartment buildings on West 135th Street whose purchase by St. Philip's had generated front page headlines in the black press continued to generate income for the church while also serving as a symbol of black ownership. By the time Father Bishop retired in 1933 and was succeeded by his son, Shelton Hale Bishop, St. Philip's was well known for its wealth and for its community programs.

The stock market crash of 1929 and the Great Depression of the 1930s were tremendous obstacles to the development of Harlem into the thriving black community that people such as James Weldon Johnson hoped it would be. The vision of A. Philip Randolph and Chandler Owen, of a Harlem that served poor people, became much more relevant during the Depression. Many of the black ownership gains that had been made there in the 1910s and 1920s were lost as the entire nation suffered from record unemployment and a disastrous economy. The black elite real estate firm of Nail and Parker, one of the largest firms in Harlem, went bankrupt. Although John Nail started another firm, the old prominence was never regained. African Americans continued to move to Harlem, which became increasingly overcrowded, and with limited job prospects, increasingly poor. [20]

The 1935 riot on 125th Street in which blacks went on a rampage, sparked by the unfounded rumor that a young boy had been killed by a department store security guard, created a marker for the era of Harlem as a problem-ridden community. Dr. Charles Roberts, the Harlem dentist who along with newspaper editor George W. Harris in 1919 became New York City's first black alderman, was asked by Mayor Fiorello La Guardia to chair the Mayor's Commission on Conditions in Harlem, exploring the causes of the riot. The report, never officially released, found that discrimination, racism, and poverty were the underlying causes of the disturbance. [21]

Long before anyone could have imagined a black riot on West 125th Street, in 1891 Henry C. F. Koch moved his dry goods store to Harlem from Sixth Avenue. The store flourished there and the community continued to grow as a predominantly white, middle-class enclave. Over the next three decades Harlem was transformed into the largest black community in the nation. Most other northern cities experienced variations of the changes experienced in New York City. While whites have typically described these transformations as "invasions" by blacks countered with "resistance" by whites, the changes in Harlem, and most likely in the other cities as well, were more complex. On both sides of the color line, class, ethnicity, politics, and economics dictated a range of strategies that could either facilitate or forestall racial change in Harlem. The ownership and occupancy of real estate, long the symbol of citizenship in the United States, was the critical element in implementing and understanding these strategies.

NOTES

INTRODUCTION

1. "A Volley of Rocks," *Harlem Local Reporter,* July 26, 1893, 1.
2. Ibid.; "Harlem Shaken by Dynamite," *New York Times,* July 23, 1893; "Trying to Fix the Blame," *New York Times,* July 24, 1893; Nancy Foner, *From Ellis Island to JFK: New York's Two Great Waves of Immigration* (New Haven, CT: Yale University Press, 2002), 224–227.
1. Mary Rankin Cranston, "The Housing of the Negro in New York City," *Southern Workman* 31, no. 6 (June 1902): 329; the journal was published by the Hampton Institute, a school for black students in Hampton, Virginia.
2. Jeffrey Gurock, *When Harlem Was Jewish* (New York: Columbia University Press, 1979); "Harlem Real Estate," *Harlem Local Reporter,* March 1, 1890, 2; "Harlem Gossip," *Harlem Local Reporter,* March 1, 1890, 4.
3. Twelfth Census of the United States, Population, 1900, City of New York, Borough of Brooklyn, Enumeration District 398, 18.
4. Cranston, "Housing of the Negro in New York City," 329.
5. Thomas J. Sugrue, *The Origins of the Urban Crisis: Race and Inequality in Postwar Detroit* (Princeton, NJ: Princeton University Press, 1996), 22–23; Thirteenth Census of the United States, Population: New York, 3, 43–45 (1910).
6. Gilbert Osofsky, *Harlem: The Making of a Ghetto: Negro New York, 1890–1930,* 2nd ed. (Chicago: Ivan R. Dee, 1996); Kenneth Mjagkij, *A Ghetto Takes Shape: Black Cleveland, 1870–1930* (Urbana: University of Illinois Press, 1978); William M. Tuttle, Jr., *Race Riot: Chicago in the Red Summer of 1919* (Urbana: University of Illinois Press, 1970); Seth M. Scheiner, *Negro Mecca: A History of the Negro in New York City, 1865–1920* (New York:

New York University Press, 1965); Irma Watkins-Owens, *Blood Relations: Caribbean Immigrants and the Harlem Community, 1900–1930* (Bloomington: University of Indiana Press, 1996).

7. George A. Hillery, Jr., "Definitions of Community: Areas of Agreement," *Rural Sociology* 20 (June 1955): 111.

8. "More Property Owners Agree to Exclude Negroes," *Harlem Home News*, July 10, 1913; "Harlem's Black Belt Is a Growing Menace," *Harlem Home News*, July 24, 1913; "Harlem Property Owners Discuss Negro Problem," *Harlem Home News*, July 31, 1913; "Negro Invasion Has Cut Property Values in Half," *Harlem Home News*, August 7, 1913.

9. Studies of racial change such as Karl Teuber and Alma Teuber's *Residential Segregation and Neighborhood Change* (Piscataway, NJ: Transaction Publishers, 1965), 21–22, indicate that while property values declined as whites began to exit communities, as more blacks entered, values usually rose again, sometimes exceeding the original prices since the limited choices available to blacks beyond the neighborhood in transition had the effect of concentrating black demand for housing in the transitional neighborhood.

10. Sugrue, *Origins of the Urban Crisis*, 22; Twelfth Census, Schedule No. 1, Population, Manhattan, Enumeration Districts 614, 616, 878, 875, 876; Thirteenth Census, 1910, Population, Manhattan, Enumeration Districts 532, 533 (Washington, DC: Department of Commerce and Labor Bureau of the Census, 1900, 1910); Allan H. Spear, *Black Chicago: The Making of a Negro Ghetto, 1890–1920* (Chicago: University of Chicago Press, 1967); "$20,000 to Keep Negroes Out," *New York Times*, December 8, 1910; "Status of Harlem Negroes," *New York Times*, March 26, 1913.

11. Booker T. Washington, *The Negro in Business* (Wichita, KS: DeVore and Sons, 1907), 152–154; "New York Loses Pioneer Undertaker, James Thomas," *Chicago Defender* (National Edition), June 3, 1922; Maceo Crenshaw Dailey, Jr., "John E. Nail," in Rayford W. Logan and Michael R. Winston, eds., *Dictionary of Negro Biography*, 469–470 (New York: W. W. Norton, 1982).

12. David Dunlap, *From Abyssinian to Zion: A Guide to Manhattan's Houses of Worship* (New York: Columbia University Press, 2004); Twelfth Census, Schedule No. 1 Population, Manhattan, Enumeration Districts 614, 616, 878, 875, 876; Thirteenth Census 1910, Population, Enumeration Districts 532, 533; Henry K. Carroll, *Report on Statistics of Churches in the United States at the Eleventh Census: 1890* (Washington, D.C., Department of the Interior, Census Office, 1894), 38, 91; Campbell Gibson and Kay Jung, *Origin, 1970 to 1990, for the United States, Regions, Divisions, and States*, Working Paper Series No. 56 (Washington, DC: U.S. Census Bureau, Population Division, September 2002), Table 1, "United States—Race and Hispanic Origin: 1790 to 1990."

13. Thirteenth Census , 1910 Bulletin, Population: New York "Composition and Characteristics of the Population," Table V, New York City, 45; "Negroes Rally Around Royall," *New York Age*, October 2, 1913; "Editor Anderson Is Certain of One Vote for Alderman," *Harlem Home News*, September 28, 1913.

14. "Negro Invasion Threat Angers Flat Dwellers," *New York Times*, July 27, 1906; "Free Renting: Organizations Formed to Kill This Practice," *Real Estate Record and Builders'*

Guide, August 25, 1900, 235; "$20,000 to Keep Negroes Out," *New York Times*, December 8, 1910.

15. Patricia Gurin, Shirley Hatchett, and James Sidney Jackson, *Hope and Independence: Blacks' Response to Electoral and Party Politics* (New York: Russell Sage Foundation, 1989), 212–213; Bruce Sinclair, *Technology and the African-American: Needs and Opportunities for Study* (Cambridge, MA: MIT Press, 2004), 133; Evelyn Higginbotham, *Righteous Discontent: The Women's Movement and the Black Baptist Church, 1880* (Cambridge, MA: Harvard University Press, 1993), 41.

16. "Status of Harlem Negroes," *New York Times*, March 26, 1913.

17. "Harlem Property Owners Discuss Negro Problem," *Harlem Home News*, July 24, 1913.

18. "Manhattan Tenement Apartments and Estimated Population by District, December 31, 1916." *Eighth Report of the Tenement House Department of the City of New York. Report for the Years 1915 and 1916*, 66, 90; "More Harlem Homes for Colored People," *New York Times*, March 26, 1911; *Tenement House Department*, 1916, 90; "The Real Estate Field," *New York Times*: August 21, 1918; March 14, 1918; September 28, 1917; July 28, 1917; Fourteenth Census of the United States, Population; Thirteenth Census, Population; "Bronx Cars to Come to Harlem, Colored Question Taken Up by Board," *Harlem Magazine*, April 1913, 21–22; Osofsky, *Harlem*, 92–104; "Payton Closes Harlem Realty Deal Involving Million and a Half Dollars," *New York Age*, July 12, 1917; "World's Finest Housing Proposition," *New York Age*, August 16, 1917.

19. Spear, *Black Chicago*, 211–213.

1. BLACK AND WHITE NEW YORKERS

1. National Archives and Records Administration (NARA), Washington, D.C., *Passport Applications, 1795–1905*; ARC Identifier 566612/MLR Number A1 508; NARA Series: *M1372*; Roll #*235*, June 26, 1880; "Mr. H. C. F. Koch Talks," *Harlem Local Reporter*, September 21, 1892; "Death of H. C..F. Koch," *New York Tribune*, September 6, 1900; John G. Taylor Identification Card, New York City Police Department; United States Federal Census, *1900*; Census Place: *Manhattan, New York, New York*; Roll: *T623_1085*; Page: *2A*; Enumeration District 100; John H. Hewitt, Jr., *Protest and Progress: New York's First Black Episcopal Church Fights Racism* (London: Taylor and Francis, 2000), 130–133; Washington, *The Negro in Business*, 199–201.

2. U.S. Census, Total and Foreign-Born Population New York City, 1790–2000, http://www.nyc.gov/html/dcp/pdf/census/1790-2000_nyc_total_foreign_birth.pdf.

3. "The New Colossus," in Emma Lazarus, *The Poems of Emma Lazarus in Two Volumes* (New York: Houghton, Mifflin, 1888), 1:202–203.

4. Ira Rosenwaike, *Population History of New York City* (Syracuse, NY: Syracuse University Press, 1972), 42; Stanley Nadel, *Little Germany: Ethnicity, Religion, and Class in New York City, 1845–80* (Urbana: University of Illinois Press, 1990).

5. "Death of H.C.F. Koch," *New York Tribune*, September 6, 1900.

6. Norval White, Elliot Willensky, and Fran Leadon, *AIA Guide to New York City*, 5th ed. (New York: Oxford University Press, 2010), 229.

7. "Death of H.C.F. Koch," *New York Tribune*, September 6, 1900; Office of the City Register, Section 7, Liber 3, pp. 427–429; Liber 318, pp. 480–482; "Koch & Co." display advertisement, *Harlem Local Reporter*, March 7, 1891; "Ready for the Opening," *Harlem Local Reporter*, March 21, 1891; "H.C.F. Koch & Co.," display advertisement, *Harlem Local Reporter*, March 28, 1891. http://www.measuringworth.com/uscompare/relative value.php.

8. James Riker, *Revised History of Harlem (City of New York), Its Origin and Early Annals* (New York: New Harlem Publishing Co., 1904), 170.

9. Ibid., 119.

10. E. Willensky and N. White, *AIA Guide to New York City*, 3rd ed. (New York: Harcourt Brace, 1988), 433, 461.

11. The Real Estate Record Association, *A History of Real Estate, Building, and Architecture in New York City During the Last Quarter of a Century* (New York: Record and Guide, 1898; reprint, Arno Press, 1967), 33; Elizabeth Blackmar, *Manhattan for Rent, 1785–1850* (Ithaca: Cornell University Press, 1989), 98.

12. "Mr. H.C.F. Koch Talks," *Harlem Local Reporter*, September 21, 1892; "Business Is Good," *Harlem Local Reporter*, June 21, 1893; "Caution," Special Notice, *New York Evening Telegraph*, July 1, 1898.

13. "H.C.F. Koch & Co.," display advertisement, *Harlem Local Reporter*, March 28, 1891.

14. Willensky and White, *AIA Guide to New York City*,187; "Erduin Koch, 56, Merchant and Horseman, Dies," *New York Herald Tribune*, December 4, 1928, 25; "Koch & Co.," display advertisement, *Harlem Local Reporter*, March 7, 1891, 3; "Ready for the Opening," *Harlem Local Reporter*, March 21, 1891, 1; "H.C.F. Koch & Co.," display advertisement, *Harlem Local Reporter*, March 28, 1891.

15. "Business Is Good," *Harlem Local Reporter*, June 21, 1893; Census of 1900, New York City, Enumeration District 863, Sheet 19.

16. James Lardner and Thomas Reppetto, *NYPD: A City and Its Police* (New York: Macmillan, 2001), 59–60.

17. Office of the City Register (New York), Section 2, Liber 14, p. 96; Twelfth Census, Schedule No. 1- Population, New York County, Enumeration District 1, Sheet B3; Enumeration District 696, Sheet B8; http://www.measuringworth.com/uscompare/relativevalue .php; Abyssinian Baptist Church 90th Anniversary Program (1898), Abyssinian Baptist Church Archives.

18. Lucille Genevieve Lomax, "Social History of the Negro Population Living in the Section of New York City known as Greenwich Village" (master's thesis, Columbia University, 1929), 4–30.

19. Leslie Harris, *In the Shadow of Slavery: African Americans in New York City, 1626–1863* (Chicago: University of Chicago Press, 2003), 23–27, 36; Graham Russell Hodges, *Root and Branch: A Comprehensive History of African Americans in New York City and East Jersey, 1613–1863* (Chapel Hill: University of North Carolina Press, 1999), 31.

20. Lomax, "Social History," 4–30; David Nathaniel Gellman and David Quigley, eds., *Jim Crow New York: A Documentary History of Race and Citizenship, 1777–1877* (New York: New York University Press, 2003), 13–22, 52–55.

21. Hewitt, *Protest and Progress*, 125, 135–138.

22. Rhoda Golden Freeman, *The Free Negro in New York City in the Era Before the Civil War* (New York: Garland Publishing, 1994), 6; Jonathan Greenleaf, *History of the Churches of All Denominations in the City of New York From Settlement to the Year 1846* (New York: E. French, 1846), 79–80, 240, 325.

23. Gellman and Quigley, *Jim Crow New York*, 77; Craig Wilder, *In the Company of Black Men: The African Influence on African American Culture in New York City* (New York: New York University Press, 2001), 74; J. H. Pease and W. H. Pease, "Samuel Eli Cornish," in R. W. Logan and M. R. Winston, eds., *Dictionary of American Negro Biography* (New York: W. W. Norton, 1982), 134–135.

24. Gellman and Quigley, *Jim Crow New York*, 90–200.

25. Wilder, *In the Company of Black Men*, 74; Charlotte Augusta Burroughs Ray, *Sketch of the Life of Rev. Charles B. Ray* (New York: J. J. Little, 1887), 7–18.

26. Freeman, *The Free Negro in New York City*, 213, 235–265.

27. Hewitt, *Protest and* Progress, 13–30.

28. Blackmar, *Manhattan for Rent*, 101–135; Clifton Hood, *722 Miles: The Building of the Subways and How They Transformed New York* (New York: Simon & Schuster, 1993), 38.

29. Hewitt, *Protest and Progress*, xvi.

30. Tyler Anbinder, *Five Points: The 19th-Century New York City Neighborhood That Invented Tap Dance, Stole Elections, and Became the World's Most Notorious Slum* (New York: Free Press, 2001), 7–13; Hodges, *Root and Branch*, 112–113.

31. Hodges, *Root and Branch*, 232–236.

32. Roy Rosenzweig and Elizabeth Blackmar, *The Park and the People: A History of Central Park* (Ithaca, NY: Cornell University Press, 1992), 65–73; Wilder, *In the Company of Black Men*, 101–102; the churches were Mother AME Zion, African Union Church, and All Angels Church.

33. Lomax, "Social History," table 3, "Negro and White Population New York City by Wards"; Anbinder, *Five Points*, 97–105; Hewitt, *Protest and Progress*, 125.

34. Lomax, "Social History," 92; Blackmar, *Manhattan for Rent*, 93–103; Scheiner, *Negro Mecca*, 15–19.

35. Anbinder, *Five Points*, 7–13; Freeman, *The Free Negro in New York City*, 72–73; Herman D. Bloch, *The Circle of Discrimination: An Economic and Social Study of the Black Man in New York* (New York: New York University Press, 1969), 19–46; Hewitt, *Protest and Progress*, 97–103.

36. Hudson Realty Company Corporate Documents, New York County Archives, Seventh Census of the United States, Population, Statistics of the United States, "Nativities of the White Population," table XL, 61.

37. Iver Bernstein, *The New York City Draft Riots: Their Significance for American Society and Politics in the Age of the Civil War* (New York: Oxford University Press, 1990), 143.

38. Ibid., 17–42.

39. Ibid.

40. Tenth Census, Population, "Population by Race, Sex, and Nativity," 402; Rosenwaike, *Population History of New York City*, 77.

41. David Quigley, *Second Founding: New York City, Reconstruction, and the Making of American Democracy* (New York: Hill and Wang, 2006), 39–69.

42. Ibid., 74–76; Freeman, *The Free Negro in New York City*, 107.

43. Osofsky, *Harlem*, 18.

44. Ninth Census, Population; Tenth Census, Population.

45. Rosenzweig and Blackmar, *The Park and the People*, 379–381; James Weldon Johnson, *Black Manhattan* (New York: DaCapo Press, 1991), 58–145.

46. Scheiner, *Negro Mecca*, 18–19.

47. Hewitt, *Protest and Progress*, 125, 135–138.

48. Ibid., 131–133.

49. Ibid., 133.

50. Dunlap, *From Abyssinian to Zion*, 6, 91, 148, 243, 262; *Trow's New York City Directory*, 1880 (New York: Trow Directory, Printing, and Bookbinding Co., 1880–1920).

51. "Prejudices of Landlords," *New York Times*, April 14, 1889; "The Northern Color Line," *New York Times*, April 28, 1889; Daniel E. Bigham, *On Jordan's Banks: Emancipation and Its Aftermath in the Ohio River Valley* (Lexington: University of Kentucky Press, 2005), 156.

52. Nancy C. Curtis, *Black Heritage Sites: An African American Odyssey and Finder's Guide* (Chicago: American Library Association, 1996), 185; Reginald W. Brown, "Some Livingstone College History," www.rowancountync.gov/Government/Departments/Rowan PublicLibrary/HistorRoom/TheoBuerbaumSalisbury/LivingstoneCollege.aspx.

53. Washington, *The Negro in Business*, 197–200; *Westfield Directory*, 1874, 35; 1875, cover; 1878–1879, 16; 1880–1881, 76; 1885, 19; 1888, 37; 1893, 45; 1894, 45; 1896, 67; 1897, 57.

54. Brown, "Some Livingstone College History."

55. Washington, *The Negro in Business*, 200–201.

56. Ibid., 200–203.

57. Ibid., 202–204.

58. Twelfth Census, Schedule No. 1- Population, New York, Enumeration District 870, Sheet 15.

59. "Harlem Real Estate," *Harlem Local Reporter*, March 1, 1890.

60. Office of the City Register, Section 7, Liber 88, p. 60; Section 2, Liber 112, pp. 330–331. The description of the exterior of the home is based on the author's view of the house, which does not appear to have been altered; Twelfth Census, Schedule No. 1- Population, New York County, Enumeration District 100, Sheet A2.

61. "Death of H.C.F. Koch," *New York Tribune*, September 6, 1900, 7; "Henry C.F. Koch Buried," *New York Times*, September 8, 1900.

2. THE END OF THE AFRICAN AMERICAN
WELCOME IN HARLEM

1. Charity Organization Society of the City of New York, Tenement House Committee, *Housing Reform in New York City: A Report of the Tenement House Committee of the Charity Organization Society of the City of New York 1911, 1912, 1913* (New York: M. B. Brown Printing & Binding Co., 1914), 4.
2. Twelfth Census, Schedule No. 1- Population, Enumeration District 617, Sheets 7A–13A; *Trow's New York City Directory*, 1895, 1896, 1897, 1898, 1899, 1900; Osofsky, *Harlem*, 11; Lomax, "A Social History," table 3B; Frederick M. Binder and David M. Reimers, *All Nations Under Heaven: An Ethnic and Racial History of New York City* (New York: Columbia University Press, 2013), 158.
3. Twelfth Census, Schedule No. 1- Population, New York City Enumeration District 614, Sheets 7A–13B.
4. Blackmar, *Manhattan for Rent*.
5. Twelfth Census, New York, Ward 12, Enumeration District 617, Sheet 10B; the occupation noted for Marcellina is illegible; the occupation of "jobber" could have referred to a person who sold wholesale merchandise or a meat packer; *Trow's New York City Directory*, 1900.
6. Twelfth Census, Enumeration District 617, Sheets 10A, 10B.
7. Vital Statistics, Twelfth Census, Census Bulletin No. 88, "Population by Sex, General Nativity, and Color, by Groups of States and Territories, 1900" (Washington, DC: U.S. Census Bureau, 1901), 9.
8. Twelfth Census, Enumeration District 617, Sheets 10B, 11A, 7A, 7B.
9. Twelfth Census, Enumeration District 617, Sheets 9A, 9B.
10. Osofsky, *Harlem*, 75; *Real Estate Record and Builders' Guide, Harlem Local Reporter, New York Times*, 1890s.
11. Sections 6, 7, and 8, Map of New York City, G. W. Bromley & Co., 1897, New York Public Library.
12. Ibid.
13. Hood, *722 Miles*, 24–28, 60.
14. John S. Billings, MD, "Population of New York, June 1, 1890, By Wards and Sanitary Districts," in *Vital Statistics of New York City and Brooklyn Covering Six Years Ending May 31, 1890* (Washington, DC: Department of the Interior, Census Office), 230–233; "Population by Sex, General Nativity, and Color by Groups of States and Territories: 1900," Twelfth Census, 1900- Population, Department of Commerce and Labor, Bureau of the Census, No. 88, 9; W. E. B. Du Bois, *The Black North* (1901; reprint, New York: Arno Press, 1969), 1–18.
15. Allan H. Spear, *Black Chicago*, 11–27; Kusmer, *A Ghetto Takes Shape*, 53–65; Roger Lane, *Roots of Violence in Black Philadelphia, 1860–1900* (Cambridge, MA: Harvard University Press, 1989), 6–44.
16. Vital Statistics, Twelfth Census, Census Bulletin No. 88, "Population by Sex, General Nativity, and Color, by Groups of States and Territories, 1900," 9; Marcy Sacks, *Before*

2. THE END OF THE AFRICAN AMERICAN WELCOME IN HARLEM

Harlem: The Black Experience in New York City Before World War I (Philadelphia: University of Pennsylvania Press, 2006), 22–23.

17. Ida Wells-Barnett, *Crusade for Justice: The Autobiography of Ida B. Wells*, ed. Alfreda Duster (Chicago: University of Chicago Press, 1970), 18–20; Osofsky, *Harlem*, 15, 36.

18. Ida B. Wells, *A Red Record: Tabulated Statistics and Alleged Causes of Lynchings in the United States, 1892–1893–1894* (Chicago: Donohue and Henneberry, 1895); W. E. B. Du Bois, *The Souls of Black Folk: Essays and Sketches* (Chicago: A. C. McClurg, 1903), 13; Louis R. Harlan, *Booker T. Washington*, vol. 1, *The Making of a Black Leader, 1856–1901* (New York: Oxford University Press, 1972), 134–287.

19. Cranston, "The Housing of the Negro in New York City," 327–332; Jacob Riis, *How the Other Half Lives: Studies Among the Tenements of New York* (New York: C. Scribner's Sons, 1890), 98–101.

20. Osofsky, *Harlem*, 46–52; Johnson, *Black Manhattan*, 58–73, 126–130; Citizens Protective League, *Story of the Riot* (New York: Arno Press, 1969).

21. "Looking Into Race Riots," *New York Times*, September 8, 1900; "Police Are Exonerated," *New York Times*, December 9, 1900.

22. "Negro Families Must 'Move On,'" *New York Herald*, May 2, 1904; "Harlem Negro Colony to Fight Evictions," *New York Times*, May 2, 1904; the *New York Times* article incorrectly names the pastor as "N. S. Betts" rather than N. S. Epps; the *Herald* article names the pastor as N. F. Epps rather than N. S. Epps.

23. "Negro Families Must 'Move On,'" *New York Herald*, May 2, 1904.

24. "Harlem Negro Colony to Fight Evictions," *New York Times*, May 2, 1904.

25. Hood, *722 Miles*, 91–112.

26. In 1904, $100 was the equivalent of $2,700 in 2013 dollars, as calculated by using the Consumer Price Index, http://www.measuringworth.com/uscompare/relative value.php.

27. Manhattan Conveyances, Section 6, Liber 88, p. 183, New York City Register; *Trow's General Directory of the Boroughs of Manhattan and Bronx, City of New York*, 1907; Thirteenth Census, Population, New York City, Enumeration District 536, Sheet 4A.

28. Twelfth Census, Enumeration District 851, Sheet 15B; Conveyances, Section 6, Liber 86, pp. 346–347, 382–383; Liber 84, pp. 379–380; Liber 87, pp. 342–343; Liber 90, pp. 388–389, New York City Register; Twelfth Census, Schedule No. 1- Population, New York City, Enumeration District 851, Sheet 15, 1900.

29. Jared N. Day, *Urban Castles: Tenement Housing and Landlord Activism in New York City, 1890–1943* (New York: Columbia University Press, 1999), 32–50.

30. Conveyances, Section 6, Liber 87, p. 95, New York City Register; James Matlock Ogden, *The Law of Negotiable Instruments*, 2nd ed. (Chicago: Callaghan and Company, 1922), 72–73; Conveyances, Section 6, Liber 84, p. 261; Liber 2530, p. 113; Liber 2535, p. 448, New York City Register.

31. Conveyances, Section 6, Liber 86, p. 346, New York City Register.

32. The loan made by the Kroehles to Thomas was a mortgage loan in which the buyers received the deed for the property; if Thomas defaulted on payments, the Kroehles would

have needed to go through a foreclosure procedure to regain the property; this loan agreement is distinct from the land contract or installment loan, a lending tool that was later used in many cities with large African American populations moving into formerly white neighborhoods and unable to obtain traditional mortgage loans; in land contract purchases, the seller retained the deed of the property until all payments were made, and if one payment was missed, typically the seller had the right to reclaim the property quickly since the seller retained the deed; Fillmore W. Galaty, Wellington J. Allaway, and Robert C. Kyle, *Modern Real Estate Practice in Illinois* (Dearborn, MI: Dearborn Trade Publishing, 2001), 196. Beryl Satter, in *Family Properties: Race, Real Estate, and Exploitation of Black Urban America* (New York: Macmillan, 2009), described how the land contract became an essential tool of exploitation of black buyers in the Woodlawn neighborhood of Chicago in the 1940s and 1950s.

33. Day, *Urban Castles*, 32–56; Conveyances, Section 6, Liber 86, pp. 346–347; Liber 87, p. 95; Mortgages, Section 6, Liber 137, pp. 499–500; Liber 139; Liber 207, pp. 305–306; Liber 225, pp. 116–118, New York City Register; *Trow's General Directory of the Borough of Manhattan and Bronx City of New York, 1904–05* (New York: Trow Directory, Printing, and Bookbinding Company, 1904).

34. *New York Times*, 1904; Conveyances, Liber 119, p. 414, New York City Register; John W. Leonard, ed., *Who's Who in New York City and State* (New York: L. R. Hamersly and Company, 1907), 270; "Real Estate Transfers: Recorded Mortgages," *New York Times*, June 16, 1903; "Astor Wants Reduction," *Real Estate Record and Builders' Guide*, January 14, 1911.

35. Thirteenth Census, 1910- Population, New York City, Enumeration District 536, Sheet 4A. Information on the year that the Kroehles arrived in the United States was not included in the Census report; "Ethical Culture Fieldston School," http://www.ecfs.org; *Ethical Culture School Record* (New York: Society for Ethical Culture, 1918), 78.

36. Twelfth Census, Schedule No. 1- Population, New York City, Enumeration District 851, Sheet 15; "Society," *New York Times*, January 16, 1910; "Tammany Hall Delegates," *New York Times*, September 27, 1897.

37. Thirteenth Census, 1910- Population, New York City Enumeration District 1146, Sheet 4B; "A Feast of German Song," *New York Times*, April 21, 1895.

38. Bruce Levine, "The Migration of Ideology and the Contested Meaning of Freedom: German Americans in the Mid-Nineteenth Century" (Occasional Paper no. 7, 1992, German Historical Institute), 13.

39. Leroy Hopkins, "'Black Prussians': Germany and African American Education from James W. C. Pennington to Angela Davis," in D. McBride, L. Hopkins, and C. Berkshire-Belay, eds., *Crosscurrents: African Americans, Africa, and Germany in the Modern World* (Rochester, NY: Boydell and Brewer, 1998), 68–70; Bruce Levine, "Against All Slavery Whether White or Black," in *Crosscurrents*, 56–60.

40. "Ethical Culture Fieldston School," http://www.ecfs.org; Twelfth Census, New York, Statistics of Population, table 35, "Foreign Born Population, Distributed According to Country of Birth" (Washington, DC: Bureau of the Census, 1900), 800–803; Nadel, *Little Germany*, 9–35.

41. Conveyances, Section 6, Liber 68, pp. 181–182; Liber 86, pp. 414–415; Liber 87, pp. 342–343, New York City Register.

42. Conveyances, Section 6, Liber 68; Liber 86, p. 414; Liber 87, pp. 241–242, 342 , New York City Register; Osofsky, *Harlem*, 94; "The Father of Harlem Called it Home," *New York Times*, June 16, 1991.

43. Lerone Bennett, Jr., "What's in a Name? Negro vs. Afro-American vs. Black," *Ebony* 23, (November 1967), 46–54.

44. Afro-American Realty Company prospectus (undated), 2.

45. Ibid.

46. Unsigned letter to Philip Payton, May 3, 1904, Booker T. Washington Papers, reel 248, box 245; the letter could have been written by Booker T. Washington or his assistant, Emmett J. Scott; Scott often wrote letters on Washington's behalf, and was also a friend of Payton's; in correspondence to Payton he addressed him as "Mr. Payton."

47. Maceo Crenshaw Dailey, Jr., "Booker T. Washington and the Afro-American Realty Company," *Review of Black Political Economy* 8, no. 2 (Winter 1978): 184–188.

48. "To Make Color Line Costly in New York," *New York Times*, July 26, 1904; "Afro-American Realty," *New York Times*, July 27, 1904.

49. James McCague, *The Second Rebellion: The Story of the New York City Draft Riots of 1863* (New York: Dial Press, 1968), 107, 178–179; Ernest A. McKay, *The Civil War and New York City* (Syracuse, NY: Syracuse University Press, 1990), 308; "New York Loses Pioneer Undertaker, James Thomas," *Chicago Defender* (National Edition), June 3, 1922.

50. In 1855 fewer than 100 men met the voting requirement for African American men that they own real estate valued at $250. McKay, *The Civil War and New York City*, 11; Junius Henri Browne, *The Great Metropolis: A Mirror of New York* (New York: Arno Press, 1869, 1975), 25; Cranston, "The Housing of the Negro in New York City."

51. "To Make Color Line Costly in New York," *New York Times*, July 26, 1904; "Afro-American Realty," *New York Times*, July 27, 1904.

52. Johnson, *Black Manhattan*, 148–149; Hudson Realty Company Certificate of Incorporation, February 9, 1893, Hudson Realty Company Annual Meeting Minutes, January 13, 1902.

53. Conveyances, Section 6, Liber 85, p. 198; Liber 84, p. 307, New York City Register.

54. Twelfth Census, Enumeration District 617, Sheets 12A, 12B, 13A.

55. Afro American Realty Company pamphlet, 3.

56. Conveyances, Liber 96, pp. 4–5; Liber 96, pp. 9–10, New York City Register.

57. Thirteenth Census, Population, New York City, Department of Commerce, Enumeration District 1146, Sheet 4B; Enumeration District 536, Sheet 4A; Enumeration District 493, Sheet 7B; "A Feast of German Song," *New York Times*, April 21, 1895; "Society," *New York Times*, December 26, 1909; "The Swabian Saengerbund," *New York Times*, June 17, 1894; Hudson Realty Company Certificate of Incorporation, February 9, 1893.

3. FROM EVICTION TO CONTAINMENT

1. Charles Lockwood, *Bricks and Brownstones: The New York Row House, 1783–1929. An Architectural and Social History* (New York: McGraw-Hill, 1972), 242.
2. Elizabeth Hawes. *New York, New York: How the Apartment House Transformed the Life of the City (1869–1930)* (New York: Alfred A. Knopf, 1993), 153–154.
3. Hood, *722 Miles*, 13–26.
4. *Real Estate Record and Builders' Guide*, January 7, 1906, 1.
5. Ibid. It is not clear whether Harlem was considered a less expensive district of Manhattan; it was when compared to areas such as Fifth Avenue, a portion of which was still lined with mansions of millionaires, or the Upper West Side, where apartment buildings for wealthier people were being built.
6. Conveyances, Section 7, Liber 125, pp. 4–9, New York City Register. "Negro Invasion Threat Angers Flat Dwellers," *New York Times*, July 27, 1906.
7. Anbinder, *Five Points*, 95–102.
8. Conveyances, Section 7, Liber 125, p. 7, New York City Register; if the building was sold after August 1907, the lease would have been canceled and Payton would have received a payment of $750; Conveyances, Section 7, Liber 118, pp. 81–82, New York City Register.
9. http://www.measuringworth.com/uscompare/relativevalue.php.
10. Afro-American Realty Company pamphlet, 2.
11. Conveyances, Section 7, Liber 125, p. 7, New York City Register; Conveyances, Section 7, Liber 118, pp. 81–82, New York City Register; http://www.measuringworth.com/calculators/compare/- calculation based on the Consumer Price Index calculation method.
12. Willford Isbell King, *The Valuation of Urban Realty for Purposes of Taxation: With Certain Sections Especially Applicable to Wisconsin* (Madison: University of Wisconsin, 1914), 54–59.
13. "Correspondence: Colored Tenants," *Real Estate Record and Builders' Guide*, January 26, 1907, 198, 230.
14. Twelfth Census, Schedule No. 1 Population, Enumeration District 619, Sheets 17A–19B; Thirteenth Census, Population, Enumeration District 528, Sheets 1A–6B.
15. Twelfth Census, Schedule No. 1 Population, New York, Manhattan Borough, Enumeration District 619, Sheets 17A–19B.
16. Conveyances, Section 7, Liber 128, p. 147, New York City Register; "mulatto"—one white parent, one African American parent; "quadroon"—one-quarter African American; "octoroon"—one-eighth African American; these terms were commonly used in the South, particularly during the period when slavery was legal; use of the terms in the North was much less common.
17. Conveyances, Section 7, Liber 128, p. 146, New York City Register.
18. Manhattan Conveyances, Section 7, Liber 108, pp. 204–205; Liber 120, p. 425; Liber 120, p. 427; Liber 121, p. 473; Liber 121, p. 474; Liber 128, pp. 145–150, New York City Register.
19. Conveyances, Section 7, Liber 128, p. 146, New York City Register.
20. Ibid.; "Afro-American Realty," *New York Times,* July 27, 1904.

21. Evan McKenzie, *Privatopia: Homeowner Associations and the Rise of Residential Private Government* (New Haven, CT: Yale University Press, 1994), 31–36.

22. Section 7, Liber 128, pp. 145–150, New York City Register; in 1895 New York State passed a civil rights bill that prohibited race discrimination in places of public accommodations; private homeowners were typically considered exempt since they could declare that their homes were not places of public accommodation but were available to people whom the homeowner desired to accommodate, as guests, renters, or purchasers.

23. Section 7, Liber 127, pp. 365–367, New York City Register.

24. John G. Taylor Identification Card, New York City Police Museum; Twelfth Census, Schedule No. 1 Population, Enumeration District 100, Sheet 1; Manhattan Conveyances, Section 7, Liber 88, pp. 60–61, New York City Register; Twelfth Census, Schedule No. 1 Population, Enumeration District 620, Sheets 9–10.

25. John G. Taylor Identification Card.

26. "Free Renting: Organizations Formed to Kill This Practice," *Real Estate Record and Builders' Guide*, August 25, 1900, 235; "$20,000 to Keep Negroes Out," *New York Times*, December 8, 1910.

27. "$20,000 to Keep Negroes Out," *New York Times*, December 8, 1910.

28. The Assembly District boundaries were redrawn after every decennial federal census; Twelfth Census, Census Bulletin No. 88, "Population by Sex, General Nativity, and Color, By Groups of States and Territories, 9; Thirteenth Census, 1910, Bulletin, Population: "Composition and Characteristics of the Population," New York, 43–45.

29. Thirteenth Census, Enumeration District 533, Sheets 8A–10B; Enumeration District 504, Sheets 1A–8B; Conveyances, Section 7, Liber 128, pp. 145–150.

30. Conveyances, Section 7, Liber 151, pp. 134–146, New York City Register.

31. Conveyances, Section 7, Liber 152, pp. 297–300; Liber 156, pp. 365–372; Liber 159, pp. 7–15, New York City Register.

32. "Status of Harlem Negroes," *New York Times*, March 26, 1913.

33. Janet L. Abu-Lughod, *Race, Space, and Riots in Chicago, New York, and Los Angeles* (New York: Oxford University Press, 2007), 134–135; Gregory Mixon, *The Atlanta Riot: Race, Class, and Violence in a New South City* (Gainesville: University Press of Florida, 2004); Lois A. Carrier, *Illinois: Crossroads of a Continent* (Chicago: University of Illinois Press, 1999), 184–185; Twelfth Census, Schedule No. 1- Population, Enumeration District 864, Sheet No. 19A.

34. "Bronx Cars to Come to Harlem, Colored Question Taken Up by Board," *Harlem Magazine*, April 1913, 21–22; Osofsky, *Harlem*, 117–118.

35. "Status of Harlem Negroes," *New York Times*, March 26, 1913. The majority of African Americans of this time were aligned with the Republican Party, then just over fifty years old. They considered that party more receptive than the Democratic Party to the needs of African Americans, as they had since its founding. Harlem did have an African American Republican Club, but a political connection to the Board of Commerce or its members is not clear.

36. "Many Injured When Young Rioters Battle on Bridge," *Harlem Home News*, March 20, 1913.

37. "Court Pleads to Jurors to Be Fair to Negro," *New York Age*, October 9, 1913; New York County District Attorney, Record of Cases, 1913.

38. Charles W. Anderson to Booker T. Washington, January 26, 1904, General Correspondence, Reel 248, Booker T. Washington Papers, Library of Congress; Booker T. Washington to Hubert Astley Paris, May 7, 1904, General Correspondence, Reel 248, Washington Papers.

39. Emmett J. Scott to Bertha Ruffner, November 29, 1913, General Correspondence, Reel 358, Washington Papers.

40. Ruffner to Scott, General Correspondence, Reel 358, Washington Papers.

41. James W. Loewen, *Sundown Towns: A Hidden Dimension of American Racism* (New York: New Press, 2005), 80.

42. "Ask Sage Company to Buy Church to Keep Away Negroes," *Harlem Home News*, June 19, 1913; "More Property Owners Agree to Exclude Negroes," *Harlem Home News*, July 10, 1913; "Harlem's Black Belt Is a Growing Menace," *Harlem Home News*, July 24, 1913; "Harlem Property Owners Discuss Negro Problem," *Harlem Home News*, July 31, 1913.

43. "Harlem's Black Belt Is a Growing Menace." The panicked environment undoubtedly hurt real estate prices, but this instability also occurred amid a general downturn in the real estate market; in looking at the year 1913, the *Real Estate Record and Builders' Guide* of January 3, 1914, described it as "a year of uninterrupted and almost unprecedented stagnation."

44. "Harlem Property Owners Discuss Negro Problem."

45. "To Create a Demand for Harlem Property," *Harlem Magazine*, August 1913, 17.

46. "Give Lie to White Realty Men's Charges," *New York Age*, August 7, 1913.

47. *Trow's New York City Directory*, 1913; Census of 1910, New York, Manhattan Borough, Enumeration District 528, Sheet 5B.

48. *Raphael Greenbaum against Caroline Morlath*, Supreme Court of the State of New York, County of New York, 2; "Property Owners Contribute Funds to Fight Invasion," *Harlem Home News*, August 28, 1913.

49. "Property Owners Contribute Funds to Fight Invasion," *Harlem Home News*, August 28, 1913.

50. Ibid.

51. "'Equal Rights' Law in Effect Monday," *New York Times*, August 30, 1913; the fines of $100 and $500 are comparable to $2,400 and $12,000 in 2012 dollars (www.measuringworth.com/uscompare/relativevalue.php).

52. Garrett Power, "Apartheid Baltimore Style: The Residential Segregation Orders of 1910–1913," *Maryland Law Review* 42 (1983): 304–313. The Court ruled the ordinance unconstitutional because it could have prevented an owner of property from occupying it if the surrounding neighborhood was occupied by people of the opposite race. The revised law applied to owners who purchased property after the date of the law's enactment. In 1917 in the *Buchanan v. Warley* case from Louisville, Kentucky, the Supreme Court found that such residential segregation laws were unconstitutional and that "'the difficult problem arising from a feeling of race hostility' [was] an insufficient basis for depriving citizens of their constitutional rights to acquire and to use property without

state legislation discriminating against them on the sole basis of color." The Harlem restrictive covenants were considered private agreements and therefore were not affected by this decision.

53. "White Property Owners Quarrel," *New York Age*, August 14, 1913.
54. *Raphael Greenbaum against Caroline Morlath.*
55. Section 7, Liber 135, p. 136; Liber 128, pp. 145–150.
56. *Raphael Greenbaum against Caroline Morlath*, Caroline Morlath deposition, September 4, 1913.
57. *Raphael Greenbaum against Caroline Morlath*, John G. Taylor deposition, August 1, 1913, 1.
58. Taylor deposition, August 1, 1913, 1–2; Taylor deposition, September 10, 1913, 1–5.
59. Morlath deposition, September 11, 1913, 1–5.
60. *Raphael Greenbaum against Caroline Morlath*, October 1, 1913; J. Delany Memorandum, October 14, 1913, Supreme Court, New York County.
61. Rebecca Kobrin, "Destructive Creators: Sender Jarmulowsky and Financial Failure in the Annals of American Jewish History," *American Jewish History* 97 (April 2013): 105–137.
62. African Americans and others periodically mounted challenges, and in 1948 in the restrictive covenant cases, the Supreme Court ruled that racial restrictive covenants were unconstitutional and violated the equal protection rights ensured by the Fourteenth Amendment. Clement Vose, *Caucasians Only: The Supreme Court, the NAACP, and the Restrictive Covenant Cases* (Berkeley: University of California Press, 1959; reprint, 1967).
63. *Trow's New York City Directory*, 1913; "Status of Harlem Negroes," *New York Times*, March 26, 1913.
64. *Trow's General Directory of the Boroughs of Manhattan and Bronx, City of New York, 1901*; Twelfth Census, Schedule No. 1- Population, Enumeration District No. 100, Sheet 2A; "The Migration of Abyssinian Baptist Church," diagram by Christopher Moore in "A Brief History of the Abyssinian Baptist Church" pamphlet, 1, Abyssinian Baptist Church Archives.

4. THE BATTLE FOR CHURCH PROPERTIES

1. Carroll, *Report on Statistics of Churches in the United States at the Eleventh Census: 1890*, 38, 91. Gibson and Jung, *Origin*, Table 1, "United States—Race and Hispanic Origin: 1790 to 1990"; the total U.S. population in 1890 was 62,622,250; total 1890 population in New York State was 556,954. Kenneth A. Scherzer, *The Unbounded Community* (Durham, NC: Duke University Press, 1999), 185–189; "Dedicating the New Church," *New York Times*, December 1, 1890.
2. C. Eric Lincoln and Lawrence H. Mamiya, *The Black Church in the African American Experience* (Durham, NC: Duke University Press, 1990), 56; Adam Clayton Powell, Sr.,

Upon This Rock (New York: Abyssinian Baptist Church, 1949); Hewitt, *Protest and Progress*, 13–21.

3. Ray, *Life of Rev. Charles B. Ray*, 50, 51; Vincent Colyer, *Report of the Committee of Merchants for the Relief of Colored People, Suffering From the Late Riots in the City of New York* (New York: G. A. Whitehorne, 1863), 11.

4. Osofsky, *Harlem*, 83; Dunlap, *From Abyssinian to Zion*, 91.

5. Gurock, *When Harlem Was Jewish*, 7–21; Oscar Israelowitz, *Synagogues of New York City: A Pictorial Survey in 123 Photographs* (Mineola, NY: Dover Publications, 2007), 12.

6. Penelope Tuttle, *History of St. Luke's Church* (New York: Appeal Printing Co., 1926), 208–255.

7. Ibid., 282. St. Luke's Hudson Street building was operated as a chapel by Trinity until 1976 when it again became an independent congregation called St. Luke in the Fields, the original name of St. Luke's when it was founded. www.stlukeinthefields.org.

8. "The Real Estate Sellers," *New York Times*, October 30, 1887; "Real Estate in Demand," *New York Times*, January 15, 1888; "Some Sales Reported by Brokers," *New York Times*, February 22, 1895; "The Real Estate Field," *New York Times*, March 1, 1896; Willensky and White, *AIA Guide to New York City*, 431–433.

9. "Race Row Started in St. Luke's Church," *Harlem Home News*, April 17, 1913.

10. Ibid.

11. Hewitt, *Protest and Progress*, 125, 135–138.

12. Jill Jonnes, *Conquering Gotham: A Gilded Age Epic—The Construction of Penn Station and Its Tunnels* (New York: Viking), 67, 84–86, 127–129, 154–155.

13. Conveyances, Section 7, Liber 124, p. 449; Liber 127, p. 15; Liber 125, p. 470; Liber 127, p. 44; Liber 124, p. 500, New York City Register; "In the Real Estate Field," *New York Times*, March 15, 1907; Conveyances, Section 7, Liber 128, p. 146, New York City Register.

14. "Wants No Negroes in St. Andrews," *New York Times*, March 3, 1907; President Roosevelt had been criticized for inviting Washington to dinner at the White House in 1901.

15. "Criticize Dr. Van De Water," *New York Times*, March 4, 1907; "Says Stand Is Unchristian," *New York Times*, March 4, 1907; "Supports by Dr. Van De Water," *New York Times*, March 5, 1907; "Whites and Blacks in Church," *New York Times*, March 5, 1907.

16. Conveyances, Section 7, Liber 143, pp. 410–411, New York City Register; Notes of the Standing Committee of the Episcopal Diocese of New York 1907, 71–77; "Church Sale Is Confirmed," *New York Age*, November 9, 1909.

17. "A Memorable Easter at St. Philip's," *New York Age*, April 7, 1910; Hewitt, *Protest and Progress*, 138–143; Willensky and White, *AIA Guide to New York City*, 448.

18. Hewitt, *Protest and Progress*, 138–139; Conveyances, Section 7, Liber 150, pp. 281–282, New York City Register; newspaper accounts note different sales figures.

19. "More Harlem Homes for Colored People," *New York Times*, March 26, 1911; Hewitt, *Protest and Progress*, 138–139.

20. Hewitt, *Protest and Progress*, 144.

21. Lawson Purdy (Warden of Church of the Redeemer) to Rev. E. C. Chorley, October 27, 1914, Church of the Redeemer Collection, Episcopal Diocese of New York Archives; "Church of the Redeemer," *New York Times*, October, 11, 1897; "A Rectorship in Dispute," *New York Times*, November 30, 1897.

22. Notes—Standing Committee of the Diocese of New York, March 3, 1910, 75, and April 7, 1910, 87, Episcopal Diocese of New York Archives.

23. Theodore Fiske Savage, *The Presbyterian Church in New York City* (New York: Presbytery of New York, 1949), 154–155, 194–195; Dunlap, *From Abyssinian to Zion*, 212.

24. *In the Matter of the Application of the Church of the Redeemer in the City of New York for leave to sell its Real Estate*, June 13, 1910, Supreme Court of the State of New York, New York County.

25. Conveyances, Section 7, Liber 151, pp. 134–146, New York City Register, June 7, 1910.

26. *Application of the Church of the Redeemer*; Notes—Standing Committee of the Diocese of New York, June 13, 1910, 99.

27. "Redeemer Church to Move," *New York Times*, June 26, 1910.

28. "Cornerstone Laid Despite the Rain," *New York Age*, June 23, 1910.

29. Lawson Purdy to Rev. E. C. Chorley, October 27, 1914.

30. Vestry Minutes, Church of the Redeemer, October 13, 1910, Episcopal Diocese of New York Archives.

31. Vestry Minutes, Church of the Redeemer, December 14, 1910.

32. Tuttle, *History of St. Luke's Church*, 357.

33. Ibid.

34. Vestry Minutes, Church of the Redeemer, March 27, 1913, April 14, 1913, June 5, 1913.

35. "Ask Sage Company to Buy Church to Keep Away Negroes," *Harlem Home News*, June 19, 1913; "Church of the Stranger," *New York Times*, November 21, 1898.

36. Vestry Minutes, Church of the Redeemer, December 17, 1913; Notes of the Standing Committee, January 12, 1914, 262; "High Church Sells Out," *New York Times*, January 21, 1914.

37. "Fate of Redeemer Church Arouses Property Owners," *Harlem Home News*, January 25, 1914; "High Church Sells Out," *New York Times*, January 21, 1914.

38. "Fate of Redeemer Church Arouses Property Owners," *Harlem Home News*, January 25, 1914.

39. Conveyances, Section 7, Liber 169, pp. 149–150, New York City Register, January 22, 1914; *Richmond's Fifteenth Annual Directory of Yonkers, Westchester County, N.Y.* (Yonkers: W. L. Richmond, 1914), 396.

40. Conveyances, Section 7, Liber 144, p. 425; Section 6, Liber 160, pp. 303, 317; Liber 172, p. 37; Liber 125, p. 236; Liber 3028, p. 391; Section 7, Liber 169, p. 149; Liber 180, p. 431; Section 6, Liber 180, p. 492; Section 7, Liber 181, p. 175; Liber 3036, p. 94; as the founding church of the national African Methodist Episcopal Zion denomination, Zion Church was known as Mother AME Zion Church.

41. Israelowitz, *Synagogues of New York City*, 3; Dunlap, *From Abyssinian to Zion*, 26, 162, 260; Conveyances, Section 6, Liber 3283, p. 205; Liber 3912, p. 375, New York City Reg-

ister; Kerry M. Olitzky, *The American Synagogue* (Westport, CT: Greenwood, 1996), 235–236; "Temple Stone Laid by Ansche Chesed," *New York Times*, September 19, 1927.

42. Gurock, *When Harlem Was Jewish*, 137–156; Census of 1910; Census of 1920.

43. "Accused of Clubbing the Rev. N.S. Epps," *New York Times*, September 10, 1901.

44. Section 7, Liber 181, p. 175; Liber 3044, p. 77, Liber 3068, p. 367; "Real Estate Field," *New York Times*, December 3, 1918; Liber 3115, p. 119, Conveyances; Willensky and White, *AIA Guide to New York City*, 447.

45. Dunlap, *From Abyssinian to Zion*, 91; Liber 160, p. 317, Conveyances, New York City Register.

46. Conveyances, Liber 144, p. 425; Liber 172, p. 37; Liber 3028, p. 391; Liber 3036, p. 94, New York City Register; Dunlap, *From Abyssinian to Zion*, 213.

47. "Status of Harlem Negroes," *New York Times*, March 26, 1913.

5. AFRICAN AMERICAN YOUTH IN HARLEM

1. *Charles J. Crowder against Afro-American Realty Company*, Supreme Court of the State of New York, County of New York, November 9, 1908; Osofsky, *Harlem*; "Mrs. B. P. Parker, Welfare Employee, Succumbs at 59," *New York Amsterdam News*, July 24, 1954.

2. Milton C. Sernett, *African American Religious History: A Documentary Witness* (Durham, NC: Duke University Press, 1999); Silas Xavier Floyd, *The Life of Charles T. Walker, D.D.: ("The Black Spurgeon")*, *Pastor Mt. Olivet Baptist Church, New York City* (Nashville: National Baptist Publishing Board, 1902) ,101.

3. Floyd, *The Life of Charles T. Walker*, 108.

4. Ibid.

5. Nina Mjagkij, *Light in Darkness: African Americans and the YMCA, 1852–1946* (Louisville: University of Kentucky Press, 2003), 8–10.

6. Paula Lupkin, *Manhood Factories: YMCA Buildings and the Making of Modern Urban Culture* (Minneapolis: University of Minnesota Press, 2010), 37.

7. Ibid., 38.

8. YMCA of the City of New York, An Inventory of Its Records, http://special.lib.umn.edu/findaid/html/ymca/ygny0020.phtml.

9. http://www.ymca.net/history/1800–1860s.html.

10. "Colored Young Men's Association," *New York Times*, April 2, 1867.

11. Terry Donoghue, *An Event on Mercer Street: A Brief History of the YMCA of the City of New York* (New York City: Privately printed, 1952), 78.

12. Johnson, *Black Manhattan*, 118–119; Eric Homberger, *The Historical Atlas of New York City: A Visual Celebration of Nearly 400 Years of New York City's History* (New York: Macmillan, 2005), 138.

13. Harlem Branch YMCA, *Harlem Branch's 50 Years of Progress in the North American YMCA Century, 1851–1951* (New York: Harlem Branch YMCA, 1951), 2.

14. Ibid.

15. "Old Timers Will Recall W. 53rd St Y," *New York Amsterdam News*, May 16, 1953.

16. *The Crisis*, December 1916, 75; Alelia Bundles, *On Her Own Ground: The Life and Times of Madam C. J. Walker* (New York: Simon and Schuster, 2001), 114–115.

17. Pamela Bayless, *The YMCA at 150: A History of the YMCA of Greater New York, 1852–2002* (New York: YMCA of Greater New York, 2002); Harlem Branch YMCA, *Harlem Branch's 50 Years of Progress*, 2–3.

18. Donoghue, *An Event on Mercer Street*, 78.

19. Charity Organization Society, *New York Charities Directory* (New York: Charity Organization Society, 1907), 380; Dunlap, *From Abyssinian to Zion*, 212; Judith Weisenfeld, *African American Women and Christian Activism: New York's Black YWCA, 1905–1945* (Cambridge, MA: Harvard University Press, 1997), 44–45.

20. Weisenfeld, *African American Women and Christian Activism*, 37.

21. Ibid., 49.

22. Ibid., 37–39.

23. Ibid., 58.

24. Clifford Putney, *Muscular Christianity: Manhood and Sports in Protestant America, 1880–1920* (Cambridge, MA: Harvard University Press, 2003), 153; Weisenfeld, *African American Women and Christian Activism*, 27–33.

25. Annetta Louise Gomez-Jefferson, *The Sage of Tawawa: Reverdy Cassius Ransom, 1861–1959* (Kent, OH: Kent State University Press, 2003), 96, 116; Conveyances, Liber 159, pp. 7–15, New York City Register.

26. Weisenfeld, *African American Women and Christian Activism*, 100–102; "New York Loses Pioneer Undertaker, James Thomas," *Chicago Defender*, June 3, 1922.

27. Wiesenfeld, *African American Women and Christian Activism*, 119.

28. Ibid., 102–114, 154.

29. Claude Johnson, *Black Fives: The Alpha Physical Culture Club's Pioneering African American Basketball Team, 1904–1923* (Greenwich, CT: Black Fives Publishing, 2012).

30. Cary D. Wintz and Paul Finkelman, *Encyclopedia of the Harlem Renaissance* (New York: Taylor and Francis, 2004), 182, 291–292; Linda A. Reynolds, Salem U.M.C. History Committee, *Salem United Methodist Church: A Chronicle, 1902–1992* (New York: Salem United Methodist Church, 1992), 82–83; Bob Kuska, *Hot Potato: How Washington and New York Gave Birth to Black Basketball and Changed America's Game Forever* (Charlottesville: University of Virginia Press, 2004), 23.

31. Hewitt, *Protest and Progress*, 138–143; Kuska, *Hot Potato*, x–xii.

32. Hewitt, *Protest and Progress*, 138; Ralph E. Luker, *The Social Gospel in Black and White: American Racial Reform, 1885–1912* (Chapel Hill: University of North Carolina Press, 1998), 171–172.

33. National Recreation Association, "Public Schools Athletic League," *Recreation* 11 (April 1917), 86.

34. Ibid., 87–88.

35. Ibid., 81.

36. Ibid., 84.

37. Diane Ravitch, *The Great School Wars: New York City, 1805–1973: A History of the Public Schools as Battlefield of Social Change* (Baltimore: Johns Hopkins University Press, 2000), 6.
38. Ibid., 82–83.
39. Ibid., 25.
40. Frances Blascoer, *Colored School Children in New York* (1915; reprint, New York: Negro Universities Press, 1970), 11–12.
41. Ibid., 12; Blascoer served as the NAACP's first secretary, from 1910 to 1911. http://myloc .gov/Exhibitions/naacp/earlyyears/ExhibitObjects/BlascoersStrategyforAppeal.aspx.
42. Ibid., 11–12.
43. "Grammar School No. 89," *School* 2, no. 22 (January 29, 1891): 173.
44. Ibid.; "Elijah Alvord Howland," *New York Times*, January 1, 1896.
45. "Some Facts About P.S. 89," *New York Age*, January 17, 1920; Theobald's son John would become chancellor of the New York City schools, serving from 1958 to 1962.
46. Adam Clayton Powell, Jr., *Adam by Adam* (New York: Kensington Publishing, 2001), 22.
47. Kenneth Bright and Inez Cavanaugh, "'That Harmful Little Armful': Fats Waller in His Formative Years," *The Crisis*, April 1944, 109.
48. "Find City Schools Cold to Negroes," *New York Times*, April 30, 1915, 9.
49. Powell, *Adam by Adam*, 23–24.
50. Ibid., 24.
51. "The First Black Policeman Remembers," http://c250.columbia.edu/c250_celebrates/ harlem_history/battle.html.
52. Eleanor Touroff Glueck, *The Community Use of Schools* (Baltimore: Williams and Wilkins, 1927), 30.
53. "Lenox Community Center," *New York Age*, October 28, 1915.
54. Glueck, *Community Use of Schools*, 30; Jeffrey Babcock Perry, *Hubert Harrison: The Voice of Harlem Radicalism, 1883–1919* (New York: Columbia University Press, 2008), 258.
55. *The Crisis*, January 1920; Census of Population, 1920, New York City, Enumeration District 19, Sheet 9B.
56. Nat Hentoff, *Our Children Are Dying* (New York: Viking, 1966), 4.
57. Gertrude Ayers, "Looking in Harlem Schools," *New York Amsterdam News*, April 26, 1941.
58. "Harriet A. Tupper," *New York Amsterdam News*, May 6, 1925; Ayer, "Looking in Harlem Schools," 8; Census of Population, 1910, New York City, Enumeration District 208, Sheet 1A; Census of Population, 1920, New York City, Enumeration District 912, Sheet 8B; "Parents' Association of P.S. 119 Holds Meeting and Hears Dr. A. C. Garner," *New York Age*, November 29, 1924.
59. Public Notice, *New York Tribune*, January 4, 1902, 6; *City Record* 34 (December 1906): 11824.
60. Joan Abelack, "The Library Media Center in a Specialized Secondary School: Stuyvesant High School," in Ellis Mount, *Libraries Service Science-Oriented and Vocational*

High School (New York: Psychology Press, 1989), 12; Eileen F. LeBow, *The Bright Boys: A History of Townsend Harris High School* (Westport, CT: Greenwood, 2000), 10; Public Notice, *New York Tribune*, January 4, 1902, 6; Erica Judge, "De Witt Clinton High School," in Kenneth Jackson, ed., *The Encyclopedia of New York City* (New Haven: Yale University Press, 1995), 332.

61. "Vocational Schools Aid Boys' Life Work," *New York Times*, October 19, 1911.
62. Census of 1910; Social Security Death Index; "Mrs. B. P. Parker, Welfare Employee Succumbs at 59," *New York Amsterdam News*, July 24, 1954.
63. William M. Clements, "The 'Offshoot' and the 'Root': Natalie Curtis and Black Expressive Culture in Africa and America," *Western Folklore* 54, no. 4 (October 1995): 283.
64. David Mannes, *Music Is My Faith: An Autobiography* (Whitefish, MT: Kessinger Publishing, 2008), 125.
65. Michelle Wick Patterson, *Natalie Curtis Burlin: A Life in Native American and African American Music* (Omaha: University of Nebraska Press, 2010), 222–223; Jean Ashton, *Harriet Beecher Stowe: A Reference Guide* (New York: Houghton Mifflin, 1977), 62.
66. Patterson, *Natalie Curtis Burlin*, 223–226; J. Rosamond Johnson, "A Treasury of American Negro Music" (unpublished manuscript, 1947); Lester A. Walton, A. W. K. White, and Lucien H. White, "Black-Music Concerts in Carnegie Hall, 1912–1915," *The Black Perspective in Music* 6, no. 1 (Spring 1978), 71.
67. Patterson, *Natalie Curtis Burlin*, 223.
68. Johnson, "Treasury of American Negro Music"; Gdal Saleski, *Famous Musicians of a Wandering Race* (Whitefish, MT: Kessinger Publishing, 2006), 150.
69. Walton, White, and White, "Black-Music Concerts," 71; "News of Greater New York," *New York Age*, September 17, 1914.
70. Stephen G. N. Tuck, *We Ain't What We Ought to Be: The Black Freedom Struggle from Emancipation to Obama* (Cambridge, MA: Harvard University Press, 2010), 125; Roberta Senechal de la Roche, *In Lincoln's Shadow: The 1908 Race Riot in Springfield, Illinois* (Urbana: Southern Illinois University Press, 2008), 1; Charles Flint Kellog, *NAACP: A History of the National Association for the Advancement of Colored People*, vol. 1 (Baltimore: Johns Hopkins University Press, 1973), 9.

6. REAL ESTATE AND POLITICS

1. Frank Lincoln Mather, ed., *Who's Who of the Colored Race: A General Biographical Dictionary of Men and Women* (Chicago: Memento Edition Half-Century Anniversary of Negro Freedom in U.S., 1915), 234; Census of 1880, Halifax County, Virginia, Enumeration District 115, 24–25.
2. Horst Dippel, *Constitutions of the World from the Late 18th Century to the Middle of the 19th Century: Sources on the Rise of Modern Constitutionalism*, vol. 1, *America* (Boston: Walter de Gruyter, 2006), 86; Gellman and Quigley, *Jim Crow New York*, 25.
3. Zita Dyson, "Gerrit Smith's Effort in Behalf of the Negroes in New York," *Journal of Negro History* 3 (October 1918): 354–359.

4. Rosenzweig and Blackmar, *The Park and the People*, 64–73.

5. Wilder, *In the Company of Black Men*, 102.

6. Gellman and Quigley, *Jim Crow New York*, 201; Census of Population, 1870, 1880, 1900.

7. Harold F. Gosnell, *Negro Politicians: The Rise of Negro Politics in Chicago* (Chicago: University of Chicago Press, 1935), 65.

8. McKay, *The Civil War and New York City*, 33; Bernstein, *The New York City Draft Riots*, 112; August Meier, "The Negro and the Democratic Party, 1875–1915," *Phylon* 17, no. 2 (1956), 173–176.

9. "The Colored Republican Club," *Harlem Local Reporter*, September 24, 1892; "Colored Democratic Rally," *Harlem Local Reporter*, October 31, 1891; "Professor Greener and Charles Mellen . . . Harlem Colored Republican Club," *Harlem Local Reporter*, October 5, 1892; Michael Louis Goldstein, "Race Politics in New York City, 1890–1930: Independent Political Strategies" (Ph.D. diss., Columbia University, 1973), 75–84; John Albert Morsell, "The Political Behavior of Negroes in New York City" (Ph.D. diss., Columbia University, 1950), 5–9; Edwin R. Lewinson, *Black Politics in New York City* (New York: Twayne Publishers, 1974), 33–35, 42; "Colored Woodford and Kaufman Club," *New York Times*, September 14, 1870, 5; Christopher Robert Reed, *Black Chicago's First Century*, vol. 1, *1833–1900* (Columbia: University of Missouri Press, 2005), 420–424.

10. Ralph Bunche, *The Political Status of the Negro* (New York: International Microfilm Press, 1945), 1335–1336.

11. Ira Katznelson, *Black Men, White Cities: Race, Politics, and Migration in the United States, 1900–30 and Britain, 1948–68* (New York: Oxford University Press, 1973), 67.

12. Ralph Crowder, *John Edward Bruce: Politician, Journalist, and Self-Trained Historian of the African Diaspora* (New York: New York University Press, 2004), 72; Harlan, *Booker T. Washington*, 97.

13. Bunche, *Political Status*, 1335.

14. John Shaw Billings, *Vital Statistics of New York City and Brooklyn* (Washington, DC: U.S. Government Printing Office, 1894), 230–233.

15. Reed, *Black Chicago's First Century*, 1:421; Roger Lane, *William Dorsey's Philadelphia and Ours* (New York: Oxford University Press, 1991), 210–213; Census of 1880; Census of 1890; Harry C. Silcox, *Philadelphia Politics from the Bottom Up: The Life of Irishman William McMullen,1824–1901* (Philadelphia: Balch Institute Press, 1989), 111.

16. W. E. B. DuBois, *The Philadelphia Negro: A Social Study* (Philadelphia: University of Pennsylvania Press, 1996), 382–383; the Citizens' Municipal League was a citywide white-led reform organization that endorsed "able" candidates for office; Roger Lane, *Roots of Violence in Black Philadelphia, 1860–1900* (Cambridge, MA: Harvard University Press, 1989), 75.

17. "Gen. Miles to Negroes," *New York Times*, August 3, 1914; Booker T. Washington, *The Booker T. Washington Papers*, vol. 10, *1909–1911*, ed. Louis R. Harlan and Raymond W. Smock (Urbana: University of Illinois Press, 1981), 316; Jennifer A. Delton, *Making Minnesota Liberal* (Minneapolis: University of Minnesota Press, 2002), 62; Stephen Harris, *Harlem's Hellfighters: The African-American 369th Infantry in World War I*

(Washington, DC: Potomac Books, 2003), 16. When World War I started, the regiment became the 15th Regiment and was sent to Europe attached to a French battalion when Americans refused to be associated with the black unit. The unit, which was eventually renamed the 369th Regiment, had great successes in battle and was awarded the Croix de Guerre by the French; Sacks, *Before Harlem*, 100; Roger Abel, *The Black Shields* (Bloomington, IN: Author House, 2006), 16.

18. "Roosevelt in Night Tour with Stinson," *New York Times*, November 8, 1910.

19. "Dix Is Elected Governor; Sweeps State by 64,074," *New York Times*, November 9, 1910; "Dix Inaugurated, Promises Economy," *New York Times*, January 3, 1911; "Next Legislature Safely Democratic," *New York Times*, November 9, 1910; "City Sends Albany Few Republicans," *New York Times*, November 10, 1910.

20. New York City Board of Elections, 1912 District Maps; "Mithel Attacks Murphy and Mc-Call," *New York Times*, October 1, 1913.

21. "Apartments to Let" classified advertisement, *New York Age*, October 2, 1913; Washington, *The Booker T. Washington Papers*, 12:315 n.3; Raymond W. Smock, ed., *Booker T. Washington in Perspective: Essays of Louis R. Harlan* (Jackson: University Press of Mississippi, 1988), 98–99; Joseph J. Boris, ed., *Who's Who in Colored America* (New York: Who's Who in Colored America Corp., 1929), 316–317.

22. Classified advertisement, *New York Age*, February 13, 1913.

23. "Oscar Igstaedter, Customs Lawyer," *New York Times*, September 28, 1937; Jervis Anderson, *A. Philip Randolph: A Biographical Portrait* (Berkeley: University of California Press, 1986), 64–65.

24. "Royall Indorsed for Alderman," *New York Age*, September 25, 1913; Lewinson, *Black Politics in New York City*, 55.

25. "Crime in New York, 1850–1950," http://www.lib.jjay.cuny.edu/crimeinny/trials/browse_defense_attorney.php?letter=L.

26. Ibid.

27. "New York City Boundaries and Districts," *Brooklyn Daily Eagle*, 1910.

28. "Negroes Rally Around Royall," *New York Age*, October 2, 1913.

29. Ibid.

30. "John M. Royal[l] at Minister's Meeting," *New York Age*, October, 9, 1913.

31. Form letter from John Royall Campaign, October 25, 1913, Booker T. Washington Papers, General Correspondence, Reel 358.

32. Lewinson, *Black Politics in New York City*, 55.

33. Anderson, *A. Philip Randolph*, 64–66.

34. "Editor Anderson Is Certain of One Vote for Alderman," *Harlem Home News*, September 28, 1913.

35. Ibid.

36. Sharon DeBartolo Carmack, *Family Tree Guide to Finding Your Ellis Island Ancestors* (Iola, WI: Writer's Digest Books, 2005), 9; *The World Almanac & Book of Facts* (New York: Newspaper Enterprise Association, 1914), 716.

37. "Police Are Exonerated," *New York Times*, December 9, 1900, 14; Anderson, *A. Philip Randolph*, 65.

38. *Annual Report of the Board of Elections of the City of New York for the Year Ending December 31st, 1913*, 57–59; "Vote for Board of Aldermen, 1913," *Tribune Almanac and Political Register* (New York: Tribune Association, 1914), 743.

39. Bunche, "Political Status of the Negro," 1335–1336; This would change in 1915 when Rev. Richard Bolden, pastor of First Emanuel Baptist Church, ran unsuccessfully for alderman, and in 1917 when Rev. Reverdy Ransom, pastor of Bethel A.M.E., ran unsuccessfully for Congress.

40. Osofsky, *Harlem*, 20–24.

41. Royall's residence is listed in the *New York City Directory* as 21 West 134th Street, just south of the Thirty-First District boundary; it is not clear why he did not run in the Twenty-First District again or how, if the address is accurate, he was able to run in the Thirty-First even though he did not live in the district; *Annual Report of the Board of Elections of the City of New York for the Year Ending December 31, 1915*, 38; "Alderman McKee Dead," *New York Times*, August 3, 1917; Charles W. Anderson to Emmett Jay Scott, December 4, 1915, *The Booker T. Washington Papers*, 13:475, University of Illinois Press, http://www.press.UIllinois.edu; Perry, *Hubert Harrison*, 247.

42. Mark H. Haller, "Policy Gambling, Entertainment, and the Emergence of Black Politics in Chicago from 1900 to 1940," *Journal of Social History* 24, no. 4 (Summer 1991): 724–725.

43. "Thomas and Johnson Win in New York Primaries," *Chicago Defender*, September 29, 1917; "Low, Dix, and Straus Led Delegate Vote," *New York Times*, December 8, 1914, 17.

44. Marsha Hurst Hiller, "Race Politics in New York City, 1890–1930" (Ph.D. diss., Columbia University, 1972), 242.

45. Ibid., 240; Boris, *Who's Who in Colored America*, 208.

46. "Race Candidates Are Nominated in Harlem," *New York Age*, September 27, 1917; "Thomas and Johnson Win in New York Primaries," *Chicago Defender*, September 29, 1917; Hiller, "Race Politics in New York City," 239–242.

47. "Court Orders Recount of Ballots for Alderman," *New York Age*, November 15, 1917; *In the Matter of The Application of James C. Thomas, Jr. for an examination of the ballots cast in the County of New York for the office of Alderman of the 26th Aldermanic District of the City of New York*; Supreme Court, Appellate Division—First Department, "Petition Upon Which Order Appealed From was Granted," 2; "Negro Asks to See Ballots," *New York Times*, November 23, 1917, 4.

48. "Thomas and Johnson Are Elected in Harlem," *New York Age*, November 8, 1917.

49. *In the Matter of The Application of James C. Thomas, Jr.*; "Negro Asks to See Ballots," *New York Times*, November 23, 1917.

50. "Court Orders Recount of Ballots for Alderman," *New York Age*, November 15, 1917; *In the Matter of The Application of James C. Thomas, Jr.*; "Recount for Alderman is Halted by Court," *New York Age*, December 8, 1917.

51. "Civic League Forces Thomas' Name Off of the Ballot," *Chicago Defender*, August 30, 1919; Thomas was appointed assistant U.S. attorney for the Southern District, and more than thirty years after the campaigns noted above, he did win elective office: in 1952 he was elected to the New York State Assembly representing the Eleventh District in Harlem; "Harlem Is Loyal to Stevenson; Seats Its First State Senator," *Chicago Defender* (National Edition), November 15, 1952; "National United Civic League Takes Building," *Chicago Defender*, June 15, 1918; Osofsky, *Harlem*, 171; Hiller, "Race Politics in New York City, 1890–1930," 231; "Negro Doctor, 81 'Oldest' Yet Active," *New York Times*, April 7, 1949; "Charles H. Roberts an Ex-Alderman, 94," *New York Times*, January 3, 1967; "Harris Wins in New York Primary Fight," *Chicago Defender* (Big Weekend Edition), September 6, 1919; "Alderman Harris Wins Market and Bathhouse," *Chicago Defender* (Big Weekend Edition), July 24, 1920; Perry, *Hubert Harrison*, 256; Arthur Ellis, *The Black Power Brokers* (Saratoga, CA: Century Twenty One Publishing, 1980), 191.

52. "'Father of Harlem' Called it Home," *New York Times*, June 16, 1991; "Payton Buried at Westfield," *New York Age*, September 6, 1917.

53. "Payton Buried at Westfield," *New York Age*, September 6, 1917.

7. THE GROWTH IN PROPERTY OWNERSHIP

1. "Bronx Cars to Come to Harlem, Colored Question Taken Up by Board," *Harlem Magazine*, April 1913.

2. Scheiner, *Negro Mecca*, 11–12.

3. Fourteenth Census, Population, 1920, Composition and Characteristics of the Population by States, Table 13, "Composition and Characteristics of the Population for Wards (or Assembly Districts) of Cities of 50,000 or more," 714–715.

4. "Bronx Cars to Come to Harlem, Colored Question Taken Up by Board," *Harlem Magazine*, April 1913, 21–22; T. J. Woofter, Jr., *Negro Problems in Cities* (New York: Doubleday, Doran, 1928), 141; Osofsky, *Harlem*, 119; records do not exist for the two other papers serving New York's black community during this period: the *Amsterdam News* and the *New York News*; Fourteenth Census, Population, Volume 2, Chapter 15, Table 6, "Number of Homes, Distributed According to Proprietorship and Encumbrance, for Cities Having, in 1920, 100,000 Inhabitants or More," 1286–1287.

5. "Commissioner of Tenements Chosen," *New York Times*, December 7, 1901.

6. Scheiner, *Negro Mecca*, 11–12; Milton C. Sernett, *Bound for the Promised Land: African American Religion and the Great Migration* (Durham, NC: Duke University Press, 1997), 57–86.

7. "The Problem of Housing," *Insurance*, January 2, 1920, 195.

8. Mary Rankin Cranston, "The Housing of the Negro in New York City," *Southern Workman* 31, no. 6 (June 1902): 327–331; "Agents Raise Rent on Race," *New York Age*, September 28, 1916.

9. "Agents Raise Rent on Race," *New York Age*, September 28, 1916.

10. Osofsky, *Harlem*, 66; "Agents Raise Rent on Race," *New York Age*, September 28, 1916; "Fight Against Raised Rents," *New York Age*, October 5, 1916.

11. "Negroes' Civic League," *Survey* 33 (October 1914–March 1915), 58; "Fight Against Raised Rents," *New York Age*, October 5, 1916.

12. Washington, *The Booker T. Washington Papers*, 10:316; "Negro Owners Increase Rent," *New York Age*, December 14, 1916; "High Rentals Meeting Warm," *New York Age*, December 28, 1916.

13. "High Rentals Meeting Warm," *New York Age*, December 28, 1916.

14. Osofsky, *Harlem*, 102–103.

15. *New York Age*, December 28, 1916.

16. "Historical US Inflation Rate 1914-Present," http://inflationdata.com/inflation/ Inflation_Rate/HistoricalInflation.aspx?dsInflation_currentPage=7.

17. "Historical Note," *Joint Legislative Committee on Housing Sub-Agency History Record New York (State) Legislature*, New York State Archives, http://nysl.nysed.gov/uhtbin/ cgisirsi/xUwdkrCsTX/ARCHIVES/230190139/9; "Fear City Will See House Famine Grow," *New York Times*, June 18, 1919.

18. "Historical Note." In April 1920 the committee issued recommendations that resulted in the passage of twelve laws under the rubric of the Anti-Rent Profiteering Bill (Chapters 942 through 953 of the Laws of 1920). The laws gave the courts new powers in landlord-tenant relationships. The laws required a thirty-day notice to tenants before they could be evicted, and only under certain stringent conditions could a landlord evict a tenant. The committee continued its work until 1923, eventually expanding its purview beyond landlords to include labor unions and building material suppliers, all of whom were implicated in a web of conspiracy that successfully inflated the price of housing.

19. "Negroes to Organize Tenants and Consumers' Co-operative League," *The Messenger*, January 1918, 10; "Rent Profiteering," *The Messenger*, July 1919, 6; Henry George, *Progress and Poverty* (New York: Cosimo Classics, 2006).

20. John B. Wiseman, "Fred Moore," in Rayford W. Logan and Michael R. Winston, eds., *Dictionary of American Negro Biography* (New York: W. W. Norton, 1982), 446–448; Moore would serve on the Urban League board for three decades; "Agents Raise Rent on Race," *New York Age*, September 28, 1916.

21. "J. L. Slaughter, the Real Estate Man," *Chicago Defender*, December 2, 1916; "Anderson and Terrell Lease $60,000 Flat Building," *Chicago Defender*, September 20, 1913; "They Can't Keep the Negro Down," *Chicago Defender*, February 7, 1914; "Olivet Baptist Church in Big Real Estate Deal," *Chicago Defender*, January 26, 1918.

22. "Payton Closes Harlem Realty Deal Involving Million and a Half Dollars," *New York Age*, July 12, 1917; Advertisement, *New York Age*, August 16, 1917.

23. "Rents Reduced," *New York Age*, September 27, 1917.

24. "Incorporate $750,000 Real Estate Firm," *New York Age*, January, 26, 1918; *Brockton Directory, 1917* (Boston: W. A. Greenough and Co., 1917), 639; *Trow's New York City Directory*, 1917, 1918–1919; Reid Badger, *A Life in Ragtime: A Biography of James Reese Europe* (New York: Oxford University Press, 2007), 219.

25. 135 Broadway Holding Corporation Certificate of Incorporation, New York County Archives; Census of 1920, Greenburg, NY: Enumeration District 50, Sheet 1A; New York City: Enumeration District 662, Sheet 3B, Enumeration District 1485, Sheet 229B, Enumeration District 1511, Sheet 11A; Leonia, N.J.: Enumeration District 56, Sheet 1A; "Cyril H. Burdett, Attorney, Was 74," *New York Times*, July 1, 1939; in 1934 Burdett had been appointed by President Roosevelt to the Federal Housing Administration, a New Deal agency through which the federal government supported the financing of new and existing housing; "Good Financial Year—New York Title Shows Increased Profits—Officers Elected," *New York Times*, January 19, 1913.

26. "Payton Closes Harlem Deal Involving Million and a Half Dollars," *New York Age*, July 12, 1917; "Terry Takes Over Property," *New York Age*, September 27, 1917; 135 Broadway Holding Corporation, Certificate of Incorporation, New York County Archives; "World's Finest Housing Proposition," *New York Age*, August 1917.

27. Osofsky, *Harlem*, 119; "Incorporate $750,000 Real Estate Firm," *New York Age*, January 26, 1918; *Brockton City Directory* (Boston: W. A. Greenough, 1917), 639.

28. "New Syndicate Takes Over Harlem Property," *New York Age*, March 9, 1918; Payton Apartments Corporation Certificate of Incorporation, New York County Archives; Fourteenth Census, Philadelphia, PA, Enumeration District 982, Sheet 2A, New York City, ED 1523, Sheet 18B; Juliet E. K. Walker, *The History of Black Business in America: Capitalism, Race, Entrepreneurship* (New York: Macmillan Library Reference USA, 1998), 189; R. L. Polk & Company's 1918 *Trow's New York City Directory for Manhattan and the Bronx*, vol. 131 (New York: Trow's Directory Publishing Co., 1918), 429, 434, 819.

29. "New Syndicate Takes Over Harlem Property," *New York Age*, March 9, 1918; "Emmett J. Scott," in Logan and Winston, *Dictionary of Negro Biography*, 549–551; Walker, *History of Black Business in America*, 189.

30. "New Syndicate Takes Over Harlem Property," *New York Age*, March 9, 1918; Conveyances, Liber 3061, pp. 455–456, New York City Register.

31. Hewitt, *Protest and Progress*, 137–144.

32. *New York Age*, June 5, 1920.

33. "Moton Co. Acquires 139th Street Houses," *New York Age*, June 5, 1920; Moton Realty Company Certificate of Incorporation, New York County Archives; Anne Herrmann, *Queering the Moderns: Poses/Portraits/Performances* (New York: Palgrave Macmillan, 2000), 130.

34. Fourteenth Census, Brooklyn, N.Y., Enumeration District 1019, Sheet 5A; New York, N.Y., Enumeration District 1425, Sheet 15B; Moton Realty Company Certificate of Incorporation, New York County Archives.

35. "Negroes Buy More Harlem Property," *New York Age*, December 6, 1919.

36. Penelope Tuttle, *History of Saint Luke's Church*, 357; "Colored Tenants in Harlem Are Praised by City Officials," *New York Age*, April 19, 1919.

37. *New York Age*, December 6, 1919.

38. Willensky and White, *AIA Guide to New York City*, 447–448; Bernard L. Peterson, Jr., *The African American Theatre Directory, 1816-1960: A Comprehensive Guide to Early*

Black Theatre Organizations, Companies, Theatres, and Performing Groups (Westport, CT: Greenwood Publishing Group, 1997), 119–120; Bruce Kellner, *Harlem Renaissance: A Dictionary of the Era* (New York: Methuen, 1987), 214.

39. "Wage Earners' Bank of Savannah, Ga. Buys Valuable 7th Avenue Corner," *New York Age*, March 3, 1920.

40. "Facts About Development of Harlem Realty Business: Millions of Dollars in Harlem Realty," *New York Age*, July 21, 1920.

41. "Another Downtown Church Plans to Move to Harlem; Abyssinian Church to Erect $200,000 Building," *New York Age*, April 10, 1920; "St. Marks M.E. Church Has Purchased Harlem Property; Will Erect Commodious and Modern House of Worship," *New York Age*, December 4, 1920.

42. Walker, *History of Black Business in America*, 182–183; Kathleen Wolgemuth, "Woodrow Wilson and Federal Segregation," *Journal of Negro History* 44, no. 2 (April 1959): 158–173.

43. "Says Glass Plans to Float New Loan," *New York Times*, June 7, 1919.

44. Deloitte, Plender, Griffiths & Co., "Report on Administration, Part II, Investment-Real Estate, New York," Mutual Life Insurance Company of New York, 1906, 36, Equitable/AXA Archives.

45. "President's Report to the Board of Directors of the Equitable Life Assurance Society of the United States, February 17, 1921," Equitable/AXA Archives, 3.

46. Abstract Index, Mortgages, Blocks 2023, 2024, 2025; Mortgages, Liber 3157, p. 470; Liber 3122, p. 108, New York City Register.

47. R. Carlyle Buley, *Equitable Life Assurance Society of the United States, 1859–1964* (New York: Appleton-Century-Crofts, 1967), 377; Willensky and White, *AIA Guide to New York City*, 450.

48. Conveyances, Section 7, Liber 4, p. 405; Liber 10, p. 63; Liber 2362, p. 237; Liber 10, p. 63, New York City Register; New York City Landmarks Preservation Commission, St. Nicholas Historic District, Manhattan, Designation Report, March 16, 1967, Number 2, LP-0322, 3–5; Kenneth T. Jackson, ed., *The Encyclopedia of New York City* (New Haven, CT: Yale University Press), 712.

49. New York City Landmarks Preservation Commission, St. Nicholas Historic District, Manhattan, Designation Report, March 16, 1967, Number 2, LP-0322, 3–5.

50. Paula Deitz, "In Harlem's Elegant Strivers' Row," *New York Times*, April 16, 1982; Equitable Life Assurance Society, *Home Office and Agency Management, 1885–1899*, 377; George W. Bromley map of Manhattan, 1897; June Hall McCash, *The Jekyll Island Cottage Colony* (Athens: University of Georgia Press, 1998), 158; Conveyances, Section 7, Liber 34, p. 9; Liber 31, p. 492; Liber 31, p. 498, New York City Register; Dunlap, *From Abyssinian to Zion*, 287; Willensky and White, *AIA Guide to New York City*, 450.

51. "Testimony of Gerald R. Brown," Armstrong Committee, p. 3604; Thirteenth Census, Population, Enumeration District 525, Sheets 4B–11B.

52. "Latin-Americans in Harlem Block," *New York Times*, August 24, 1913.

53. Abstract Index, Mortgages, New York County, Blocks 2023, 2024, 2025, New York City Register; Fourteenth Census, Population, Enumeration District 1415, Sheets 7B–10A.

54. "Recent Sales," *Real Estate Record and Builders' Guide*, December 20, 1919, 636; "Recent Sales," *Real Estate Record and Builders' Guide,* June 26, 1920, 843; "Recent Sales," *Real Estate Record and Builders' Guide*, January 3, 1920, 13; "Recent Sales," *Real Estate Record and Builders' Guide*, February 14, 1920, 173; "Many Dwellings Sold for Occupancy," *New York Times*, April 16, 1920; "$65,000 Apartment to Be Opened; Pickens Buys Home in Harlem," *New York Age*, February 28, 1920.

55. William J. Collins and Robert A. Margo, "Race and Home Ownership, 1900–1990," January 2000, http://eh.net/Clio/Conferences/ASSA/Jan_00/margo.shtml; Woofter, *Negro Problems in Cities*, 136–151; Fourteenth [1920] Census,, State Compendium, New York Statistics of Population, Occupations, Agriculture, Manufactures and Mines, "Ownership of Homes for Counties Having 10,000 Inhabitants or More," 86.

56. Woofter, *Negro Problems in Cities*, 136–151; Abstract Index, Mortgages, Blocks 2023, 2024, 2025, New York City Register.

57. Woofter, *Negro Problems in Cities*, 136–151.

58. "Recent Sales," *Real Estate Record and Builders' Guide*, December 20, 1919, 636; "Recent Sales," *Real Estate Record and Builders' Guide*, June 26, 1920, 843; "Recent Sales," *Real Estate Record and Builders' Guide*, January 3, 1920, 13; "Recent Sales," *Real Estate Record and Builders' Guide*, February 14, 1920, 173; "Many Dwellings Sold for Occupancy," *New York Times*, April 16, 1920; Kellner, *Harlem Renaissance*, 343; Osofsky, *Harlem*, 118; Correspondence, John E. Nail Collection, Beinecke Library.

59. "Real Estate Firm a Factor in Development of Harlem," *New York Age*, December 20, 1919; Kellner, *Harlem Renaissance*, 259; Logan and Winston, *Dictionary of American Negro Biography*, 469–470; "Status of Harlem Negroes," *New York Times*, March 26, 1913.

60. "$65,000 Apartment to Be Opened; Pickens Buys Home in Harlem," *New York Age*, February 28, 1920.

61. Annual Statement of the Equitable Life Assurance Society of the United States, Schedule A—Part 3, 1919; Equitable AXA Archives; "Weds Three Days After Burial of Her Mother," *New York Age*, June 14, 1919.

62. Abstract Index, Mortgages, Blocks 2023, 2024, 2025; Mortgages, Liber 3157, p. 470; Liber 3122, p. 108, New York City Register; Minutes of the Finance Committee, Equitable Life Assurance Society of the United States, vol. 13 (October 1, 1918–August 26, 1919), vol. 14 (September 2, 1919–April 27, 1920), vol. 15 (May 4, 1920–November 20, 1920).

63. Fourteenth Census, Population, New York City, Enumeration District 1435; "$65,000 Apartment to Be Opened; Pickens Buys Home in Harlem," *New York Age*, February 28, 1920; Bruce Kellner, *The Harlem Renaissance: A Historical Dictionary for the Era* (New York: Methuen, 1984), 343. In the 1920s the area was sometimes pejoratively referred to as "Strivers' Row," the home of black snobs. With the passage of time the pejorative

nature of the name faded and the term "Strivers' Row" became a term of pride for the blocks' residents and for many other Harlem residents.

64. William M. Tuttle, Jr., *Race Riot*, 157–183; "St. Nicholas Historic District Designation Report," New York City Landmarks Preservation Commission.

65. "N.A.A.C.P. Elects Johnson to New Place," *New York Age*, December 21, 1916; Kellner, *Harlem Renaissance*, 257.

66. James Weldon Johnson, "The Future of Harlem," *New York Age*, January 10, 1920.

67. *New York Age*, January 10, 1920; in Johnson's 1930 book *Black Manhattan* he moderated his prediction of permanent African American residency in Harlem, suggesting that a move would occur at some point in the future but that African American property ownership would allow them to reap benefits through property sales that would enable them to move with resources

68. "Rent Profiteering," *The Messenger*, July 1919.

CONCLUSION

1. Cranston, "Housing of the Negro in New York City"; Ninth Census, Population; Tenth Census, Population; Eleventh Census, Population; Twelfth Census, Population.

2. *New York Age*, April 7, 1888, regarding 2350 Second Avenue, 120th Street Station; *New York Age*, February 16, 1889, regarding 211 East 97th Street; *New York Age*, March 30, 1889, regarding 366 126th Street near Eighth Avenue; "Negro Invasion Threat Angers Flat Dwellers," *New York Times*, July 27, 1906; Conveyances, Section 7, Liber 128, p. 147, New York City Register; "Afro-American Realty," *New York Times*, July 27, 1904.

3. Osofsky, *Harlem*, 105–123; Watkins-Owens, *Blood Relations*, 41; "Harlem Negro Colony to Fight Evictions," *New York Times*, May 2, 1904; Manhattan Conveyances, Section 6, Liber 88, p. 183; Liber 86, p. 382; Stanley Nadel, *Little Germany*, 9–35.

4. Osofsky, *Harlem*, 105–110; *Trow's General Directory of the Boroughs of Manhattan and Bronx, City of New York* (New York: Trow Directory Co., 1907), 1097; Twelfth Census, Population, New York City, Enumeration District 851, Sheet 15, 1900.

5. Osofsky, *Harlem*, 127–149; Spear, *Black Chicago*, vii–27; Mjagkij, *A Ghetto Takes Shape*, xi–xiii, 35–65.

6. Osofsky, *Harlem*, 92–104; "Bronx Cars to Come to Harlem, Colored Question Taken Up by Board," *Harlem Magazine*, April 1913, 21–22; Conveyances, Section 6, Liber 86, pp. 346–347; Liber 86, pp. 382–383; Liber 84, pp. 379–380; Liber 87, pp. 432–343; Liber 90, pp. 388–389, New York City Register; Conveyances, Section 6, Liber 87, p. 95, New York City Register.

7. "Status of Harlem Negroes," *New York Times*, March 26, 1913; "Negro Invasion Has Cut Property Values in Half," *Harlem Home News*, August, 7, 1913; "Fight Against Raised Rents," *New York Age*, October 5, 1916; Scheiner, *Negro Mecca*, 11–12.

8. "Payton Closes Harlem Realty Deal Involving Million and a Half Dollars," *New York Age*, July 12, 1917; "Incorporate $750,000 Real Estate Firm," *New York Age*, January 26, 1918;

James Weldon Johnson, "The Future of Harlem," *New York Age*, January 10, 1920; Osofsky, *Harlem*,127–149, 189–201.

9. Penelope Tuttle, *History of St. Luke's Church*, 208–255; Notes, Standing Committee of the Diocese of New York, March 3, 1910, 75, April 7, 1910, 87, Episcopal Diocese of New York Archives; *In the Matter of the Application of the Church of the Redeemer in the City of New York for leave to sell its Real Estate*, June 13, 1910, Supreme Court of the State of New York, County of New York.

10. Nineteenth Census, Population: New York Composition and Characteristics of the Population, Table V, New York City, 45; "Negroes Rally Around Royall," *New York Age*, October 2, 1913; "Editor Anderson Is Certain of One Vote for Alderman," *Harlem Home News*, September 28, 1913; "Race Candidates Are Nominated in Harlem," *New York Age*, September 27, 1917; "Thomas and Johnson Are Elected in Harlem," *New York Age*, November 8, 1917; "Harris Wins in New York Primary Fight," *Chicago Defender* (Big Weekend Edition), September 6, 1919; "Alderman Harris Wins Market and Bathhouse," *Chicago Defender* (Big Weekend Edition), July 24, 1920.

11. Woofter, *Negro Problems in Cities*, 136–141; "Payton Closes Harlem Realty Deal Involving Million and a Half Dollars," *New York Age*, July 12, 1917; Advertisement, *New York Age*, August 16, 1917; "Incorporate $750,000 Real Estate Firm," *New York Age*, January 26, 1918; "More Harlem Homes for Colored People," *New York Times*, March 26, 1911; "Real Estate Field," *New York Times*, July 28, 1917; "Real Estate Field," *New York Times*, September 28, 1917; "Negro Apartments," *New York Times*, November 18, 1917; "Real Estate Field," *New York Times*, March 14, 1918; "Real Estate Field," *New York Times*, August 21, 1918.

12. Abstract Index, Mortgages, Blocks 2023, 2024, 2025; Mortgages, Liber 3157, p. 470; Liber 3122, p. 108, New York City Register; Conveyances, Section 7, Liber 4, p. 405; Liber 10, p. 63; Liber 2362, p. 237; Liber 10, p. 63, New York City Register; New York City Landmarks Preservation Commission, St. Nicholas Historic District, Manhattan, Designation Report, March 16, 1967, Number 2, LP-0322, 3–5.

13. James Weldon Johnson, "The Future of Harlem," *New York Age*, January 10, 1920; "Rent Profiteering," *The Messenger*, July 1919; "Why Negroes Should Be Socialists," *The Messenger*, October 1919; "How to Reduce High Rents," *The Messenger*, November 1919; "Rent Boosting," *The Messenger*, April–May 1920.

14. Johnson, "The Future of Harlem," *New York Age*, January 10, 1920; Rufus Schatzberg and Robert J. Kelly, *African American Organized Crime: A Social History* (New Brunswick, NJ: Rutgers University Press, 1997), 93–94; Sacks, *Before Harlem*, 97–100.

15. "Distribution of Negro in Harlem, 1913, 1920, 1926," Maps of the NY Urban League; Philip A. Klinkner and Roger M. Smith, *The Unsteady March: The Rise and Decline of Racial Equality in America* (Chicago: University of Chicago Press, 2002), 144–145; Jesse Hoffnung-Garskof, *A Tale of Two Cities: Santo Domingo and New York After 1950* (Princeton, NJ: Princeton University Press, 2008), 99–100.

16. "Payton Closes Harlem Realty Deal Involving Million and a Half Dollars," *New York Age*, July 12, 1917; Advertisement, *New York Age*, August 16, 1917; "Payton Buried at

Westfield," *New York Age*, September 6, 1917; "John G. Taylor, Foe of Harlem Negro Has Passed Away," *Harlem Home News*, February 8, 1914; Conveyances, Section 7, Liber 159, pp. 36–38; Liber 3196, pp. 151–152.

17. "Erduin Koch, 56, Merchant and Horseman, Dies," *New York Herald Tribune*, December 4, 1928; "Koch Store Sold," *New York Amsterdam News*, August 27, 1930.

18. Mark Naison, *Communists in Harlem During the Depression* (Chicago: University of Illinois Press, 1983), 118; "Harlem's Pioneer Department Store Sold," *New York Times*, August 22, 1930; "Koch Store Sold," *New York Amsterdam News*, August 27, 1930.

19. Peterson, *African American Theater Directory*, 61–62; "The Dunbar Theater," http://www.explorepahistory.com/hmarker.php?markerId=538; "Private Bank Loss Runs in High Figures," *Chicago* Defender, February 28, 1925; "Hold Funeral Services for Noted Banker," *Chicago Defender*, January 28, 1928.

20. Logan and Winston, *Dictionary of American Negro Biography*, 469–470.

21. Klinkner and Smith, *The Unsteady March*, 145. Former Harlem alderman Dr. Charles Roberts chaired the mayoral commission investigating the 1935 riots; "Harlem Riot Laid to Economic Ills," *New York Times*, March 26, 1935; Nina Mjagkij, *Organizing Black America* (London: Taylor & Francis, 2001), 521.

BIBLIOGRAPHY

MANUSCRIPT COLLECTIONS

Abyssinian Baptist Church Archives. New York City.

Episcopal Diocese of New York Archives. Church of the Redeemer, Vestry Minutes.

Equitable/AXA Archives. New York City.

Johnson, James Weldon, and Grace Nail Johnson. Papers. Beinecke Library, Yale University, New Haven.

New York City Register. Office of the New York City Register.

Schomburg Center for Research in Black Culture, Philip Payton/Afro-American Realty File. New York City.

Washington, Booker T. Papers. Library of Congress.

GOVERNMENT DOCUMENTS

Annual Report of the Board of Elections of the City of New York for the Year Ending December 31st, 1913.

Annual Report of the Board of Elections of the City of New York for the Year Ending December 31, 1915.

Billings, John S., M.D. "Population of New York, June 1, 1890, By Wards and Sanitary Districts." In *Vital Statistics of New York City and Brooklyn Covering Six Years Ending May 31, 1890.* Washington, DC: Department of the Interior, Census Office, 1890.

Carroll, Henry K. *Report on Statistics of Churches in the United States at the Eleventh Census: 1890.* Washington, DC: Department of the Interior, Census Office, 1894.

Fourteenth Census of the United States. State Compendium, New York Statistics of Population, Occupations, Agriculture, Manufactures and Mines. "Ownership of Homes for Counties Having 10,000 Inhabitants or More." Washington, DC: Bureau of the Census, 1924.

Gibson, Campbell, and Kay Jung. *Origin, 1970 to 1990, for the United States, Regions, Divisions, and States*. Working Paper Series No. 56. Table 1, "United States—Race and Hispanic Origin: 1790 to 1990." Washington, DC: U.S. Census Bureau, Population Division, September 2002.

Hudson Realty Company Corporate Documents. New York County Archives Seventh Census of the United States, Population, Statistics of the United States. "Nativities of the White Population," Table XL.

"Manhattan Tenement Apartments and Estimated Population by District, December 31, 1916." *Eighth Report of the Tenement House Department of the City of New York. Report for the Years 1915 and 1916*.

Map of New York City. G. W. Bromley & Co., 1897. New York Public Library.

National Archives and Records Administration (NARA). *Passport Applications, 1795–1905*.

New York County District Attorney. Record of Cases, 1913.

New York Department of Finance. City Register's Office, Manhattan Conveyances, Sections 6–7, 1880–1925.

New York Urban League Map. New York Municipal Archives, Ninth Census of the United States, Population. 1880.

135 Broadway Holding Corporation Certificate of Incorporation, New York County Archives.

St. Nicholas Historic District, Manhattan. Designation Report, March 16, 1967. Number 2, LP-0322. New York City Landmarks Preservation Commission.

Supreme Court of the State of New York, County of New York. *Charles J. Crowder against Afro-American Realty Company*. November 9, 1908.

——. *In the Matter of the Application of the Church of the Redeemer in the City of New York for leave to sell its Real Estate*. June 13, 1910.

——. *In the Matter of the Application of James C. Thomas, Jr. for an examination of the ballots cast in the County of New York for the office of Alderman of the 26th Aldermanic District of the City of New York*. 1917.

——. *Raphael Greenbaum against Caroline Morlath*. 1913.

Tenth Census of the United States. Population. "Population by Race, Sex, and Nativity." Washington, DC: U.S. Department of Commerce and Labor, 1890.

Thirteenth Census of the United States. Population: New York. "Composition and Characteristics of the Population for Wards (Or Assembly Districts) of Cities of 50,000 or More." Washington, DC: U.S. Department of Commerce and Labor, 1910.

Twelfth Census of the United States. Population. Washington, DC: U.S. Department of Commerce and Labor, 1900.

NEWSPAPERS

Brooklyn Daily Eagle. 1910.
Chicago Defender. 1902–1922.

Harlem Home News. 1913–1914.

Harlem Local Reporter. 1891–1893.

New York Age. 1888–1920.

New York Amsterdam News. 1922–1954.

New York Evening Telegraph. 1898.

New York Herald. 1904.

New York Herald Tribune. 1928.

New York Times. 1887–1991.

New York Tribune. 1900.

BOOKS AND ARTICLES

Abel, Roger. *The Black Shields.* Bloomington, IN: Author House, 2006.

Abu-Lughod, Janet L. *Race, Space, and Riots in Chicago, New York, and Los Angeles.* New York: Oxford University Press, 2007.

Ackerman, Kenneth D. *Boss Tweed: The Rise and Fall of the Corrupt Pol Who Conceived the Soul of Modern New York.* New York: Carroll and Graf Publisher, 2005.

Afro-American Realty Company prospectus. Undated.

Anbinder, Tyler. *Five Points: The 19th-Century New York City Neighborhood That Invented Tap Dance, Stole Elections, and Became the World's Most Notorious Slum.* New York: Free Press, 2001.

Anderson, Jervis. *A. Philip Randolph: A Biographical Portrait.* Berkeley: University of California Press, 1986.

——. *This Was Harlem: A Cultural Portrait, 1900–1950.* New York: Farrar, Straus, and Giroux, 1982.

Ashton, Jean. *Harriet Beecher Stowe: A Reference Guide.* New York: Houghton, Mifflin, 1977.

Badger, Reid. *A Life in Ragtime: A Biography of James Reese Europe.* New York: Oxford University Press, 2007.

Bayless, Pamela. *The YMCA at 150: A History of the YMCA of Greater New York, 1852–2002.* New York: YMCA of Greater New York, 2002.

Bennett, Lerone, Jr. "What's in a Name? Negro vs. Afro-American vs. Black." *Ebony* 23 (November 1967): 46–54.

Bernstein, Iver. *The New York City Draft Riots: Their Significance for American Society and Politics in the Age of the Civil War.* New York: Oxford University Press, 1990.

Bingham, Daniel E. *On Jordan's Banks: Emancipation and Its Aftermath in the Ohio River Valley.* Lexington: University of Kentucky Press, 2005.

Billings, John Shaw. *Vital Statistics of New York City and Brooklyn.* Washington, DC: U.S. Government Printing Office, 1894.

Binder, Frederick M., and David M. Reimers. *All Nations Under Heaven: An Ethnic and Racial History of New York City.* New York: Columbia University Press, 2013.

Blackmar, Elizabeth. *Manhattan for Rent, 1785–1850.* Ithaca, NY: Cornell University Press, 1989.

Blascoer, Frances. *Colored School Children in New York*. 1915. Reprint, New York: Negro Universities Press, 1970.

Bloch, Herman D. *The Circle of Discrimination: An Economic and Social Study of the Black Man in New York*. New York: New York University Press, 1969.

Boris, Joseph J., ed. *Who's Who in Colored America*. New York: Who's Who in Colored America Corp., 1929.

Boyle, Kevin. *Arc of Justice: A Saga of Race, Civil Rights, and Murder in the Jazz Age*. New York: Macmillan, 2005.

Brockton Directory, 1917. Boston: W. A. Greenough and Co., 1917.

"Bronx Cars to Come to Harlem, Colored Question Taken Up by Board." *Harlem Magazine*, April 1913, 21–22, 30.

Browne, Junius Henri. *The Great Metropolis: A Mirror of New York*. New York: American Publishing Co., 1869. Reprint, New York: Arno Press, 1975.

Buley, R. Carlyle, *Equitable Life Assurance Society of the United States, 1859-1964*. New York: Appleton-Century-Crofts, 1967.

Bunche, Ralph. *The Political Status of the Negro*. New York: International Microfilm Press, 1945.

Bundles, A'lelia. *On Her Own Ground: The Life and Times of Madam C. J. Walker*. New York: Simon and Schuster, 2001.

Carmack, Sharon DeBartolo. *Family Tree Guide to Finding Your Ellis Island Ancestors*. Iola, WI: Writer's Digest Books, 2005.

Carrier, Lois A. *Illinois: Crossroads of a Continent*. Urbana: University of Illinois Press, 1999.

Charity Organization Society of the City of New York. *New York Charities Directory*. New York: Charity Organization Society, 1907.

——. Tenement House Committee. *Housing Reform in New York City: A Report of the Tenement House Committee of the Charity Organization Society of the City of New York, 1911, 1912, 1913*. New York: M. B. Brown Printing & Binding Co., 1914.

Citizens Protective League. *Story of the Riot*. New York: Arno Press, 1969.

Clements, William M. "The 'Offshoot' and the 'Root': Natalie Curtis and Black Expressive Culture in African and America." *Western Folklore* 54, no. 4 (October 1995): 277–301.

Colyer, Vincent. *Report of the Committee of Merchants for the Relief of Colored People, Suffering From the Late Riots in the City of New York*. New York: G. A. Whitehorne, 1863.

"Correspondence: Colored Tenants." *Real Estate Record and Builders' Guide*, January 26, 1907.

Cranston, Mary Rankin. "The Housing of the Negro in New York City." *Southern Workman* 31, no. 6 (June 1902): 327–332.

The Crisis. 1911–1920.

Crowder, Ralph. *John Edward Bruce: Politician, Journalist, and Self-Trained Historian of the African Diaspora*. New York: New York University Press, 2004.

Curtis, Nancy C. *Black Heritage Sites: An African American Odyssey and Finder's Guide*. Chicago: American Library Association, 1996.

Dailey, Maceo Crenshaw, Jr. "Booker T. Washington and the Afro-American Realty Company." *Review of Black Political Economy* 8, no. 2 (Winter 1978): 184–188.

——. "John E. Nail." In Rayford Logan and Michael R. Winston, eds., *Dictionary of American Negro Biography*, 469–470. New York: W. W. Norton, 1982.

Day, Jared N. *Urban Castles: Tenement Housing and Landlord Activism in New York City, 1890–1943.* New York: Columbia University Press, 1999.

Deloitte, Plender, Griffiths & Co. "Report on Administration. Part II, Investment-Real Estate," 24–82. New York: Mutual Life Insurance Company of New York, 1906.

Delton, Jennifer A. *Making Minnesota Liberal.* Minneapolis: University of Minnesota Press, 2002.

Dippel, Horst. *Constitutions of the World from the Late 18th Century to the Middle of the 19th Century: Sources on the Rise of Modern Constitutionalism.* Vol. 1, *America.* Berlin Walter de Gruyter, 2007.

Donoghue, Terry. *An Event on Mercer Street: A Brief History of the YMCA of the City of New York.* New York City: Privately printed, 1952.

Du Bois, W. E. B. *The Black North.* 1901. Reprint, New York: Arno Press, 1969.

——. *The Philadelphia Negro: A Social Study.* 1899. Philadelphia: University of Pennsylvania Press, 1996.

——. *The Souls of Black Folk: Essays and Sketches.* Chicago: A. C. McClurg, 1903.

Dunlap, David W. *From Abyssinian to Zion: A Guide to Manhattan's Houses of Worship* (New York: Columbia University Press, 2004).

Dyson, Zita. "Gerrit Smith's Effort in Behalf of the Negroes in New York." *Journal of Negro History* 3 (October 1918): 354–359.

Ellis, Arthur. *The Black Power Brokers.* Saratoga, CA: Century Twenty One Publishing, 1980.

Floyd, Silas Xavier. *The Life of Charles T. Walker, D.D.: ("The Black Spurgeon"), Pastor Mt. Olivet Baptist Church, New York City.* Nashville: National Baptist Publishing Board, 1902.

Foner, Nancy. *From Ellis Island to JFK: New York's Two Great Waves of Immigration.* New Haven, CT: Yale University Press, 2002.

Freeman, Rhoda Golden. *The Free Negro in New York City in the Era Before the Civil War.* New York: Garland Publishing, 1994.

"Free Renting: Organizations Formed to Kill This Practice." *Real Estate Record and Builders' Guide*, August 25, 1900.

Galaty, Fillmore W., Wellington J. Allaway, Robert C. Kyle. *Modern Real Estate Practice in Illinois.* Chicago: Dearborn Real Estate Education, 2001.

Gellman, David Nathaniel, and David Quigley, eds. *Jim Crow New York: A Documentary History of Race and Citizenship, 1777–1877.* New York: New York University Press, 2003.

George, Henry. *Progress and Poverty.* New York: Cosimo Classics, 2006.

Glueck, Eleanor Touroff. *The Community Use of Schools.* Baltimore: Williams and Wilkins Co., 1927.

Goldfield, David R., ed. "Blockbusters." In *Encyclopedia of American Urban History.* Thousand Oaks, CA: Sage Publications, 2006.

Goldstein, Michael Louis. "Race Politics in New York City: Independent Political Behavior, 1890–1930: Independent Political Strategies." Ph.D. diss., Columbia University, 1973.

Gomez-Jefferson, Annetta Louise. *The Sage of Tawawa: Reverdy Cassius Ransom, 1861–1959*. Kent, OH: Kent State University Press, 2003.

Gosnell, Harold F. *Negro Politicians: The Rise of Negro Politics in Chicago*. Chicago: University of Chicago Press, 1935.

Greenleaf, Jonathan. *History of the Churches of All Denominations in the City of New York From Settlement to the Year 1846*. New York: E. French, 1846.

Gurin, Patricia, Shirley Hatchett, and James Sidney Jackson. *Hope and Independence: Blacks' Response to Electoral and Party Politics*. New York: Russell Sage Foundation, 1989.

Gurock, Jeffrey. *When Harlem Was Jewish*. New York: Columbia University Press, 1979.

Hale, Grace Elizabeth. *Making Whiteness: The Culture of Segregation in the South, 1890–1940*. New York: Random House Digital, 2010.

Haller, Mark H. "Policy Gambling, Entertainment, and the Emergence of Black Politics in Chicago from 1900 to 1940." *Journal of Social History* 24, no. 4 (Summer 1991): 719–739.

Harlan, Louis, ed. "Emmett J. Scott." In Rayford W. Logan and Michael R. Winston, eds., *Dictionary of Negro Biography*. New York: W. W. Norton, 1982.

——. *Booker T. Washington*. Vol. 1, *The Making of a Black Leader, 1856–1901*. New York: Oxford University Press, 1972.

Harlem Branch YMCA. *Harlem Branch's 50 Years of Progress in the North American YMCA Century, 1851–1951*. New York: Harlem Branch YMCA, 1951.

Harris, Leslie. *In the Shadow of Slavery: African Americans in New York City, 1626–1863*. Chicago: University of Chicago Press, 2003.

Harris, Stephen. *Harlem's Hellfighters: The African-American 369th Infantry in World War I*. Washington, DC : Potomac Books, 2003.

Hawes, Elizabeth. *New York, New York: How the Apartment House Transformed the Life of the City (1869–1930)*. New York: Alfred A. Knopf, 1993.

Henry, George. *Progress and Poverty*. New York: Cosimo Classics, 2006.

Hentoff, Nat. *Our Children Are Dying*. New York: Viking, 1966.

Herrmann, Anne. *Queering the Moderns: Poses/Portraits/Performances*. New York: Palgrave Macmillan, 2000.

Hewitt, John H., Jr. *Protest and Progress: New York's First Black Episcopal Church Fights Racism*. London: Taylor and Francis, 2000.

Higginbotham, Evelyn. *Righteous Discontent: The Women's Movement and the Black Baptist Church, 1880*. Cambridge, MA: Harvard University Press, 1993.

Hiller, Marsha Hurst. "Race Politics in New York City, 1890–1930." Ph.D. diss., Columbia University, 1972.

Hillery, Jr., George A. "Definitions of Community: Areas of Agreement." *Rural Sociology* 20 (June 1955): 111–123.

Hodges, Graham Russell. *Root and Branch: A Comprehensive History of African Americans in New York City and East Jersey, 1613–1863*. Chapel Hill: University of North Carolina Press, 1999.

Hoffnung-Garskof, Jesse. *A Tale of Two Cities: Santo Domingo and New York After 1950*. Princeton, NJ: Princeton University Press, 2008.

Homberger, Eric. *The Historical Atlas of New York City: A Visual Celebration of Nearly 400 Years of New York City's History*. New York: Macmillan, 2005.

Hood, Clifton. *722 Miles: The Building of the Subways and How They Transformed New York*. New York: Simon & Schuster, 1993).

Hopkins, Leroy. "'Black Prussians': Germany and African American Education from James W. C. Pennington to Angela Davis." In D. McBride, L. Hopkins, and C. Berkshire-Belay, eds., *Crosscurrents: African Americans, Africa, and Germany in the Modern World*, 65–81. Rochester, NY: Boydell and Brewer, 1998.

Israelowitz, Oscar. *Synagogues of New York City: History of a Jewish Community*. Brooklyn, NY: Israelowitz Publishing, 2000.

——. *Synagogues of New York City: A Pictorial Survey in 123 Photographs*. Mineola, NY : Dover Publications, 2007.

Jackson, Kenneth T., ed. *The Encyclopedia of New York City*. New Haven, CT: Yale University Press, 1995.

Johnson, Claude. *Black Fives: The Alpha Physical Culture Club's Pioneering African American Basketball Team, 1904–1923*. Greenwich, CT: Black Fives Publishing, 2012. Kindle edition.

Johnson, J. Rosamond. "A Treasury of American Negro Music." Unpublished manuscript, 1947.

Johnson, James Weldon. *Black Manhattan*. 1930. Reprint, New York: Da Capo Press, 1991.

Jonnes, Jill. *Conquering Gotham: A Gilded Age Epic—The Construction of Penn Station and Its Tunnels*. New York: Viking, 2007.

Katzman, David M. *Before the Ghetto: Black Detroit in the Nineteenth Century*. Urbana: University of Illinois Press, 1973.

Katznelson, Ira. *Black Men, White Cities: Race, Politics, and Migration in the United States, 1900–30 and Britain, 1948–68*. New York: Oxford University Press, 1973.

Kellner, Bruce. *Harlem Renaissance: A Historical Dictionary for the Era*. New York: Methuen, 1984.

Kellog, Charles Flint. *NAACP: A History of the National Association for the Advancement of Colored People*. Vol. 1. Baltimore: Johns Hopkins University Press, 1973.

Kelly, Robert. *African American Organized Crime: A Social History*. New Brunswick, NJ: Rutgers University Press, 1997.

King, Willford Isbell. *The Valuation of Urban Realty for Purposes of Taxation: With Certain Sections Especially Applicable to Wisconsin*. Madison: University of Wisconsin, 1914.

Klinkner, Philip A., and Roger M. Smith. *The Unsteady March: The Rise and Decline of Racial Equality in America*. Chicago: University of Chicago Press, 2002.

Kobrin, Rebecca. "Destructive Creators: Sender Jarmulowsky and Financial Failure in the Annals of American Jewish History." *American Jewish History* 97 (April 2013): 105–137.

Kuska, Bob. *Hot Potato: How Washington and New York Gave Birth to Black Basketball and Changed America's Game Forever*. Charlottesville: University of Virginia Press, 2004.

Lane, Roger. *Roots of Violence in Black Philadelphia, 1860–1900.* Cambridge, MA: Harvard University Press, 1989.

———. *William Dorsey's Philadelphia and Ours.* New York: Oxford University Press, 1991.

Lardner, James, and Thomas Reppetto. *NYPD: A City and Its Police.* New York: Macmillan, 2001.

Lazarus, Emma. Introductory biographical sketch by Josephine Lazarus. *The Poems of Emma Lazarus in Two Volumes.* Vol. 1. New York: Houghton Mifflin, 1888.

LeBow, Eileen F. *The Bright Boys: A History of Townsend Harris High School.* Westport, CT: Greenwood Publishing Group, 2000.

Leonard, John W., ed. *Who's Who in New York City and State.* New York: L. R. Hamersly and Co., 1907.

Levine, Bruce. "Against All Slavery Whether White or Black." In D. McBride, L. Hopkins, and C. Berkshire-Belay, eds., *Crosscurrents: African Americans, Africa, and Germany in the Modern World,* 53–64. Rochester, NY: Boydell and Brewer, 1998.

———. "The Migration of Ideology and the Contested Meaning of Freedom: German Americans in the Mid-Nineteenth Century." Occasional Paper no. 7, German Historical Institute, 1992.

Lewinson, Edwin R. *Black Politics in New York City.* New York: Twayne Publishers, 1974.

Lewis, David Levering. *When Harlem Was in Vogue.* New York: Random House, 1981.

Lincoln, C. Eric, and Lawrence H. Mamiya. *The Black Church in the African American Experience.* Durham, NC: Duke University Press, 1990.

Lockwood, Charles. *Bricks and Brownstones: The New York Row House, 1783–1929. An Architectural and Social History.* New York: McGraw-Hill, 1972.

Loewen, James W. *Sundown Towns: A Hidden Dimension of American Racism.* New York: New Press, 2005.

Logan, Rayford W., and M. R. Winston. *Dictionary of American Negro Biography.* New York: W. W. Norton, 1982.

Lomax, Lucille Genevieve. "A Social History of the Negro Population Living in the Section of New York City known as Greenwich Village." Master's thesis, Columbia University, 1929.

Luker, Ralph E. *The Social Gospel in Black and White: American Racial Reform, 1885–1912.* Chapel Hill: University of North Carolina Press, 1998.

Lupkin, Paula. *Manhood Factories: YMCA Buildings and the Making of Modern Urban Culture.* Minneapolis: University of Minnesota Press, 2010.

Mannes, David. *Music Is My Faith: An Autobiography.* Whitefish, MT: Kessinger Publishing, 2008.

Mather, Frank Lincoln, ed. *Who's Who of the Colored Race: A General Biographical Dictionary of Men and Women.* Chicago: Memento Edition Half-Century Anniversary of Negro Freedom in U.S., 1915.

McCague, James. *The Second Rebellion: The Story of the New York City Draft Riots of 1863.* New York: Dial Press, 1968.

McCash, June Hall. *The Jekyll Island Cottage Colony.* Athens: University of Georgia Press, 1998.

McKay, Ernest A. *The Civil War and New York City*. Syracuse, NY: Syracuse University Press, 1990.

McKenzie, Evan. *Privatopia: Homeowner Associations and the Rise of Residential Private Government*. New Haven, CT: Yale University Press, 1994.

Meier, August. "The Negro and the Democratic Party, 1875–1915." *Phylon* 17, no. 2 (1956): 173–191.

Minutes of the Finance Committee, Equitable Life Assurance Society of the United States. Vol. 13 (October 1, 1918–August 26, 1919). Vol. 14 (September 2, 1919–April 27, 1920). Vol. 15 (May 4, 1920–November 20, 1920).

I Mjagkij, Kenneth. *A Ghetto Takes Shape: Black Cleveland, 1870–1930*. Urbana: University of Illinois Press, 1978.

Mjagkij, Nina. *Light in Darkness*: *African Americans and the YMCA, 1852-1946*. Louisville: University of Kentucky Press, 2003.

——. *Organizing Black America*. London: Taylor and Francis, 2001.

Mixon, Gregory. *The Atlanta Riot: Race, Class, and Violence in a New South City*. Gainesville: University Press of Florida, 2004.

Morsell, John Albert. "The Political Behavior of Negroes in New York City." Ph.D. diss., Columbia University, 1950.

Mount, Ellis. *Libraries Service Science-Oriented and Vocational High Schools*. New York: Psychology Press, 1989.

Nadel, Stanley. *Little Germany: Ethnicity, Religion, and Class in New York City, 1845-80*. Urbana: University of Illinois Press, 1990.

Naison, Mark. *Communists in Harlem During the Depression*. Urbana: University of Illinois Press, 1983.

"Negroes' Civic League." *Survey* 33 (October 1914–March 1915).

Negroes to Organize Tenants and Consumers' Co-operative League." *The Messenger*, January 1918.

Ogden, James Matlock. *The Law of Negotiable Instruments*. 2nd ed. Chicago: Callaghan and Company, 1922.

Olitzky, Kerry M. *The American Synagogue*. Westport, CT: Greenwood, 1996.

Osofsky, Gilbert. *Harlem: The Making of a Ghetto: Negro New York, 1890–1930*. 2nd ed. Chicago: Ivan R. Dee, 1996. Originally published in 1966 by Harper & Row.

Patterson, Michelle Wick. *Natalie Curtis Burlin: A Life in Native American and African American Music*. Omaha: University of Nebraska Press, 2010.

Pease, J. H., and W. H. Pease. "Samuel Eli Cornish." In R. W. Logan and M. R. Winston, eds., *Dictionary of American Negro Biography*, 134–135. New York: W. W. Norton, 1982.

Perry, Jeffrey Babcock. *Hubert Harrison: The Voice of Harlem Radicalism, 1883–1918*. New York: Columbia University Press, 2008.

Peterson, Bernard L. *The African American Theater Directory, 1816–1960: A Comprehensive Guide to Early Black Theatre Organizations, Companies, Theatres, and Performing Groups*. Westport, CT: Greenwood Publishing Group, 1997.

Powell, Adam Clayton, Jr. *Adam by Adam*. New York: Kensington Publishing, 2001.

Powell, Adam Clayton, Sr. *Upon This Rock*. New York: Abyssinian Baptist Church, 1949.

Power, Garrett. "Apartheid Baltimore Style: The Residential Segregation Orders of 1910–1913." *Maryland Law Review* 42 (1983): 304–313.

Pritchett, Wendell. *Brownsville, Brooklyn: Blacks, Jews, and the Changing Face of the Ghetto*. Chicago: University of Chicago Press, 2002.

"The Problem of Housing." *Insurance*, January 2, 1920.

"Public Schools Athletic League." *Recreation* 11 (April 1917): 80–93.

Putney, Clifford. *Muscular Christianity: Manhood and Sports in Protestant America, 1880–1920*. Cambridge, MA: Harvard University Press, 2003.

Quigley, David. *Second Founding: New York City, Reconstruction, and the Making of American Democracy*. New York: Hill and Wang, 2006.

Ravitch, Diane. *The Great School Wars: New York City, 1805–1973: A History of the Public Schools as Battlefield of Social Change*. Baltimore: Johns Hopkins University Press, 2000.

Ray, Charlotte Augusta Burroughs. *Sketch of the Life of Rev. Charles B. Ray*. New York: J. J. Little, 1887.

Real Estate Record Association. *A History of Real Estate, Building, and Architecture in New York City During the Last Quarter of a Century*. New York: Record and Guide, 1898. Reprint, New York: Arno Press, 1967.

"Recent Sales." *Real Estate Record and Builders' Guide*, December 20, 1919.

"Recent Sales." *Real Estate Record and Builders' Guide*, February 14, 1920.

"Recent Sales." *Real Estate Record and Builders' Guide*, June 26, 1920.

Reed, Christopher Robert. *Black Chicago's First Century*. Vol. 1, *1833–1900*. Columbia: University of Missouri Press, 2005.

"Rent Profiteering." *The Messenger*, July 1919.

Reynolds, Linda A. Salem U.M.C. History Committee. *Salem United Methodist Church: A Chronicle, 1902–1992*. New York: Salem United Methodist Church, 1992.

Richmond's Fifteenth Annual Directory of Yonkers, Westchester County, N.Y. Yonkers: W. L. Richmond, 1914.

Riess, Steven A. "Madison Square Garden." In Kenneth T. Jackson, ed., *The Encyclopedia of New York City*. New Haven, CT: Yale University Press.

Riis, Jacob. *How the Other Half Lives: Studies Among the Tenements of New York*. New York: C. Scribner's Sons, 1890.

Riker, James. *Revised History of Harlem (City of New York), Its Origin and Early Annals*. New York: New Harlem Publishing Co., 1904.

Rosenwaike, Ira. *Population History of New York City*. Syracuse, NY: Syracuse University Press, 1972.

Rosenzweig, Roy, and Elizabeth Blackmar. *The Park and the People: A History of Central Park*. Ithaca, NY: Cornell University Press, 1992.

Sacks, Marcy. *Before Harlem: The Black Experience in New York City Before World War I*. Philadelphia: University of Pennsylvania Press, 2006.

Saleski, Gdal. *Famous Musicians of a Wandering Race*. Whitefish, MT: Kessinger Publishing, 2006.

Satter, Beryl. *Family Properties: Race, Real Estate, and Exploitation of Black Urban America.* New York: Macmillan, 2009.

Savage, Theodore Fiske. *The Presbyterian Church in New York City.* New York: Presbytery of New York, 1949.

Schatzberg, Rufus, and Robert J. Kelly. *African American Organized Crime: A Social History.* New Brunswick, NJ: Rutgers University Press, 1997.

Scheiner, Seth. "The Negro in New York City, 1865–1910." Ph.D. diss., New York University, 1963.

——. *Negro Mecca: A History of the Negro in New York City, 1865–1920.* New York: New York University Press, 1965.

Scherzer, Kenneth A. *The Unbounded Community.* Durham, NC: Duke University Press, 1999.

Senechal de la Roche, Roberta. *In Lincoln's Shadow: The 1908 Race Riot in Springfield, Illinois.* Urbana: Southern Illinois University Press, 2008.

Sernett, Milton C. *African American Religious History: A Documentary Witness.* Durham, NC: Duke University Press, 1999

——. *Bound for the Promised Land: African American Religion and the Great Migration.* Durham, NC: Duke University Press, 1997.

Silcox, Harry C. *Philadelphia Politics from the Bottom Up: The Life of Irishman William McMullen, 1824–1901.* Philadelphia: Balch Institute Press, 1989.

Sinclair, Bruce. *Technology and the African-American: Needs and Opportunities for Study* Cambridge, MA: MIT Press, 2004.

Smith, Mortimer. *William Jay Gaynor, Mayor of New York.* Chicago: Henry Regnery Co., 1951.

Smock, Raymond W., ed. *Booker T. Washington in Perspective: Essays of Louis R. Harlan.* Jackson: University Press of Mississippi, 1988.

Society for Ethical Culture. *Ethical Culture School Record.* New York: Society for Ethical Culture, 1918.

Spear, Allan H. *Black Chicago: The Making of a Negro Ghetto, 1890–1920.* Chicago: University of Chicago Press, 1967.

Sugrue, Thomas J. *The Origins of the Urban Crisis: Race and Inequality in Postwar Detroit.* Princeton, NJ:: Princeton University Press, 2005.

"Testimony of Gerald Brown." In *Testimony taken Before the Joint Committee of the New York State Senate and Assembly of the State of New York to Investigate and Examine into the Business and Affairs of Life Insurance Companies Doing Business in the State of New York,* 4:3592–3735. Albany: J. B. Lyon Company Printers, 1906.

Teuber, Karl, and Alma Teuber. *Residential Segregation and Neighborhood Change.* Piscataway, NJ: Transaction Publishers, 1965.

Thomas, Lately. *The Mayor Who Mastered New York: The Life and Opinions of William J. Gaynor.* New York: William Morrow, 1969.

"To Create a Demand for Harlem Property." *Harlem Magazine,* August 1913.

Tribune Almanac and Political Register. New York: Tribune Association, 1914.

Trotter, Joe William, Jr. *Black Milwaukee: The Making of an Industrial Proletariat,1915–45.* Urbana: University of Illinois Press, 1985.

Trow's General Directory of the Boroughs of Manhattan and Bronx, City of New York, 1901.

Trow's New York City Directory. New York: Trow Directory, Printing, and Bookbinding Co., 1880–1920.

Tuck, Stephen G. N. *We Ain't What We Ought to Be: The Black Freedom Struggle from Emancipation to Obama.* Cambridge, MA: Harvard University Press, 2010.

Tuttle, Penelope. *History of St. Luke's Church.* New York: Appeal Printing Co., 1926.

Tuttle, William, Jr. *Race Riot: Chicago in the Red Summer of 1919.* Urbana: University of Illinois Press, 1970.

Vose, Clement. *Caucasians Only: The Supreme Court, the NAACP, and the Restrictive Covenant Cases.* Berkeley: University of California Press, 1959; reprint, 1967.

Walker, Juliet E. K. *The History of Black Business in America: Capitalism, Race, Entrepreneurship.* New York: Macmillan Library Reference USA, 1998.

Walton, Lester A., A. W. K. White, and Lucien H. White. "Black-Music Concerts in Carnegie Hall, 1912–1915." *The Black Perspective in Music* 6, no. 1 (Spring 1978): 71–88.

Washington, Booker T. *The Booker T. Washington Papers.* Vol. 10, *1909–1911,* and Vol. 12, *1912–1914.* Edited by Louis R. Harlan and Raymond W. Smock. Urbana: University of Illinois Press, 1981, 1982.

——. *The Negro in Business.* Wichita, KS: DeVore and Sons, 1907.

Watkins-Owens, Irma. *Blood Relations: Caribbean Immigrants and the Harlem Community, 1900–1930.* Bloomington: University of Indiana Press, 1996.

"Watt Terry." *Brockton Directory, 1917,* 639. Boston: W. A. Greenough & Co., 1917.

"Watt Terry." *Trow's New York City Directory.* New York: Trow Publishing Co., 1917, 1918–1919.

Wells, Ida B. *A Red Record: Tabulated Statistics and Alleged Causes of Lynchings in the United States, 1892–1893–1894.* Chicago: Donohue and Henneberry, 1895.

Wells-Barnett, Ida. *Crusade for Justice: The Autobiography of Ida B. Wells.* Edited by Alfreda Duster. Chicago: University of Chicago Press, 1970.

Weisenfeld, Judith. *African American Women and Christian Activism: New York's Black YWCA, 1905–1945.* Cambridge, MA: Harvard University Press, 1997.

Westfield Directory. Westfield, MA, 1874–1897.

White, Norval, Elliot Willensky, and Fran Leadon. *AIA Guide to New York City.* 5th ed. New York: Oxford University Press, 2010.

Wilder, Craig. *In the Company of Black Men: The African Influence on African American Culture in New York City.* New York: New York University Press, 2001.

Willensky, E., and N. White. *AIA Guide to New York City.* 3rd ed. New York: Harcourt Brace, 1988.

Wintz, Cary D., and Paul Finkelman. *Encyclopedia of the Harlem Renaissance.* New York: Taylor and Francis, 2004.

Wiseman, John B. "Fred Moore." In Rayford W. Logan and Michael R. Winston, eds., *Dictionary of American Negro Biography,* 446–448. New York: W. W. Norton, 1982.

Wolgemuth, Kathleen. "Woodrow Wilson and Federal Segregation." *Journal of Negro History* 44, no. 2 (April 1959): 158–173.

Woofter, T. J., Jr. *Negro Problems in Cities.* New York: Doubleday, Doran, 1928.

The World Almanac & Book of Facts. New York: Newspaper Enterprise Association, 1914.

INDEX